THE ABBEY PAPERS

First Published by The Inner Light Publishing Co.

This edition published 2002 by SIL Trading Ltd.

ISBN 1 899585 80 X
© Society of the Inner Light 2002

All rights reserved. No reproduction, copy or transmission of this publication may be made without written permission. No paragraph of this publication may be reproduced, copied or transmitted save with written permission or in accordance with the provision of the Copyright Act 1956 (as amended).
Any person who does any unauthorised act in relation to this publication may be liable to criminal prosecution and civil claims for damages.

A CIP catalogue record for this book is available from the British Library.

Design, Typesetting & Printing by
Clinton Smith Design Consultants, London, NW3 2BD

Printed and bound in Great Britain.

The Society of the Inner Light has no branches nor authorised representatives and expresses no opinion on other groups.

SIL Trading Ltd is the commercial extension of The Society of the Inner Light -

Registered Charity No; 207213

Its aims and objectives include the propagation of theology and metaphysical religion.

THE ABBEY PAPERS

Inner Teachings Mediated
by Gareth Knight

S.I.L.(Trading) Ltd
38 Steeles Road
London, NW3 4RG

Other books by Gareth Knight

A Practical Guide to Qabalistic Symbolism
Esoteric Training in Everyday Life
Evoking the Goddess (*aka* The Rose Cross and the Goddess)
Experience of the Inner Worlds
Magic and the Western Mind (*aka* A History of White Magic)
Magical Images and the Magical Imagination
Merlin and the Grail Tradition
Occult Exercises and Practices
Tarot and Magic (*aka* The Treasure House of Images)
The Secret Tradition in Arthurian Legend
The Magical World of the Inklings
The Magical World of the Tarot
The Occult: an Introduction
The Practice of Ritual Magic
The Magic of JR Tolkien
The Magical World of C.S Lewis
Pythoness: The Life and Work of Margaret Lumley Brown

Books by Dion Fortune with Gareth Knight

The Magical Battle of Britain
An Introduction to Ritual Magic
The Circuit of Force
Principles of Hermetic Philosophy
Spiritualism and Occultism
Principles of Esoteric Healing

CONTENTS

1. The Approach to Magical Images
   (Received 24.7.1993 – 7.8.1993)   9

2. A Guide to the Inner Abbey
   (Received 8.8.1993 – 3.10.1993)   47

3. The Magical Vortex
   (Received 4.10.1993 – 21.10.1993)   192

FOREWORD

The Abbey Papers, which comprise this book, came to me over a period of ninety days, apparently stimulated by some editorial work I had been doing upon the War Letters of Dion Fortune, subsequently published as Dion Fortune's Magical Battle of Britain. I had not particularly sought to set up as a channel of communication in this way but the initiative seemed to come from within, nagging away at me compulsively, much as I believe some poets are pressured by their muse, until I sat down and did something about it – if only to prove to myself it was all nonsense or of no great consequence. To my surprise it all started to flow quite readily and the fact that it now appears in print means that at least I and the publishers feel that there is something within it all that is worth sharing.

The source of the communications seemed to come from three inner plane communicators who worked with Dion Fortune for much of her life or later with her successor Margaret Lumley Brown. Both these ladies were adept at trance mediumship at various levels. My own technique was less dramatic, being simply to sit with a receptive mind tuned in to the communicators involved and to write down what came into my head, either as dictated words or as sequential ideas. I was fully conscious in all of this, it not being a species of automatic writing, where the recipient is unconscious of what the hand holding the pen may be doing. The only difference from normal writing was that it "came through" at twice or three times the speed at which I can normally write. That is to say, about 1200 words per hour as opposed to some 500.

I make no claims as to their assumed identity and prefer to refer to them in what follows simply as the Chancellor, the Philosopher and the Soldier. In my own mind I had a clear image of each one, respectively a Tudor statesman, an ancient Greek, and a young army officer of the 1st World War but I see no point in being more specific than this. The scripts must stand by themselves on their own intrinsic merit rather than claim to have any authority deriving from an assumed source. I am not inclined to enter into debate as to whether this source is my own subconscious mind or wise and influential friends upon the inner planes – although I must confess that I would prefer that it be the latter.

The scripts provide a fair amount of practical advice upon occult and mystical techniques and so it is open to the dedicated reader to follow up on any of this in order to discover his or her own way into the Inner Abbey and come to a personal judgement as to the relative merits of a subjective or objective explanation of its experiential validity.

Gareth Knight

PART ONE: THE APPROACH TO MAGICAL IMAGES

1

Magic is a sacred art. Let no-one persuade you that it is anything less. It is the means whereby man can attain contact with and expression of his "higher" roots. For man is like a tree, whose flowering may be seen on Earth and yet whose roots are in the heavens.

Magic is the deliberate cultivation of the stem between root and flower, for without the passing of the sap along that stem no flowering will be seen on Earth. The Earthly Paradise will remain but a vision of that which has not been achieved, a potentiality that is lost, and the present a waste land.

So you see the Earth in which you live, or rather in which you are divinely decreed to express yourselves, is a spiritual garden. Although to you, the reality appears up-side down. You have heard of the hanging gardens of Babylon - one of the ancient wonders of the world. Within that wonder of ancient science and botanic art there is a useful image, an image that resonates with an inner truth. For the world you know is a hanging garden, dependent on its roots within the heavens.

Therefore magic is the science and art of heavenly horticulture, as it was of the primal human archetypal pair, known in the Bible as Adam and Eve. Adam was the man of the true Earth; Eve, the springing forth of new life from him.

It was she who, instructed by the Serpent of Wisdom, caused what is known as the Original Fall, and their expulsion from the Garden. This was a fall indeed, and one whose consequences may well seem to be the bitter rewards of sin. But the original Garden of Eden, with its four rivers, and firmament above and below, was made by God. The Garden that will be planted beyond Eden, in the lands watered by the four primeval rivers of Elemental expression, will be the Garden of Man and Woman, of Adam and Eve.

The early dreams of Adam, of the female form Lilith, were a foreshadowing of Eve. A glimmering intuition within the spiritual soul of man of that which was to come. His cosmic destiny was manifested by the coming of Eve, and her creation from within himself, from the outer cage of his heart. There is an inner meaning to the creation of Eve from Adam's rib, just as in Adam having been created from the dust of the Earth.

"What dust?" you may ask yourselves. "What form of rib? Are not these no more than idle tales, the fantasies of a primitive race striving to explain human existence?" They may have been this too, in their original mode of expression, but beyond them lies a deeper realisation of the truth and reality of God.

"The Fall then," you may say, "was a fall upwards? Another instance of the manifest world having an inverted appearance - where what is up and down in Heaven is down and up in Earth?"

Yes, in part. But there was also an element of sin, of real Cosmic Fall – together with the gift of the Freedom of Will, and the very expression of that gift. For remember that God created the Tree of the Knowledge of Good and of Evil. It thus also came from God, even though its existence and its power were indicated by the Serpent.

By reason of that "sin", the human couple were expelled from the Paradise Garden, for they had been invested with the power and knowledge to become "as gods". Thus were they thrust from the Garden by an angelic power.

That same angelic power who guards and prevents the way back in. For to return would be a regression, a creeping back into the cradle. An attempt to put on again the swaddling bands of cosmic childhood - rather than to go out into the world of spiritual growth, in "coats of skin", and there to till the Earth to make of it a garden, like unto the paradisal one they had left behind.

And the Serpent also fell. The expression is in terms of sin and retribution in the Book of Genesis, although the conditions are also those of opportunity and consequence. The serpent was to become the lowliest beast, crawling on its belly. It becomes however, in the way of the world, the potential of life. The expression of organic life within the barren rocks of elemental creation - which was the best that could be done by the angelic powers before the cosmic event of the Fall.

The highest expression of form to that date could only be the crystal. The arrangement of inanimate form that man later discovers and names as the laws of physics and chemistry. A hard beautiful expression of heavenly principles, that is based upon divine mathematics.

In the Serpent we have the first manifestation of life. The primeval worms that move and live in the warm seas, whose contents constitute a mixture of the elements of the Earth, that are warmed and enlivened by the rays of the Sun. These very primary forms of life that still exist in the human body. That are to be found in the vital being of all living matter.

All matter that lives, lives with the energy of the Serpent. It is in the sap that rises in the stems of plants and trees, and the flow of blood and lymph in every animal organism, the pulse of life that creates the structure of all the bodies that exist on Earth. And the Serpent also exists in the human body in the higher form of the upright skeleton, the upright spine, that aspires toward the Sun. And the aspiring inner power within that column of earthly manifest life is known in the East as the "serpent power" - or *kundalini*.

The raising of that Serpent Power, in certain forms of yoga known to the East, is a way of spiritual enlightenment. For at the apex of its journey, the power and aspiration of the Earth is conjoined with the power and aspiration of the Heavens, and great is the celebration and glory thereof, whether it occur in the human heart, the human throat, (the organ of expression and creation), or the human head - the supreme expression in the material creation of the creative powers of Heaven.

The human head is indeed a mighty creation. The material expression, *in potentia*, of "the Head Which is Not" - the Qabalistic name for the Ultimate Power and Glory of God within the Heavens.

The head however, as with that of the rest of the body, is dependent for its physical being upon the chemical elements and compounds of the primal creators. And the later organic organisation and expression of those elements into animate form. These are the powers of the Serpent, who is otherwise known as the Lord of this World, or to those who see a dichotomy between spirit and matter, as the Adversary.

But the Lord of this World returns to the Kingdom of Heaven as a mighty prince, when enlightened human beings, the achieved, the redeemed Adam and Eve, shall enter their own glory. When they have built Jerusalem in the pleasant lands of the outer heavens, expanding Heaven into what was a primeval chaos set apart (even though within the power and body of God) in the beginning.

However, there is also the question of sin, of the evil created by the mis-expression of divinely given free will. That must also be taken into our vision and into our calculations. Without that expression, that existence of sin, the principles of evolutionary life would be simple indeed, and harmonious. But we have to take into account war and pestilence, pride and greed, and all the darker aspects of creation, so dark and stained indeed, that some holy men have been led to believe that there is eternal war between spirit and matter. But such is not the case. It is only an appearance. An appearance that comes from a partially sighted spiritual vision.

{*The Chancellor, 24.7.93*}

2
As soon as free will became a gift, then Adam and Eve became "as gods", with all the responsibility that this implies. And moreover "gods" who had experienced form. In this they would be higher than the angels - who have not experienced life in form, even

though a large proportion of them may have created it, for creation of form is an angelic function at various levels.

Form, as you know it, is the creation of the created. God creates the Primal Divine Sparks. These units of the children of God then set about form creation, rather like children building sand castles, but with this difference. The angels, (or earlier swarms, to use a phrase from *The Cosmic Doctrine*), created according to patterns laid down, or inspired within them, by the loving regard and intuitive direction of God. This is an action of the Holy Spirit at work, the angelic inspirer.

You may wonder about comparisons between *The Cosmic Doctrine* and other "received" writings. Each is an attempt at teaching from the inner levels by inspirational communication. Some are more successful than others. Often the flow is marred by fixed ideas already in brain consciousness, like pebbles in a silted stream.

Sometimes it may be done by direct use of trance - a means of communication that gives a less impeded flow, but one that is susceptible to being *too* free, for it implies a lowering, or absence, of the critical faculties of enlightened waking consciousness.

This function may be left to another, and may be performed with good intention and integrity, but this is not, by its very nature, conducive to complete accuracy. This might be obtained if the dual function were exercised within the same consciousness but this requires a rare combination of sensitivity and a well trained mind. A mind with access to much data yet not overburdened thereby. And data that tends to fact rather than to opinion, particularly should this apply to formerly misunderstood, misrepresented or misapplied teaching.

So there is ever a tendency for error to grow, and a channel to become silted up. A tradition that was once freely flowing, like a hill stream, between firm but malleable banks may cease to flow. It may break its banks, lose form and become a marsh. Although there is always a chance it may retain pools within it, perhaps even a small lake, which can reflect the heavens from which the stream originated.

For the water of the stream comes from heaven. This is an aspect of the holy symbol of the "dew", (sometimes called the sweat, or even the tears, of the stars). And the natural circulation of water, when regarded as an image of human consciousness, is like the distillation process of the alchemists.

The vapour rises from the sea, warmed by the sun from the contemplative mass of the sea of human consciousness. It is held within the air, sometimes visible as clouds, either black or white, or in various forms that denote the expression and the intention of consciousness within the heavens. And in this the winds play a part, for the wind is an expression of the Holy Spirit, "that bloweth where it listeth". Although in some respects, as in nature, it may also be configured by the conditions of Earth itself, its hills and valleys, its times and seasons governed by its position and direction in space. Then come the rains, in torrent or in gentle mist, but in whatever the condition it falls, essential to life. For by this continuous recirculation life is enabled to develop, to maintain its hold. The life giving water, circulated by the sun, fructifies the earth.

Another form of water is the living water of consciousness, and in this lies the divine idea behind the rite of baptism, for water also washes clean. Pure water provides drink, essential to life more directly even than food. And so does the circuit of consciousness.

The seas themselves represent man in the mass, whether it be by race or by nation. Such is the nature of national and tribal consciousness, the group minds and group souls of the nations. And in lesser degree it applies to any group.

A group is like a hollowed basin within the Earth. The process is automatic, much as in the analogy of the rubber sheet that demonstrates the idea of curved space and time caused by the mass of objects in the universe, as conceived by Einstein. A group, or basin, is therefore a "trap", or container, a "centre of gravity" for consciousness.

It is awareness of this principle that is a factor in higher magic. For magic in its higher sense is the diverting of streams to flow into different channels and basins. It is a process of divine irrigation so to speak. For this reason the Tarot card of Temperance is, in its way, an alternative form for the Magician. And this image too is, appropriately, one of the Cardinal Virtues. The Star also, in the form of the maiden, kneeling between land and sea, pouring water beneath the stars, is a most holy, and deeply Rosicrucian (*ros* (dew) + *crucis* (cross)) emblem.

{The Chancellor, 25.7.93}

3
We have begun to describe the principle of the four elements in action as truly understood.

The *Earth* is the basis for all growth and life and living experience upon the material plane.

The *Waters* of consciousness, as higher consciousness are attracted up by the heat of the sun. Yet with their life giving properties they also flow down upon and into the Earth. They play a part in the deeps of the seas, the ocean currents and tides, which are the affairs of men and of nations. And also in the flow and the network of rivers, (esoterically understood), and of lakes, holy lakes of inspired consciousness, reflecting the heavens.

The *Air*, which is the higher, more volatile element into which the waters of consciousness can be borne, bring the character of climate, that is to say the different expressions of "planetary character" upon earth. Weather in this sense represents a mode of the inner or unseen destiny of nations, and the applications of the Holy Spirit.

As for *Fire*, it is the heat, the warmth, the radiation of the Sun. That which raises the water into the air, and fructifies the Earth and the life impulses therein. Without it all would be darkness, and cosmic death. It is therefore the most direct agent of the power and love of God.

The Moon, pursuing this elemental analogy, is a body active only at the level of gravity, affecting the flow of earthly tides, although through the inner tides, also with a certain effect upon growth. It is not a higher principle, for it has no Air or Water of its own and is therefore unresponsive to the Sun-Fire.

So is it with the Planets. They are expressions of the Primal Swarms, the Creative Hierarchies of Flame and Form. They are the patterns of the geophysical expression of Spirit in Matter, but they have no gardens, no bearers of higher life - at any rate not in the form that can be conceived and perceived by you on Earth, in normal consciousness. They may be organs of experience for certain types of elemental life but that is not of current human concern.

The Stars are as the Sun, each of them a lamp of God, with the potential for giving life, of forming arenas of life expression such as your own. But in their most basic form and level of necessity they are the conditioners and sustainers of physical form, the creators of the patterns of the chemical forms of the elements, in which the higher life forces can play.

From this you may see that the Archangelic creators of organic life are at a higher level of operation than that of the primal creators - the Lords of Form and Flame. Biblically represented by the serpent, these are Lords of Mind, and the later Biblical account of the coming of angels to the daughters of men to breed a race of giants, is an account of their leadership by incarnation into the lower forms.

The Messiah was therefore akin to this function of the Lords of Mind, in the nearest analogy to the process that you can understand. Although he was far greater, in that he uniquely embodied the pattern of the human goal, that of a Lord of Civilisation or Lord of Humanity.

And this embodied and exemplified a shift to the tilt of the Earth, symbolically speaking. It restored a Pattern, cracked by Original Sin. Although the sin is "original", not in terms of being inherent from the beginning of physical creation, but of having its origin in the heart and the expressed free will of man. Thus it originates in man and those of the angels that fell with him.

In this function the Lords of Mind were Ray Exemplars, but treading the Earth "as giants" only in "those days". They might, in our analogy of the seas of human consciousness, be likened to the leaders of shoals of fishes, with a knowledge of the tides. Or at a higher level, on the tides of the air, representative of the innate intelligence or spiritual instinct of migrating birds.

Remember we speak, in all of this, in terms of analogy. That is, in pictorial form imagery of the forces at work. Patterns to be discerned in aspects of the lower world about you today, that in their form are similar to primal actualities. This is the function of symbol. To represent an aspect of an earlier or interior reality, in another plane or another time, by a pattern that forms on the surface of expressed creation now. We look at eddies in the stream, and draw our figures of teaching from them. Do not mistake the symbols for the reality.

We are concerned with the here and the now. How the waters of consciousness, and of higher consciousness in particular, can be channelled and directed. This is the work of magic. It is an art and a science, and no different, in intention or application, from the manipulation of electricity.

{The Chancellor, 26.7.93}

4

Each incarnate individual is a pool of consciousness. This pool being formed - as in a rock or garden pool - by the physical body. In the case of animals the pool is somewhat shallower. However in the case of animals there is a certain connection between them, as of underground channels. One could call it a sort of telepathic link although the terminology is inappropriate because it assumes distance between those so connected by like thought.

In fact any two persons are conjoined by like thought. And when two or three are gathered together there is a combining of the waters, temporarily, into one pool. And in the case of an invocatory intention, the enlarging of the pool enables a larger entity from another plane to bathe in it, so to speak.

The figure I use may seem somewhat bizarre, but is accurate enough in its way. The bigger the pool you provide, the greater the entity, the spiritual being, that can swim in it. In the case of a very small pool it may be only large enough for the washing of hands, or the dipping of the face.

It will be apparent that the larger the congregation of contributing consciousness, the bigger the pool. Although there is also an element of quality inherent in all of this. A few deeply committed souls can provide a far larger capacity for spiritual beings to disport than a much greater number of the untrained or less committed.

This is the rationale, and the purpose and the method of a magical group, as well as of a church congregation, which in turn could be compared to a small body of religious contemplatives dedicated to, and trained in prayer.

A larger crowd can provide a larger expanse of water, but one that is extensive rather than deep. And also one that may be, figuratively speaking, somewhat muddied and noisome. Thus one is unlikely to attract a more fastidious or refined kind of spiritual entity. Of such is the sporting crowd, which can have its higher elements, as in the respect and admiration for the hero, or team of heroes, but which can become besmirched by loutishness.

In spiritual terms of consciousness, like being attracted to like, this kind of pool attracts a loutish kind of entity, which leads to the kind of behaviour that might be otherwise expected from an ill intentioned poltergeist. Towns and property may be broken up, people assaulted. And at its worst this kind of thing leads to the lynch mob, in which a particularly evil type of entity might be discerned.

"By their fruits shall ye know them." You do not necessarily need the vision of the higher planes to know what type of inner creature is being given the opportunity for a vampiric feast, or a threshing about in material waters. This kind of thing does not help the evolution of the Earth, nor the education of, or example to, the lesser elemental creatures ensouled therein. Patterns are made that can, if one is not careful, be all too readily repeated. Or in *Cosmic Doctrine* terms a "track in space".

The same mechanics apply to the true and the good, of course. And the regular meeting for prayer, or for internal communion or communication.

Communion and communication are not the same, by the way, although connected. In much the same way that sexual and social intercourse are similar but not the same.

Religious or mystical communion is akin to an inner union, and its analogy is a physical act of love, although an inner kind of eroticism needs to be avoided. Through the effects of "original sin", (striking as it does, and did, at the creative faculty, and by extension, through the physical organs of creation), such analogies, appropriate though they may be, can appear bizarre, inappropriate, blasphemous even, in one light.

In another light they can portray a false trail lit by evil reflected glamour. (The inner symbolism of moonshine, and earthshine, has a bearing on this). This leads to an erotic kind of false mysticism, the communion being not with a true spiritual entity, but with a phantasm that is a reflection of thwarted physical desire. And this, if it gets beyond a kind of idolatrous onanism, so to speak, can become ensouled with larvae-like creatures of the less salubrious areas of the inner planes.

Sexual mores, you will gather, have an important bearing upon the technicalities and operation of mysticism and magic. In the directed mysticism of the church or other types of organised religion, (I speak of the Islamic, or Buddhist, Hindu and so on, as well as of the

Catholic tradition of the West), there are inbuilt safeguards. It is also true that sometimes these are overdone, so that there may develop some strange and peculiar difficulties with regard to sexual gender and its expression. Thus matters that have their foundation in truth can become overstated or distorted. This is the classic pattern of superstition, whereby the valid and the real become ossified forms, empty and hollow observance.

The cult of the Virgin is an aid toward purity in the historical church - although it can spill over into a kind of sentimentality, as can all things handled by the spiritually ill-equipped. Hence the adage of pearls before swine.

But being part of a flock of sheep is of preferred status to joining the Gaderene swine. The flock may follow its shepherd, duly and properly led, assisted perhaps by the occasional dog, who seems to threaten and bar the way to false paths. The Gaderene swine are possessed, and dash, with greater show of vitality perhaps, to their own destruction.

{The Chancellor, 27.7.93}

5
From the analogies of water that we have been using you may perhaps see a symbolic connection with the mission of Jesus, who called his disciples to be "fishers of men". And the symbol of the fish was very much a Christian icon before that of the cross became paramount.

The waters of baptism we have already mentioned. There is also the miracle of turning water into wine, at a marriage feast be it noted. This was a prediction and symbolic indication of the importance of the Messiah, of the Incarnation, and of the Resurrection Body, that brought a new mode of physical being into expression. When the "great marriage" in material and physical consciousness takes place then the water will indeed become wine.

Be it noted that this needs divine assistance and intervention. Evolutionary theories, and the principles of growth and change through aspiration and effort are all very well in their place, but there is also the profoundly important element of Divine Grace. And without this, be it remembered, there would have been no creation in the first place.

In the Old Testament the waters of life are displayed in the account of the magician/mystic Moses striking the rock in order to bring water to the wandering tribes in the wilderness. And the parting of the waters of the Red Sea is another instance of the inward significance of Biblical accounts of water. The account in Genesis of the original creation describes the Spirit of God breathing upon and stirring the waters; and then making a division between them, into the higher and lower waters.

The firmament is a place set aside by God for the works of higher creation. The waters are of the primal creation, that of the Elohim, spirits of God, the very first swarms.

In works of mysticism and of magic, therefore, the principle of water, meaning the basic principle of consciousness, is paramount. It is the prime substance, the *prima materia*, upon which all alchemical operations are performed. This concerns the making of solutions. In a sense all manifestation of life in form is a making of solutions. The passage of the waters of consciousness rubs off grains of material substance, takes them, moves them, changes them, and takes up part of them into solution. This renders the sea salt, and gives the different taste or quality to various streams of waters.

Remember however the turning of water into wine. By filtration, the grosser, unassimilated pieces of matter may be taken from the solution. By distillation, that which was dissolved in it will be precipitated. That which remains in either case is the historical record of a human life.

Filtered waters of consciousness are that which is obtained when purificatory processes are undertaken in life, either by experience or by inner disciplines. Distilled waters of consciousness are that which rises to another plane, possibly in initiation, most usually in death to the physical. In either case there remains a residue, the historical record.

However, there is also the principle of transformation or transubstantiation, the turning of water into wine. This is a question of chemical change, a deeper change than that of colloidal carrying, or bearing in solution. A change of relationships at the atomic level is involved.

In elementary changes in simple chemical compounds, this principle may be found in its basic simplicity. But there are deeper, more profound instances, where organic change is involved. For instance in the wine, where a process of fermentation of a once living organism, the grape of the vine, lies at the root of the process.

The Element of Water, in its wider sense, comes in various forms of the liquid state, be it in the sap of the plant, the spinal fluid or other fluids of the human body, and most importantly the blood.

In the principle of the blood, and the differences between it, which can hardly be chemically differentiated, you have the ties of kith and kin, of family and of race. Differentations in the blood are as distinctive as the various forms of water that are natural to any territory, and so their call gives rise to problems in the history of mankind, and of the races and nations. Blood is thicker than water, it is said. It is also more profound in its primeval and indeed spiritual pull.

The waters of intellectually based idealism, laudable in intention, are very often a gross over-simplification. Do your children ask for bread and you give them a stone? Similarly do they need a transfusion of blood and you inject them with water? Much esoteric theorising, "new age" universalism, is often a watering down.

God is found in the particular. It is the unique, and the one, and the individual that is important. The universal at its most extreme is exemplified by a flood, which covers all and takes it back to primal sources. It was Noah, the individual who obeyed the will of God, who trusted his own intuitions, and took active steps to follow them out, who survived to form the basis for a new creation.

{The Chancellor 28.7.93}

6

I want to talk today about the human aura, for it too is a human fluid, so to speak. It exists, something after the manner of frog spawn, in a sea of light. When you conduct your meetings, (I speak in particular of a magical group, although the principles are relevant to any coming together of persons), their success depends upon the quality of the immediately surrounding sea of light.

There should be an osmosis of astral light, (whose laws are analogous to the laws of physical liquid flow), between the various auras of all present. This may be experienced as, (and in part may be induced by), a feeling of fellowship and mutual love and respect. This not in any sentimental way, which lowers the quality or specific gravity of the astral light of the group as a whole. For sentimentality is more related to the solar plexus, below the diaphragm, than to the heart, the seat of the higher emotions, which is above the diaphragm.

The gentle eddy and flow of the astral light amongst all participants, (rather than a concourse of hard shells as would be the case in a more formal meeting), enables it to be moulded and caused to flow in patterns by higher beings who may be present and contacted.

Inner beings with levels of consciousness on the same level as the incarnate participants may well contribute directly themselves to the pool of astral light and assist in its circulation. But in circumstances of higher magic, or of mystical contact and intention, the higher entity contacted may not manifest at the level of the astral light - but come as a presence that irradiates and informs the pattern and substance of the group astral light. This brings about feelings of uplift, enlightenment, inspiration to those present, in their individual ways. Indeed, if the astral swirlings or patternings have been profoundly affected in this way, it can lead to some considerable feeling of change in the psychological vehicles, that will not always be comfortable. This is because the individual aura has been affected, either temporarily or more or less permanently by the experience.

It is for these reasons that group working is generally more effective than solitary working. The solitary worker is to some extent hoisting himself by his own boot straps. But not entirely, for inner help is always at hand - and aspiration, sincerely and constantly held, will bring inner help and guidance. As with a team of climbers, an individual can be helped by the presence of others, if necessary even being hauled up bodily on a rope in areas that exceed his ability or his strength. Whereas solitary working depends on the forces of the individual aura, unaided by companions of the way.

However, the actual presence and co-operation of inner beings, built up generally over time as faith, familiarity and knowledge increase, can bring about considerable progress. In extreme cases we have the witness of the mystics of the church, great and small, who have been lifted, their auras cleansed, informed, and changed, by the higher presence acting in any of the ways or the levels described for a magical group.

Ritual, be it complex or simple, hallowed by time or spontaneous, will have its part to play in all of these inner dynamics. For ritual is the expression of an inner pattern, and a pattern that is inspired by, or which represents, spiritual dynamics of a higher level.

Thus in ritual the force flows are more formalised and established, which can have a greater effect through their concentrated channelling, and one can give continuity and momentum to the self expression of a group. These patterns can also be aided by, and can attract and inform Elemental beings - which can lead to a wider dissemination of the patterns expressed within the ritual. This wider dissemination on the inner levels happens with any magical working, including *ad hoc* spontaneous rites, but these will not generally have the same power as regular formal rites, which gain strength through repetition.

As before said, these principles apply to the meetings of any human group, whether or not they realise, or intend, the involvement of inner plane beings. The world is a wider place than many realise, and incarnate spirits, if truth be told, are rather in the minority. Thus any meeting of people has its quota of inner participants, for better or for ill. All present have their auras with them, whether they realise it or not, and which are not, like ritual robes, put on and taken off for special circumstances. Like the physical body, the aura is there all the time. Emotional, or intellectual interchange will therefore be taking place.

Before the meeting starts these will be like eddy currents, of no uniform flow or purpose. But once proceedings commence, hearts and minds are formed into patterns, and a unified group mind is formed. This can be as effective upon the auras of all participants as any magical ritual.

In the case of musical or theatrical performance this can be a spiritual or up-lifting experience, making profound changes in the individual aura. A person can be changed by a moving performance. It will stay in the heart and mind for a very long time, affecting actions and attitudes to life itself.

Performances of mere entertainment, light music or a comedy show are harmless diversions, that can also lighten or lift the spirits, increase humanity and human awareness.

However, you may judge for yourself the kind of inner entity that is attracted to the salacious, the pornographic, the destructive, and the depressive. Do those who take part in it come out up-lifted or besmirched? Indeed it can be akin to what is conceived in popular imagination to be a "black magic" ritual.

{The Chancellor 29.7.93}

7

It is an ambience of trust, of the family grouped about the fireplace, that is the condition conducive to successful magic. Such was the atmosphere of the extended group, in cottage, in baronial hall, or tribe around a communal fire, listening to extempore telling of tales that led to the building of the myths and legends of the race.

The astral light is pooled in such a circumstance and directed by the leader, the story teller, or bard. The communal hearth acts as a focus, and indeed is the origin from which the meaning of the word "focus" derives.

You will thus appreciate that the fundamental requirements of magic are very simple. Whether it be verbal communication between the planes, or activity of the astral light that teaches or inspires. It is upon this basis that all else follows, no matter how complex the ritual, or extensive the organisation. It is when this fact is lost sight of, that desiccation or ossification sets in. When that which was once a living fire, shared by a few friends or fellow workers, followers of a similar ideal, becomes organised into an impersonal structure. Into an edifice instead of an organism. A robot, a machine, rather than a living being.

But by virtue of the simplicity of their basic needs lies the strength of the mysteries, and of intercommunication between the planes. If in any burgeoning group the contact should be lost; corroded like the terminals of a battery that will no longer pass power; or limed like the mouth of a tap that will give only a meagre trickle of water; there is always the opportunity for others, commencing from basic structures, to start again from scratch.

Such a situation is of course unfortunate - that a large and hitherto successful group inhibit the very things that it set out to demonstrate. Again it is like a spring that comes up in boggy ground that cannot provide a flow for it. The inspiration has been materialised, the waters silted up. It can be very difficult indeed to make the waters flow again in such a situation, and a new spring must be tapped at some other spot. A new rock struck with the wand of the magus to give forth a living flow.

{The Chancellor, 30.7.93}

8
How then is a new spring, a new source of living water to be found? How the rock struck? With which wand, and under what mandate?

It is by the gathering of a few friends with a common purpose. And with a faith in the reality and good will of those in the spiritual world whom they seek to make contact, and from whom they will receive protection, enlightenment and teaching. This gathering of friends in common purpose and respect is the natural warmth that is spoken of in alchemy. To warm the alchemical still of the "first matter", the prima materia. To hatch the cosmic egg of higher consciousness and contact - so that a live chick shall be born. The alchemical bird, that at first needs careful nourishing, but which will grow by due care and process into a powerful creature indeed, an immortal phoenix.

And this element of the alchemical bird being a phoenix is a further indication to you how the spark of the Mysteries, once lit, is passed on. For the original fire, even if largely smothered, banked up by its own ash so that it hardly gives out further light or heat or living flame, can burst forth again. Any ember from that source of inner fire can be fanned by those who know and care, into a new manifestation of the phoenix - which will rise in a blaze of wonder and glory as powerful as ever it was when first hatched, induced and evoked.

This is a natural path of progress in the Mysteries over the course of time. It is to be seen in the history of many occult and esoteric fraternities, indeed in the larger area of religious bodies themselves. The gradual banking down of the original fire, and then resurgence of the flame by the spirit in the heart of some reformer. This can have a major effect, as for instance in the case of St Francis of Assisi, or have more special local purpose, as in St Joan of Arc, allied to political destiny and purpose, or to particular demonstrations of the power and reality of the spirit. Such were the Curé d'Ars and the Lady Julian of Norwich, simple servers of the church, whose great love and faith kindled the holy flame to visible appearance anew.

And remember that we speak of outer demonstration in the material world. A once blazing spiritual fire may have become with time no more than what seems to be a bank of ash covered embers, yet within that pyre there may well remain considerable heat. It is a holy source of power for some considerable time - that will last even while individual embers may flame, catch light but soon be extinguished, like burning straws.

We use the analogy of fire at this point, to demonstrate the power of the spirit as manifest on Earth. It is an alternative image to water, which with its life-giving flow can also demonstrate the power of the spirit. Just as Jesus used the image of seed, in the parable of the sower who went forth to sow.

These three analogues, these figures of speech, examples of life giving elements in the world of matter, are all apt analogies of the expression of the spirit, of the Holy Spirit, and are fruitful and instructional to ponder.

Just as the living seed may fall on stony ground, among weeds, on shallow soil, or in good earth and so be a successful expression of burgeoning life, so may there be different conditions pertaining for the fire, the holy fires of Pentecost, or the water, the waters of baptism and new life.

The fire may catch on the domestic hearth, or the tribal or city pyre, duly prepared with reverence and intention. Or it may be of short and flashy duration amongst a few fragments of dry tinder, that give much flame but are soon consumed, having nothing of substance to feed the transforming flame. For fire is an element of transformation, and there must needs be something to transform.

Similarly with the seed. The kingdom of heaven was likened to a mustard seed, a tiny thing, but potential miracle of life that it may be through growth to a mighty tree, it needs the required conditions to do so. Of earth for the roots, and sun and rain and irrigation, and the loving care of those who tend it - unless it grows in the wild like a free act of God amongst the elemental kingdoms.

As in the analogy of water, we see the ways in which the spirit may be expressed in Earth. Fire, water, the seed, three great instructive emblems in the study of magic, which is the science of the transformation of consciousness. All are figures of what may happen to the expression of higher consciousness in the lower world of personality and the outer affairs of men.

{The Chancellor, 31.7.93}

9

The forming of a magical, or a mystical group, is like planting, nurturing and growing a plant from a seed. In the outer world you would take your pot of earth, good fruitful loam, for that provides the source of food for the growing seed when it sends forth its roots.

The containing pot is the physical location of your group, and the earth within is the basic character of those who are associated with it. Should they be of inappropriate character, they will provide a soil that is insufficient or even hostile to the growth of the seed. In the botanic world soil may be too acid or too full of lime, in which case certain types of seed, or spiritual group or growth, will not be sustained. This concerns the mental set, the temperament of those taking part. What their expectations, their previous assumptions may be. Whether they are mystically or occultly inclined. Whether sentimental, pious, in search of proof, or proud of open minded scepticism. Some can verge on the type of soul (or soil) that is not conducive to germination or growth at all.

As in the parable, there will be those who provide soil that is too stony, or that has no nutriment in it, or is like a quagmire of shifting sand, or of impervious clay, or drained by giving all to previous growth perhaps. Or those full of poison or disease, the ill-willed and the inherently destructive. Or with needs of their own that pull energy from the good earth around, and take from rather than give to the roots of the seed itself.

So much for the conditions on the outer plane. A suitable place of meeting, and suitable people of requisite good-will, faith and character to meet there. There remain the other factors of seed, water, heat and light. All of these pertain to the inner planes.

The seed is the latent inner contact. It may be in the form of an image, an aspiration or an idea. There are three levels of being of the seed itself - the kernel, pith and rind - equivalent to intellect, emotions, and representation. Any one of these can be effective at the very start, but all three will need to manifest before growth starts to break, expressed in one or more of the members of the group who provide the germinating bed.

Remember that seed can exist on its own, waiting the right circumstances for germination for a very long time. It has even been known for wheat from ancient Egypt, entombed in a pyramid, to germinate after four thousand years. Though as with seeds, it is the more recent spiritual impulse that is more likely to find the conditions of sustainable nurture and growth.

The three factors of idea, emotion and image will be the seed from which the living roots and shoots break from the seed into the group. Idea and emotion break through the initial outer image. The emotions pertain to the roots, which pass through into the compost of the mind and soul of the group, and which in time, like a root ball in a pot, will bind all together.

And remember also the fate of a plant that is not potted on, when the roots pack tighter and tighter within until no more nutrition is possible. The wise gardener pots on to a larger container, that holds more nutritional earth. This is the analogy of the growth of a group.

But again the image also holds good for those type of seeds that, by their nature, do not go on to grow large plants. There is a difference of quality here, that is not dependant on quantity. You may grow the seed of a blushing violet, of delightful form and scent, in a small pot. But if your seed is that of an oak tree, then at some stage planting on into open ground is going to be a necessity.

This is the equivalent of a religious group, or sect, that has a presence to be seen by all in the outer world. The average esoteric group is one that grows on to be containable in a large urn, or a reasonable spot in a garden, like a rose, or lily, or fruiting plant. Here the criterion is the quality of form and expression of the fruit and flower - not the size to which it might grow. The principle we seek to show is that of appropriate size of pot to seed, of group and location to seed ideas and aspirations.

The whole pattern of growth and characteristics is in the seed, and that is God-given - from a higher plane altogether. It is the divine or archetypal spiritual mandate that is expressed in idea, emotion, and containing basic imagery.

You can have whatever pot, or earth, you like, and feed it with what water and heat and light you like, but although you will affect the health and rate and state of growth of the plant, you will not change its nature. You can turn an acorn into an oak with due care and attention and passage of time, you will never turn it into an ash or a pumpkin.

As we have said, the roots pertain to the emotions, and are that which feeds upon the consciousness of the members of the group. The means of interchange is represented by the life giving water, which comes from above, and needs to be in circulation for healthy growth of the plant.

Without the plant, coming forth from the seed, the soil within the pot would be inert. It could stand out in sun and rain, and nothing would happen. The soil would become wet with falling rain or dew, and then dry out in warmth and sun. And this, we might say, is the lot of the ordinary man or woman of the world. They, like good soil, may be responsive to the gifts of heaven in the forms of sun and rain, but without the appropriate seed sewn within, no new life can be created.

Once the plant begins to grow, the seed begins to take emotional input from the group. To take it up, with the inclusion, most importantly, of elements from the individuals involved. As every gardener knows, phosphorus, nitrogen, potassium, are needed for healthy growth of root, leaf and flower, plus an important range of trace elements. All these are contributions of the soul itself. As members of a group - its earth, its loam - you contribute of your own being, the equivalent of the potash, the nitrogen, the phosphorus, the trace elements. And this is done by idealism, by your emotional commitment, expressed as devotion, loyalty, aspiration.

The other direction of the seed's growth is upward, the green shoots that grow into air and light - the element of intellect, of intuition, of reason (in its higher and lower sense). The warmth and the light are provided by the sun. But be aware too, that not all seeds or plants require unremitting sun-light. Some are natural denizens of shade, or their just and appropriate proportion of light and shade, of heat and coolness. A fern does not flourish in the heat of the sun, a sunflower wilts in the deep shade of the forest. And so with all the species of plant from lush lowland vegetation to those of alpine conditions and rarity. So do groups correspond to a particular habitat in terms of their origin and surrounding culture. An exotic bloom does not necessarily thrive in a temperate climate.

{The Chancellor, 1.8.93}

10

We now have a new entity, the plant itself, as part of our image of the functioning of an esoteric group. Let us recapitulate what this means.

There is the pot, the soil within, the seed from which the plant has grown, putting forth root and stem and leaf. There is the sun and the rain, the environment of the plant and its container. All of this is part of a unity, a healthy organism properly functioning.

The container is that which is provided by you, on the outer plane, be it hall, temple, domestic room, or other dedicated space for the work of the group when it meets together.

The loam is yourselves, your own character, what you contribute by your own presence within the container for nurturing the seed.

The seed is the seed idea, that comes into objective existence by factors beyond your control, in times and places beyond your ken. In the case of the Mysteries it is produced, as professional seedsmen develop and breed a plant species, by a body of just men made perfect, on the inner planes, under divine direction. In its outer appearance it is a body of knowledge and teaching and belief. This establishes its roots in the hearts and minds of the members of the group who feel drawn to it. (Should any not feel sympathetic to it, then you have the situation of lime or acid soil and a plant that may be lime or acid hating, with consequent difficulties for the flourishing of the plant, or the group).

The upward growth of the plant into leaf and stem is the development of potential consciousness of the group into the higher worlds. Here elements of the higher worlds nourish it. The rain might be described as the higher equivalent of emotion. Buddhi, intuition, or love-wisdom, are various terms that describe it in part. It falls onto the earth within the container, makes it moist and fertile, able to give of its nutrients to the plant. In alchemical terms this is the alchemical stage of *solutio*. This moisture in human terms could be expressed as mutual love and friendship, and dedication to a common cause. Without that love, the soil in the pot is a dead and arid thing, unable to contribute to its potential. This love and common aspiration helps to release the quality of each group member into the root of the plant, and this goes up as sap into stem and leaf to contribute to the growing of the plant.

At the same time the warmth of the sun and its rays represent the spiritual encouragement that comes from on high to all growth and endeavour below. In the first instance it warms the Earth in the pot itself, bringing conditions of growth and germination to the seed. This represents idealism and faith and enthusiasm - without which the water of the human emotions would be relatively cold - in extreme conditions frozen, unable to flow.

However, as in the plant world, there is a complex action and reaction of photo-synthesis in response to the light of the sun. The implicit wisdom in the seed of the plant, according to its species and nature, reacts to the spiritual stimulus. This enables the plant to breathe, to survive and to act as a living organism in health and well being that extend down to the very roots of the plant.

You now see the interior conditions for the growth and well-being of a group. There are also gardeners who feed the plant, sheltering it from too much sun or rain, striving to give it its best conditions for growth. These are the Inner Plane Adepti and certain beings of the angelic hierarchies. And by your participation in the group, as providers, in your personalities in Earth, of conditions of the soil itself, the growing medium, you are participators in your own small way with these spiritual beings,

The plant itself will burst forth eventually into flower and fruiting, and later seeding into greater proliferation than before, as a spiritual demonstration of the love and design and being of the Creator, and of all the creative hierarchies that seek to serve the Creator's vision and bidding. For we are talking of the equivalent of the heavenly garden, whose primal image, as far as the Earth is concerned, is the Garden of Eden. And what reason is there for a beautiful garden, but the beauty of its own existence?

{The Chancellor, 2.8.93}

11
It may be apparent to you by now that what we have been describing, in the visual detail of a growing plant, is an example of one form of magical image.

It is the most common form, of pictorial analogy, to render simple, by specific and concrete example, that which is abstract and complex. It is a form of reasoning and demonstration that is to be found in many walks of life, from the parables of the Bible, to the pictorial diagram in science depicting the complex forces at work within the atom. Examples are legion.

This is the most common form because it is the simplest, and is used simply as a means of enlightenment, not of power. Although it would be possible to use certain aspects of an enlightening or descriptive image in an experiential or empowering way.

For instance it would be possible, in single or in group meditation to use the simple image of the plant and flower in a more active way, by visualising a specific part of the process described and identifying with it.

We may take for example the unfolding of the flower from an enclosed bud. It is a simple exercise in magical dynamics to imagine yourself as the unfolding flower. As a simple exercise of meditation, perhaps stretched over several sessions for a beginner, or undertaken as a group exercise, to feel yourself gradually unfolding to become a fully opened flower, say a rose, with all its wondrous complexity of beauty and the spiritual fragrance that comes from it.

This is an exercise that not only exercises the visualising faculties, but by image and intention opens up the latent inner faculties, so that you may perceive the inner planes as the flower perceives the sun and the light. And as no act of meditation is ever solitary, so you may become aware of the inner equivalent of the bees, attracted by your blossoming, and of other flowers besides your own that are flowering. This is a true "communion of saints" for in one, and the original, sense, all who open their senses to the inner worlds are saints.

Nor should you forget the equivalent of the flower fairies of the outer world, who are by no means a figment of sentimental fancy. These beauteous and ancient beings, the servants of the Lords of Mind in untold aeons before human time and conception. The equivalent of these elemental creatures of the outer world will come to you as ministering spirits in the inner world, giving you your contact with the angelic realms.

Whilst above all are the attentions of the gardener, who looks upon all that He has created and brought to pass, of which you, each and every one, are a small, but unique and special contributor, loved and admired in the wonder of God, equally with any other part of His creation.

Learn to blossom then, my children, for that is the true state of your existence. And this again can be referred to the instructive image of the potted plant. For you may visualise yourself not only as the blossom but as the whole of the plant as well. The analogy seen as having an individual as well as a group application.

Your own inner being is represented by leaves, and stem, and roots within the earth, a kind of interior nervous system that passes from one state of being to another. Your roots in the Earth, your leaves and flowering in the heavens. Think upon that as an example of instruction, and use it too as an image of empowerment. Feel your own true being as a creature whose faculties span the planes - for that is an overriding and distinctive human quality. See that you use it. And this is the way - through the active use of magical images, in many forms and ways.

For the imagination is a God given capacity that spans the planes. It is effective within and beyond the material world. Go to the material world for your images, but do not be limited by the bounds of that world. That is to be pot-bound, stunted, completely failing in your wondrous human and spiritual potential.

{The Chancellor, 3.8.93}

12
Your imagination corresponds to the moisture in the soil, and the sap within the roots, stem, leaves and flower of the plant. No matter

what the plant is doing or creating there is imagination at work. For this is the means of creating the forms, as well as bringing and sustaining life to them - even if it becomes an automatic and unconscious factor after a time. And once formed, as in a leaf for example, the form cannot be changed by further imagination. Only grown according to type - or if imagination is withdrawn, allowed to wither.

You will realise that there are important magical dynamics to this function of imagination. That by the direction and control of images, you can develop your talents and abilities - or let them wither on the vine. There are limitations, in that you cannot change yourself into being what you are not - the archetypal pattern of your being is held in the fertilised seed - but you can, by direction of intent and imagination, develop your latent capacities to the full.

Disease cannot necessarily be controlled simply by action of the sap. This is brought about by an external factors, although the healthful function of the imagination and emotions can to some extent alleviate. Disease - or evil in the broader sense of the word - has its roots in spiritual deviation. The coming into existence of sources of mutation or parasitic corruption, that seek out any inherent weakness in the genetic pattern within the creative seed to serve their own existence and despoil the original creation.

"The wages of sin is death" on an evangelical poster may incite some secular amusement, but the words contain a truth. For evil, manifesting as disease in its victim host, is self-destructive - its kingdom cannot cohere. It can only spread or proliferate where it finds a hold. It can be a catastrophic unbalancing of equilibrium at the most elemental levels - in flood or forest fire, landslip or tornado.

Let it not be thought that disease is a punishment for individual sin, be it past or present. It can strike anywhere, and is no respecter of persons. There is the phrase of St Paul, that "ye bear one anothers' burdens", and this is an affirmation of the love and coherence of the family, the whole human family, indeed in a wider sense the whole creation.

It may well happen, that in the more limited specific case, physical disease, and particularly accident, can occur as a direct result of personal folly, but this is by no means the whole story in the longer term. No man is an island. If one has sinned, all have sinned. And if one bears a burden, he bears it for all. In this you may find a positive way, a realisation of service, in the bearing of affliction. You do so as the ass carries the ark, for the eventual betterment of all. It is a way of service - as the poet Milton said about his blindness, "They also serve who only stand and wait." They also serve who are the victims, the afflicted.

This is not to say that evil or affliction is a condition that does not cry out to heaven for vengeance - but that reckoning will come in the latter days. When all the harvest, the fruits of creation, are gathered in.

In the meantime, the tares grow with the wheat, and may even stunt it and choke it out. And your own fruits may not necessarily show as material fulfilment in the material world, or the expression of all of which you are capable, or of all that you personally deserve - although in the perfect divine plan that would have been so. But you can serve to your best by your attitude to what you are confronted with.

The types of circumstance with which you wrestle are the golden fruits of heavenly opportunity, although they may seem far from that to you in the material world. This, as has been depicted in the Graal legends, is because the land is sick. Nothing can go as had been intended in the Waste Land. It is a despoiled garden. A decayed and fallen Eden. And this because the King is afflicted. And the King is the archetype of the human race - the human kingdom. He is Adam, Adam Kadmon. The universal man, who was created to be a king of all, of a pleasant creation. The King of Eden. But who has fallen from that state.

Again these are magical images. More complex magical images. Those of spiritually healing myth and legend. And they function by directing imagination, (image making), and emotion, (creative energy), in the right direction for healing or for well being, on a group as well as individual level.

Imagination therefore, in the magical image of the plant, is the free flow of imaginal attention from root to flower. In the roots it seeks, and brings about expansion, means of sustenance in the physical world. In the stem it provides the backbone of upward spiritual aspiration - otherwise one would be content to grovel in the earth like beasts. In the leaves it develops the means of inner transformation, and growth from the upper air, from the spiritual light. And in the leaf itself is the pattern for the flower. The flower is modified leaf, brought about to be the crowning glory of the plant, a means for effective interchange, with bees and insects, interchanging pollen.

In a sense bees, and such insects, are functions of flowers. This is to look at things for a moment from the point of view of an elemental hierarch. An elemental hierarch, in human terms, is a fairly high ranked angel.

The flower also contains the new seed, the potential for further and future abundance, be it a hundred or a thousand fold.

{The Chancellor, 4.8.93}

13

The magical image of plant as representative of the human psyche can be modified to ally it to the magical image of the human spine, and particularly the inner aspect of the human spinal column. You have the nervous system at the level of physical patterning, but there is a more complex etheric patterning beyond that. For any physical organism has a two-fold aspect, of solid and liquid, that can be discerned as a framework for manifestation and expression on the physical plane. There is also air and fire, which form the etheric patterning for that framework. This level is more complex, more extensive, in its way, than the material expression, although as you know, that can be complex enough.

The detailed processes of the builders of form are intelligent and intricate indeed, and we ever are forced to simplify them when working on the level of the astral magical images. This applies even to a so-called "inanimate" stone. With all its complexity of atomic and molecular structure it is as extensive at its internal level as the starry universe appears to human regard. How much then does this also apply to the human organism, with its greater capacity for internal and subjective reaction!

However, simplicity and clarity are the desiderata of the magical image, for it is by that means that power and comprehension can flow. Thus in terms of magical image the human organism based around the spine can be likened to the plant we have so far described.

Here the roots of the plant are the complex system of nerves at the base of the spine, and much of the autonomic nervous system for the working of the internal organs and the body itself.

The plant/spine analogy has parallels, one being the diaphragm within the human body. In the plant this corresponds to the level of the soil in which the plant grows. All below is the realm of root, all above of stem, leaves and flower.

The very bottom roots, searching in the depths of the soil for nourishment of the whole plant, are the physical senses, in their aspect of touch.

The stem itself is the link of inner consciousness between what you call the outer and inner worlds. But as appropriately shown in our image, the outer world is that of air and sun, and inner world of water and earth. The terms inner/outer, higher/lower, are relative, like mirror images - subjective and mirrored reflection being different according to which side of the mirror one's spiritual being is focussed, so to speak.

The leaves of the stem represent the inner perceptions which take nourishment from, and interact with the upper outer air, and the spiritual sun. These pertain to psychic centres above the diaphragm. And you will see that it is along these lines that the whole structure of yoga is based.

For there, in yoga, one has a complex system of contrived magical images that correspond with points upon the spinal column, and to an extent with the endocrine glands. And by sustained meditation, concentrating upon these visualised images, at their various perceived levels, the inner and higher faculties are developed. Even, in certain instances, the development of little known outer ones, which is the modus operandi of certain feats of yogic wonder working. It is, however, only wonder working in the comparative terms of being relatively little known or recognised, in the materialist experience of the west. They are perfectly natural functions of the human organism, albeit developed to an unusual degree, as a concert pianist, or tight rope walker, each in their way, has developed a particular set of dedicated and advanced skills. And of course, as in all skills and potentialities pushed to their limit of expression, of the virtuoso, the master craftsman, an element of personal gift and adaptability of the individual organism also comes into play.

The head and brain itself, with an important node at the throat, is as important in its way as the diaphragm. Here is the most "inward" discipline or spiritual flowering of the whole inner human organism, and the burgeoning of the spiritual seed, its fruiting or crop. This is the treasure stored up in heaven.

{The Chancellor, 5.8.93}

14

You have the same structure depicted in the fruitful imagery and structure of the Tree of life. What the chakras and complex system of *nadis* is to the Eastern system, the Tree of Life and the geometric formation of its spheres and paths, is to the West.

On the Tree of Life the roots are to be found in Malkuth, the Flower in Kether. The elements of growth that contribute to the transmutation or transition of leaves into flower are in Chokmah and Binah. Indeed these can be regarded as the petals of the flower of which Kether is the stamen and the pistils. And the perfume of the flower, and the element of the beings that respond to it (cosmic bees so to speak) is the Ain Soph Aur, the Limitless Light.

Coming down the Tree, the side Sephiroth of Chesed and Geburarh are as the leaves of the plant, being aware of and reacting to the light and warmth of the upper air, the vehicles of a kind of spiritual photosynthesis.

The Sephiroth of Netzach and Hod are below the ground level, which is represented by Tiphereth. They are the searching/responsive activities of the roots of the plant. Your intellectual and emotional reaction and responses to relationships - the raw data of which is fed in through the senses at Malkuth.

In Yesod is the etheric/psychic structure - the subtler nervous system, including astral or imaginative inner linkages. All that is conceptualised in psychological theories as the subconscious or unconscious.

In a similar way the psychological equivalent of Tiphereth can be regarded as the superconsciousness, where such is recognised. But you have to remember that most psychological theory is formulated by those who have very little conscious awareness of anything beyond Tiphereth.

Tiphereth, for all practical purposes as far as you are concerned, is the level of higher vision, where you can build magical images that relate to the higher worlds. The images of Yesod (and also Malkuth, which has its own subliminal images too) relate more to the wants and desires of the lower world, from sexual fantasies to dreams of material possessions. But for the most part, let it be said, to valid and healthy reactions to the everyday world as you know it.

The task of mystical or esoteric training is the raising of the focus of consciousness, the point of the ego, the "I" awareness, up the Middle Pillar. In the animal or the animal man/woman, the ego centre is toward Malkuth. In the more destiny oriented person, it approaches Tiphereth. In moving into the higher reaches above Tiphereth it aims to produce the spiritually motivated personality.

This may produce a saint, an initiate, a visionary, a prophet, even a martyr - although much will depend on the ability to change the focus of the ego at will. Someone centred permanently in the higher reaches may not be too practical in the lower worlds. Here you have the hermit, or the recluse, who may seem in terms of the outer world to verge even on madness, or at least eccentric delusions. Whereas others, capable of very high spiritual consciousness can also have a formidable effect upon the lower worlds by the spiritual power they can express at these levels. Thus you have the type represented by a Joan of Arc, or a Mother Teresa. Other examples come from religious teachers - innovators such as St Paul, although the supreme exemplar is Jesus, the Christ.

There is a certain dichotomy between the values and the abilities associated with the upper world and those of the lower. Function at all levels is rare, and in present conditions, as rare as the occurrence of a polymath - a consciousness that is equally at home in arts, sciences, languages, mathematics, and many practical skills. And just as there is diversity of outlook at even one level, the notorious lack of communication between artist and scientist for example, so is there difficulty of understanding between higher and lower worlds.

But if the saint or idealist seems incomprehensible to the worldly-wise, think also how the general activities of humankind may appear to those centred in the spiritual worlds. How the bestialities of warfare, cupidity, lust - reactions almost entirely centred at the animal level - appear to the angels. Indeed to higher vision the lower world of Earth can appear like a cosmic snake pit.

{The Chancellor, 6.8.93}

15

In much of this, the Tarot image of the Hanged Man is relevant. Here you have one whose values are in the upper world, although he appears to be in the lower world. The Tarot image of the Wheel of Fortune can also be applied. In one sense of the card it represents not simply the fortunes of the material world, but the complete cycle of the life process. From spiritual rulership at the top to slavery to the material senses to the bottom - the prodigal son among the swine. Whilst the two figures at the sides represent the soul progressing downwards or upwards. This is the path of soul experience, of involution and evolution, in terms of the progress of the soul in worldly or material experience.

Remember that the wheel continues to turn. It is a process or mechanism that is put in place by the ancient Lords of Mind. The progress of the individual soul about it goes at its own pace. Is not bound to the wheel.

Thus the point on the wheel at which the soul of a reader of these papers is likely to be, is just beyond the mid point on the upward ascending part of the cycle.

A soul completely content with the material kingdom, (and such could lead a very successful life in material terms, fully at home in the earth), with no conscious desire or knowledge of higher things, would be located at the bottom.

Those souls more concerned with the material plane are those on the downward arc, who have left the considerations of the spiritual behind, and are obsessed with material desires but not in a position to fulfil or control them as yet.

Those on the upward part of the cycle have their eyes on the heavens, but for this reason can seem to an extent impractical. The type of soul represented by the Hanged Man would be a well-functioning one placed at the left hand upper quarter, particularly as seen by someone in the lower right hand, descending quarter.

The greater part of the human race in incarnation is clustered about the lower nodal point. The more contented ones actually upon it. Others, with unfulfilled desires (which may be inflated by glamour) going down towards it. And there are those just past it, who realise that there is something more to life and the soul's desires than material possessions or power.

Some tend, because of their own position on the Wheel, to look at others on other parts of the Wheel in a certain judgmental way. However, remember that God, who sits as it were at the centre of the Wheel, and who conceived it and is ultimately responsible for its turning, loves all, whatever their stage on the way. For all are of the star seed, sparks from His own divine fire, blown into the circular swirling, to experience and progress at their own rate and according to their own insights and desires.

Another Tarot image that takes account of the upper and lower worlds is that of the Star, the maiden who kneels by the still waters of manifestation. The stars in the cosmic sky beyond her are no ordinary stars, and she kneels by no ordinary pool. The stars are cosmic potential - the mind of the Creator, constellated for the purposes of material creation. And the still waters that reflect the maiden herself and the stars are the waters of material potential.

There is a parallel in classical mythology, of Narcissus staring in the pool, enamoured of his own reflection. The Star Maiden, however, is not in such a position. She smiles benignly, the Tree of Knowledge is behind her, and upon it the bird (or butterfly) that signifies the human soul in all its potential. She is pouring water into the pool of manifestation. This is star water, star seed, the swarms of divine sparks, reflections of the stars, each one of which will pass its period of growth and evolution within the waters, before eventually bursting forth again.

This bursting forth is depicted in another image of the Tarot, that of the Last Judgement, where the dead are rising from their material graves. Thus is Osiris freed from his coffin, to be rendered free and creative again - for Osiris is a particular form (or magical image) for the whole of the human race, or swarm of divine sparks.

Osiris in this respect is also a Lucifer, or Serpent in the Garden figure - a representation of the fall into matter, aside from any evil. In the Egyptian legend, the counterpart of the serpent of Genesis is the evil Set, but in this respect the Egyptian legend is less subtle than that of the Hebraic, which if truth were told is a later refinement of the cruder Egyptian formulary of belief. Remember Moses came out of Egypt as did all the tribes of Israel, the custodians of the Holy Book. They thus developed a deeper and more subtle awareness of God than the ancient pagan spiritual teaching.

This is a natural progress in the consciousness of mankind, towards a realisation of the unified and loving nature of the one and universal God, unfragmented into pagan pantheons or multitudinous spirits of trees or locations or fetishes.

Such spirits exist, they are local spirits and gods, but are not there for human worship. They are simply fellow travellers, so to speak. The current wave of neo-paganism, and indeed the mythological and legendary element in the secret and ancient wisdom, is to maintain an awareness of what otherwise might be forgotten. Because you learn not to worship your spiritual or elemental neighbours, does not mean that you should condemn them or ignore them. You should have grown to accommodate a wider perception.

The Star Maiden is thus, in ancient Egyptian terms, a form of Isis. An embodiment of the material and feminine principle - but an Isis of the heavens, Uranian Isis. And here, ancient Egyptian legend had much, in the various legends of Isis, that is unsurpassed in any later recension of the holy wisdom. This includes the Hebraic, where it breaks in, to a degree, in the Song of Solomon. A love song that should be directed to the heights.

{The Chancellor, 7.8.93}

PART TWO: APPROACH TO THE INNER ABBEY

16

I wish now to speak about the Spirit of the Temple.

What is a temple? It is a place set apart for holy mysteries. For a conjunction, for a marriage. For it is a bridal chamber as well as a sepulchre. It is a church. An alchemical laboratory. Any point in form about which a structure is raised for the meeting of different modes or levels of being in loving concourse.

In its broadest sense it is the very universe itself, which is indeed constructed in a holy place. For it is set apart within the body of the Creator himself. Thus upon holy ground measured out from Himself by the All-encompassing Creator do the structures and forms of the worlds develop.

And the myriads of divine sparks are blown from the mind of God into this winnowing ground for the interplay of creation. For the laying out of the Garden of Eden in the first instance. And thence after the Fall, all further creation, the mighty structures of angelic beings.

All takes place within the divine "voluntary absence". The "No-Thing" of God. What in the Qabalah, on the Tree of Life, is represented by the Three Wondrous Veils of what are somewhat unsatisfactorily called "Negative Existence". But if all were known, they veil the very bosom of God, the blood and flesh of the transcendent Creator.

You will appreciate that here we are at the limits of what magical images can usefully describe or encompass. Nonetheless these disjointed fragments, like wisps of cloud, may draw your eyes to the heavens and to the Sun behind the Sun, that lies, golden and shining, with the fiery power of creative love. And the whole of the Creation depends, for its very existence and sustenance, on the Being beyond all beings, the ultimate embodiment and source of light and life and love.

You will also be aware of the great feminine imagery that is associated on the Tree of Life with the Sphere of Binah - Understanding. Here is the archetype of the great temple, "not built with hands, eternal in the heavens". And it provides the forms for all the creatures of creation to meet or give praise or thanksgiving to God.

Many of the great feminine images have been ascribed, or taken over or adapted, by the Cult of Mary: as Mother of God, Divine Bride of God, and prototypical Handmaiden of God. Here is the true server, believer and initiate; the priestess above all priests and priestesses; and to whom pertain the ideas of a building or a temple. To quote from the litany of Lareto, the Tower of David, the Tower or Gate of Ivory.

Here is the archetype of the temple itself, in whatever form it may be adapted to serve the local, lesser, limited views of mankind throughout all of time. Thus it is behind the humblest wayside shrine, or indoor sanctuary, be it permanent or transitory. Behind the lighting of a candle, the breaking of bread, the falling on one's knees with intent. All are an expression, a part of, the great primordial temple, shrine or abbey.

And this structure is the primal magical image. The magical image of which all other magical images form a part - for religious or mystical instruction, the grades of initiation, or by whatever other mode of language you wish to choose to describe the coming of the soul to its fulness. Be it as the prodigal returning, the pilgrim, the way-shower, the saint. All manner and modes of humankind and their ways of returning to God, and recognising their relationship with God, can be constructed into a journey to, and throughout, this holy and mighty edifice.

In another sense it is the body of Our Lady, the Holy Wisdom, whose head is full of the stars of Chokmah, and who kneels at the Gateway to the Heavens, of the Ain Soph Aur, being crowned by her Lover. These are the heights of love that are expressed in the mystical meaning of the Song of Solomon - the love song of God and the Bride of Creation.

It is meet however, that we use a succession of less volatile magical images as a means whereby to step-down and control the power. For entry into the direct reality of the Divine Love in action would be akin to seizing a high tension cable. It would mean your immediate destruction, your resolution back to basic fundamentals - into an "uncreate" being - in the body of God in the relatively "Unmanifest". This would truly be a Lightning Flash, a Lightning Struck Tower, to take an image from the Tarot.

In this sense the story of the Tower of Babel is not so much one of ordinary human pride and ambition upon a material level. It represents a spiritual pride, an attempt to rise up, to climb to spiritual heights too early, too irreverently, in a combination of spiritual prurience and blasphemy. You have similar dynamics in the story of those who touched the Ark of the Covenant and were struck down. And of others in pagan myth, such as Actaeon, torn apart by seeking to gaze upon the naked goddess.

As it is written of God, in the Scriptures, "You shall not look upon my face and live". So that even Moses - the archetypal wise man, priest, adept and servant of God, could only see Him indirectly - after He had passed. And there are also the ancient traditions of Isis, whom "no man has seen unveiled".

To look upon the face of God would be akin to looking with physical human eyes upon the face of the Sun, or into a laser - blindness. An overload of the carrying capacity of human consciousness, and the created structures of being.

And so to look upon Isis, or Sophia the Divine Wisdom, we see her veiled, in the structure of the archetypal temple "that is not built with hands". And this can lead us to a gradual, bearable revelation, as we grow in spiritual stature and perception. Until all our crooked ways are made straight, and in the most holy of holies we may know, even as we are known.

{The Chancellor, 8.8.93}

17

Let us take then the magical image of "the holy place". It will be apparent that when we build an edifice of praise and worship upon the physical plane, it is a fitting means and witness of affirmation and praise. It is built by dedicated effort. It is a sacrifice of time and material to the greater glory of God, to that which is beyond the material plane.

It follows that a similar structure, upon the holy ground of the dedicated and prepared imagination, will have a like effect.

Now when such a physical building is completed, it is to the honour and credit, and even the glory, of those who conceived and constructed it. However it becomes a whited sepulchre, a charnel house of dry bones, unless and until there is living and lively worship within it.

So too is it with the structures of the imagination. It is one thing to construct them, which has its reward. It is another thing to use them. This is their purpose and brings rewards far greater.

The first is like the student of the magical arts, or his brother the mystical devotee, who passes from instructor to instructor, from book to book, and system to system in search of knowledge and power - staying at no place long enough to use it as a channel of inner contact and communication. One type of these, those who are in love with the Path itself, are not true seekers of the goal to which it leads. Yet a true dedication will bring right usage, even in the most unpromising and unlikely of structures of outer belief.

The mystical and the magical may appear as strange suburbs of misrule to those who are orthodox, but the heart that is true can fly to heaven on the most unlikely of vehicles - be it witches' broomstick or the chariot of Elijah. In the enthusiasm of the most homespun philosophical sect - as transitory as a butterfly compared to the eagle of orthodoxy - there are the means for the soul's flight.

So orthodoxy of teaching is not a major criterion for the way of the soul. It is belief itself that supplies the power. Belief and faith, and the action which follows it.

This applies to the churchgoer, as it also applies to the magician and the mystic. The humblest parishioner who attends the services is greater in stature than the one who merely speculates upon theological doctrine in however informed a manner. This is an instance of the parable of the widow's mite - and of the difficulty of a rich man entering the kingdom of heaven.

The riches so represented may be intellectual ones. To have read all the holy fathers and the scriptures and their commentaries implies richness indeed, yet is nothing if it does not lead to the sanctuary. The poor widow had no learning, nor opportunity for it, but her life was wholly dedicated to what she believed in and she expressed it in action. An action that concerned sacrifice. A giving greatly of her substance and her time.

The gatherer of riches, be they material or intellectual, sacrifices his time certainly enough, but the direction of effort is inward. This is the difference from the effective worshipper, who gives out - and can then receive the gifts and the substance of the spiritual world. The acquisitive seeker draws in, but it is as of the fairy gold that turns to dust and ashes or dry leaves. He has drawn in the lesser in substitute for the greater and what he now has is of little worth.

Thus if any reach for what we have to say as a means of gathering knowledge, we say they are gathering up dry sticks and withered leaves. But those who are prepared to put into action that which we describe will be planting spiritual seeds in the Earth, that will come forth as living wood and leaf and flower.

So seek not to judge, by reference to other works, whether or not to believe what we say. But test the truth of our words by active work of the imagination. Be bridge builders between the planes. Constructors of the inner church, the inner temple. And then will come to you all manner of proof and gifts of what and whom you seek.

The way is built upon the substance of the imagination. Upon what is then learned and imparted in vision and contact can the intellectual structures be made. But the intellect itself is a superstructure. And great and towering though its edifices may be, unless they are founded upon living faith and belief they are as towers upon shifting sand. Matchstick castles in the air.

One might as well seek to write an account of foreign parts and climes without ever having been there. As with outer travel, so with inner, you have to tread the way, and you will be surprised at the reality of that which you find.

There is rarely "otherness" or "reality" in the intellect. It seeks to explain, to make familiar, to build structures around that which is found. It cannot generate its own reality - unless it come from above. For its true roots lie in intuition.

For the consciousness limited within the world this is not an easy mode of operation. The limited consciousness may spin theories or subtle philosophies - but rarely, very rarely does this lead to experience of the truth. This is a more lowly way – in a journey through images. You have eyes and ears to see and hear, and hearts and minds to interpret your senses to you. Use them - in inner and outer ways - to gain the full benefits of your incarnation.

{The Chancellor - 9.8.93}

18

We will commence by building and entering the Sacred Abbey. This is a magical image that, besides having its prototype expressed upon the physical plane in numerous examples throughout the world, is also fashioned in the world of the imagination. It is a design or pattern that was first conceived in the heavens, but is increased and contributed to by all who have worshipped, worked or walked with reverence within it.

We take as our model the pattern of the great constructions for which the High Middle Ages had a particular facility. It was indeed part of the historical mission or destiny within the Divine Plan of this period. The Divine Plan is the restitution of the fallen world back toward the original perfection, and these buildings served as bridges between Heaven and Earth. A Heaven that might be conceived as a true and real terra firma, and an Earth that is and was like a floating island, that had slipped from its attachment to the main land and which was being secured by having the links remade, by these bridges or means of access to the heavenly main land.

Each abbey or cathedral has its own unique individuality. (We shall henceforth use the term "abbey" because although cathedral fits the usage as well, an abbey has the tradition of a connection with a contemplative order - which adds far greater power and depth). It is an application of what we spoke of in the beginning, about the flow of the waters of consciousness. An abbey is like a deep pool in a garden. A pool containing life of another order of existence, that, standing in the common light of day, we may gaze upon in wonder as we look into the depths at the hints and shadows of another mode of life.

Thus the vision serves its purpose, for unlike any garden pool, here are links to a greater world, the heavens themselves. But insofar that any garden pool has its own characteristics, is an expression of its immediate milieu, so is every abbey unique in that it is a separate pool of consciousness. One in which the pilgrim soul can be immersed, cleansed, refreshed, baptised, made new.

This is sensed by the crowds who still flock to these places, despite the secular assumptions of contemporary society. These are a temporary shallows, we have to say, that will lead in time to new depths. For humankind is like a river, which will in time lead, by whatever devious meanders, to the universal encompassing sea. The modern consciousness in its present historical diversion senses its own shallowness and seeks for pilgrimage in the guise of what is now called tourism. A shallow substitute in its way, for the ancient pilgrims faced a harder journey than is found or expected today, but what it lacks in quality is made up for in quantity. And the pursuit of being "taken out of themselves" is rendered faster, more varied, than ever it could have been in olden days. The same human needs and instincts remain in search of expression. It is only the mode and means that vary, according to the climate of specific historical times.

The same applies, although in slightly different ways, to those who travel to ancient sacred sites, or to historical buildings where important events of state took place. Each of these in their way are centres of power, within the body of the human consciousness. Pools or basins hollowed out by great events, or persistent custom, or dedicated ceremony, which can still contribute to the sacred cultural heritage.

And a spring of such kind is increased by its use. This may be by the intelligent and devoted application of a few individuals, as in the upkeep of some obscure ancient site or shrine, or the wider flow of masses, uncomprehending in the main, to major public sites. Even though the conscious contact may be shallow, little realised at the time of the visit, much may be gained by the individual soul. Some resonance will remain that may in future time and in another place, (perhaps not even of this world), cause the recognition of a heavenly pattern within the soul and of its true origin.

The same applies, and particularly so perhaps, to children. Although by their very stage of growth and nature they may not be consciously attuned to the inner dynamics of a place, nonetheless they will be more open to it, on an accepting childlike level.

Did not the Christ say "Suffer little children to come unto me"? This was a lesson to the disciples that children were not necessarily "out of their depth" when being taken into serious holy things. But that "of theirs is the kingdom of heaven". That is to say, that their level of acceptance, of brightness of imagery, of make-believe if you will, provides the key whereby the soul can open heaven's gate.

To become as little children. This does not mean to revert to childish ways, but to retain, or regain, the child-like elements of wonder and of faith. Free of the restrictive structures of the mind that, originally built to give protection and shelter, now obscure the light.

{*The Chancellor* - 10.8.93}

19
Let us then picture ourselves approaching and entering the great abbey, the temple, the place set apart, that is not built with hands. For it is a place where we can meet you.

And when we say it is not built with hands, we do not mean that it is an ephemeral vision, an idealistic fantasy. Its imaginative fabric may not be of bricks and mortar and carved stone but are capable of such material appearance, as witness the many examples of the structure and pattern that have appeared on the physical plane, from Beauvais to Chartres, from Westminster to Notre Dame, from Cologne to Coventry, from Tewkesbury to Glastonbury. These are materialised visions, bridges from the spiritual and the Unseen. Examples of talismanic magic, symbols in stone, far greater in effect that any superstitious trinkets that pass, in the fancies of the foolish, for what is hidden or occult power.

What we describe, and experience now, is a magical image. Something that is held in common between material and spiritual consciousnesses. You build, hold and perceive the pattern in the imagination. We do the same, as do many elemental builders on the inner planes. And so an edifice is built by those of heaven and earth together in which all can meet.

And the same dynamics can apply if you enter a holy place upon the physical plane, one of those for example that we have mentioned. And there can be a greater ambience and opportunity there than meditating in your private chamber. You gain a great deal by visiting such holy places, even if you do not realise it at the time. But great though these opportunities are, there can also be the distraction of other visitors, whilst in your own private meditation room there can be a purity, and an individual ambience, as between family and friends, rather than a public outing.

For those of you who have the opportunity to meet in a congenial, informed, well trained and spiritually attuned and dedicated group, you have what may be close to ideal conditions. Hence the importance of the magical group, or the meeting for meditation and prayer, provided it is well run and well contacted.

But you need to get the balance right, and this takes time and skill. Nothing involving co-operation of independent spirits is ever easy, automatic, or to be taken for granted. Hence the tests and trials of the way, as you learn discretion and discernment, amongst other virtues. The goal is to be found in the images of the Tarot. Of Temperance being the first ideal, where everything is balanced, leading to the Victory procession of the Chariot once the group has gained momentum, signified also by the processing of the conjoined Lovers - those of the inner and outer planes in communication and action, celebration and a sense of direction.

So let us see ourselves upon the paving of the approach to our abbey. We approach from the North, the direction of matter and greatest symbolic darkness, and make our way towards the western end. But not for us, this day, is the great West door opened. That is for grand and special occasions of high ritual and purpose.

To our left and right are yew trees, emblematic of great age. And beyond them grave stones, also putting us in mind of the destiny of man. For death is the path which all mankind must follow, which will come as certainly, more certainly indeed, than tomorrow's sun will rise. These stones put us in mind of our ancestors. Our friends who have gone before. Our kith and kin. And of the ties, forged in flesh and blood and life experience, that go beyond the grave. For it is beyond the grave that we shall pass in our journey, and to eternal truths and realities older even than the ancient yew trees.

The doorway we approach is surrounded and protected by a porch. It is as if we approached the open side of a great stone box. There are flag stones to support our feet, and a stone ceiling above, that supports a symbolic arch, whereon is sculpted in low relief the figure of Virgin and Child. Although alternatively you may see a Risen Christ. For this is a particular feature of the Abbey that is not built with hands, its features may have a dual or even multiform appearance. One time you look and it is one thing, and the next time you look it is something else. This may be according to your need, or to give instruction in a lesson.

But by no means does it mean that this place is ethereal. Rather is it a place of very solid magical and mystical realities. An enchanted place - in the true sense of that term. For "en-chant-ment" derives from "holy singing", and that is the truth behind the conventional image of the angels singing praises about the throne of God. They sing in praise of what they see with their spiritual and unsullied eyes. And by their en-chanting they build the forms by which mortal man can climb a ladder, Jacob's ladder, to the stars. And recall that Jacob's ladder had for its base, or his pillow, a stone. And rising up and down from it were myriads of angels. This became the site of a holy place, a "Beth-el" or house of God. The archetypal one.

Upon each side of the porch as you enter you will see bench seats. These are for the weary and heavy laden, or those who simply wait without. There are notices affixed to the walls, which in this holy place are the equivalent of holy scriptures. And those who wait outside are the devout who have not yet quite mustered the strength of faith and vision to enter in. Indeed this porch is like the outer church. It provides a place for those who worship by instinct, or by convention, or even by intellectual conviction, but who have not yet developed the mystical consciousness that enables full entry to this place of the heart in open vision and instruction.

Before us is the door that leads within. It is large and is of oak, heavily studded with nails, as mighty and strong in its way as the great West door, of which it is a smaller replica. It holds the holiest of holy things within, and keeps all that is unworthy out, no matter how hard it batter against the portal by main force. The way in is small, strait or narrow, a door within a door, large enough only for one individual to pass at a time. There to pass the stern discerning eye of a guardian, protector, sacristan of these holy mysteries.

And so, lifting your feet carefully over the high step, you bow your head to go through the low and narrow door, an inevitable gesture of humility as you enter into the sacred place within. Here I shall undertake to be your guide, but later, when you have learned the means of passing about these inner ways, you may go where and as you will. (I almost said alone, but that is a misnomer, an impossible state, with only an illusory appearance upon the outer plane. As nature on Earth abhors a vacuum, so no-one is ever alone. The Spirit of God is ever with them. At a call, the holy saints and angels will be by your side.)

Let us pass within.

{The Chancellor, 11.8.93}

20

The expanse of the abbey lies before us. It is grand and magnificent, holy in the true and proper sense of the word ("wholly"), and as such beyond the dimensions of normal human consciousness. Particularly a consciousness that comes straight from the constricting and narrow limitations of the material world - from confinement in the "garments of skin". And like a diver surfacing from a great depth, your progress must be in stages, otherwise you may experience the equivalent of "the bends", brought about by different spiritual pressure.

This is an interesting parallel technically speaking. The diver's problem in the physical world is a matter of the amount of oxygen contained in the blood. In the metaphysical realm a similar condition pertains, for blood is the vehicle for the spirit (as well as life giving oxygen), although the situation is somewhat in reverse. There is more pressure spiritually the higher that you go in the heavens. There

...cally the deeper you go in the sea. Once more ...ion of inner and outer conditions.

...led from our gaze for the present by these, so high that they might almost ...ens, forms a passageway for us to our ...ckwise ambulation around this holy ...:hern aisle.

...wish, but the inner eye cannot quite ...that is supported by the pillars. Just ...1 you look upward on a clear day your ...n of colour, the colour blue - so in ...es but the sensation of gold - a kind ...ight well be the floor of heaven, but ...:ion, it is just a very high ceiling. ...is northern aisle, in a small group, ...f like-minded readers of these words, ...me is but an illusion in these inner ...sion, but this place can be entered from many points in external time.

Time is like a linear cut-out of a two-dimensional carnival pageant that can be seen curving round the external grounds of the abbey. This is difficult to describe, and more so to explain, but we do best, I fancy, simply to present you with the images, as they appear on the inner planes. Reflecting upon these images, (and "reflecting" is an accurate word), strange though they may seem, can cause you to gain another perspective upon what seems to your material consciousness to be an all-encompassing quantum. It is far from being that, you have my word. But as a young child has first to learn to come to terms with modes of perception on the physical plane, so does man have like problems when passing from physical life into the conditions of the inner planes.

And once focussed upon the inner planes, it is an additional skill to be able to look from there and see accurately and well into the outer. It is rather like staring into a dim and murky pool, with qualities that not only refract but distort the light. However these are in accordance with codifiable laws laid down by the builders of form upon the etheric sub-planes. One's sight is obscured by having to gaze through the etheric, the level of scaffolding and struts, so to speak, that hold the structures of the outer world together in coherence.

Thus communication between inner and outer worlds is a specialist task, whether one is upon the inner or the outer planes, that is to say, looking out or looking in. And why it is that sometimes one may have confusion or distorted communication, from those whose desire for service exceeds their trained or natural abilities. This is a problem which affects all. One can even have disoriented angels, as well as disoriented and confused mediums, adepts and initiates.

Thus is magic, in all its forms, a difficult and noble science. It is an intimate attempt at penetrating the Veil of Isis. It is a way that is not forbidden - only difficult. It is like a man standing at a very thick wall, with a hollow tin or glass placed to his ear, striving to receive communication from the other side. That is the situation with ordinary untrained man. As one progresses so the wall becomes thinner, more translucent and transaudient, until it is of the texture of a fine veil. But one can pass through it in full consciousness (I speak not of temporary states of trance, vision or psychic perception), only at death.

{The Chancellor, 12.8.93}

21

We proceed to a point where there stands another sacristan, a guardian. And he is demanding something of each one of us, in the form of a token or small coin. If the coin be small in size it is not small in value, for it weighs in terms of significance as much as the widow's mite. And in terms of ancient mythology it is the coin that is taken from the dead by the ferryman before he takes them across the river between the land of the living and that of the dead. It represents in one sense our right to outer life, yet it also contains an encapsulation, a sacramental recording, of all that we have experienced in life.

In the condition immediately after death known in ancient Egyptian times as the Judgement Hall of Osiris, the outer reaches of the ante-chamber of the post mortem condition, it is as if the souls listened to this recording being replayed as they reflect upon all the lessons they have to learn from their incarnation into matter. And when a Higher Self or human Soul, or Spirit of God, is represented to the inner eye in anthropomorphic form, it may be seen to bear about its neck a kind of necklace or chain of office.

In certain Tibetan Buddhist or Hindu religious images it may be depicted as a necklace of skulls. And here too is to be found the inner sacerdotal meaning of the somewhat bizarre Tibetan tradition of drinking from cups made from skulls. Putting aside the more external element you may associate with Gothic horrors - recall the holy significance of the head. Then see the significance of the skull as that which contained all the potential and capability of a soul during one earthly life. You will see it then as a kind of sacramental cup, or Graal, sacred and unique to that one spirit of God in one unit of experienced space and time, in this particular corner of the cosmos.

So the bizarre imagery should not be shied away from or found repulsive. It is the "bare bones" of experiential reality. And turning to the imagery of Tarot once again, the custodian, or figure before us, is that of Death. And in the card, what is Death exacting? He is scything or mowing down the physical elements of the bodies, so that they may return to the elements within the ground. It only seems a sinister figure, or one so full of horror, if one has so little faith as to assume that the spirit and soul are mutilated and destroyed as well.

They may sink into the after-death condition, the one that we have described, of contemplation and review of the past life. In Catholic tradition this is referred to as Purgatory, and the preparation for their sacrament of Confession plays much the same role as the internal review that esoteric schools teach their students to undertake at the end of each day. Whatever its name, it is a major and important phase by which all the spiritual and everlasting fruits of the immediate past life are gained. It is therefore like a winnowing floor, or a place of preparation and purification. Here old sins and assumptions are sloughed off as they are seen and reviewed in a spiritual and holy light. And what remains at the end are true grains of living spiritual wheat, separated from the dross or the husks by the process of the threshing floor.

In passing the figure on this occasion you are not committing yourselves to death, for you come under special custodianship, under the seal of what is known as initiation. By this means you can, in some measure, pass in and out between one world and another whilst still in incarnation. But remember you do so through the intermediary faculty of vision, and not in absolute reality. That you will experience once only, at the time of your physical death. Although the visionary experience that you gain in the meantime, during physical life, may stand you in good stead, preparing you for the reality that will eventually befall you, and through which you, as a personality, will finally pass.

It is because of this that initiation is likened to a death. And the more committed the initiate, whether occultist or mystic, the more could he or she be likened to the "living dead". This is a phrase that understandably may seem bizarre to the less spiritually discerning, whose values are focussed entirely in the outer world, but it means simply one whose sense of reality and values is on another plane - whose treasure is stored in heaven, where moth and rust cannot corrupt it. And the relevant Tarot image for this is, as we have earlier said, the Hanged Man.

Now to those whose vision is in the outer world alone, or in the more limited conventions of religious faith that are little more than watered down secular assumptions, such an attitude may well seem self-defeating, introspective and unhealthy. And of course in pathological or neurotic situations so it may be. There are indeed the weak or ailing souls who reject the joys and the responsibilities of full life in the physical world. These are the outer equivalent of what, on the inner, are referred to by the Tibetans as "hungry ghosts". Anaemic, pathetic creatures, seeking sustenance in a world that is not fully open to them. The "un-dead" seeking life, and the "un-living" seeking death. Each, in their way, attempting to avoid the immediate lesson, that of spiritual responsibility – which, if they really knew, is a call to joy and fulfilment.

On the physical plane, these are spirits reluctant to manifest. And the esoteric and artistic fringes are indeed full of them, for there they can see apparent sustenance for their illusions. On the inner planes, they are souls who will not go to the Judgement Hall to listen to their own recording, but having died unfulfilled, or inadequate, or filled with remorse, or possibly with lusts or visions of power, (which leads to another type of "hungry ghost"), they beat like moths upon a lighted window seeking an illusion of physical reality.

But you, having given your token to the Guardian of the Threshold, (and if you look at it you may see it to be of gold, imprinted with the face of the Sun), may pass by him. And you need have no fear of not returning. By the fact of being incarnate in a physical body still, you will be able to return to it. For you are here in vision, and in a guided and protected vision, and not in an ultimate and irreversible reality.

{The Chancellor, 13.8.93}

22

Having passed the Guardian, we realise that we are also at the portal to the Tower of the Great Abbey. We have the choice of continuing a circumambulation of the ground level of the mighty abbey, or of ascending the Tower. Whenever you come to this place, either option will be open to you. We shall attend to both, but first we will make an ascent of the tower.

This is at first a steep ascent, through a working area hung with bell ropes and with various types of machinery. It seems to have something to do, either with the working of the mechanism of a clock within the tower, or with the means of providing heating and lighting and other services to the whole of the building. There may well be a boiler room below us, for we feel a low rumbling as of the draught of a mighty furnace. And somewhere above our heads is the steady rhythmic ticking, like a heart beat, of a great clock.

Our present concern however is with our immediate progress, for we feel a sense of vulnerability as we climb at an inclined angle to the top of a high-roofed chamber. The ladder is of wood and iron, and seems old, and very well used. We may wonder about its strength and stability but it seems sound enough, so what we really have to be concerned about is the strength and stability, not of the ladder, but of our own will, and sense of dedication. All that prevents us from climbing through this space is a sense of vulnerable emptiness, and that is but a reflection of our own emptiness of faith, courage, and purpose. And so, realising this, we safely reach the first floor of the tower.

From here it is possible to look down, into a high ceilinged chapel, to the immediate east and beneath us. It is the equivalent of the kind of chapel which, in an abbey or cathedral frequented by tourists, has a curtain at the doorway, advising visitors that it is a place reserved for prayer and silent meditation, and where the sacred host may be reserved.

We are enabled to look down, through a small squint hole, which is by our feet, so that we have to kneel to look down. We see a fairly spacious chapel, which seems irradiated with golden light. An altar is at the north eastern corner, and above it hangs a perpetual light, in a blood- or ruby-red protective lamp, before a reliquary within the body of the altar. There is also a bag, high above the reach of ordinary man, that can be lowered by the priest or guardian when more wafers of the host are needed.

Before the altar, lining the western and southern walls, are pews or prayer desks, in which are kneeling a number of figures deep in prayer or meditation. These are the souls of the newly dead. It is perhaps partly their penitential reverence that gives the atmosphere of the chapel its golden ambience, but there is also a greater figure that builds over the altar. It is of the Christ - who stands, his hands raised in blessing upon all those who are kneeling before him.

In part this is a simulacrum built by the prayer and devotion of those who come to this place, but at the same time it is no empty chimera, or pious mirage, for it is ensouled with the presence of the Most High, and thus is a channel for divine grace. This is an example of one form of magical image at work, although here it might be better termed a mystical, or perhaps spiritual, image. This is an exemplification of the spiritual exercises discovered by a formidable soldier of the faith, Ignatius of Loyola, but it is a means and method by no means confined to him, or to his Order. It is the expression of a natural inner law, a means of grace, as natural as seeing or eating or drinking or breathing. The building of visions before the inner eye acts as a vehicle for spiritual power and divine grace. It is at the same time a means of ascent and redemption for the soul.

{The Chancellor, 14.8.93}

23

We will have more to say about the state of the souls in this chapel a little later, but first we must look to ourselves. The room that we are in is but an antechamber to the tower itself, which rises over the centre of the building, where transept crosses nave, not at the northern side where we presently are. The way across is by a narrow walkway, which is well guarded by handrails, although there is no fear of a drop, for solid masonry is all about us.

We come to a central chamber, which is furnished with small square windows at each of its four sides. If you look out of the windows you will see that we are at the level of the rooftop of the nave of the abbey. Indeed it would be possible, if we so wished, to pass onto either an interior or an exterior walkway which pass round the abbey at this height. From the interior one we could look down upon those who worship or walk about in the abbey below, and from the exterior one we could look out upon the external world beyond the environs of the abbey.

We can see a certain amount however, from the windows, and even from here the view without may seem somewhat vertiginous. Beyond the periphery of the abbey grounds, beyond a low wall towards the north, from whence we commenced, there passes a road. And upon that road there appears to be a sort of moving pageant.

Beyond the road itself there is a landscape, that appears simply put there as a kind of conventional backdrop. In the far distance is the blue and purple of rolling hills, as if we were at the centre of a circle of unpeopled green fields.

The real world (as you call it when in incarnation) is outside on the road itself, and from the standpoint of those who look upon it from within the abbey, it has the air of a certain falseness. A certain mountebank air, a somewhat shabby form of glamour and promise of good times and easy riches. In the outer world itself it would pertain to the kind of atmosphere associated with a fairground or an amusement arcade. The place is essentially artificial or false. In one sense a kind of fantasy theme-park into which many souls are attracted simply in search of diversion, to get "out of themselves", yet where only the young or the immature find themselves really diverted.

To revert to another, older type of image, it is like a procession of wagons, mobile stages or tableaux, passing down the road, although the movement is illusory. If it moves at all, it does so more slowly than those involved in it realise.

And to go within any of those tableaux is to go into a place that seems to be reality. One sees what appear to be incarnate people, real souls, moving about within, but they are no more vital than waxwork images, although images that move to a certain extent. These are archetypal figures of past, contemporary or indeed future social life, invested with qualities and activities that are very much in the eye of the beholder.

As I say, this is a caravan largely of reflections and illusions - even though most of those within it, see it and feel it and experience it as real. It is a kind of waxwork show where the exhibits may also be distorting mirrors. There are other elements too of the fairground, the cheap exhibition. A ghost train, and a chamber of horrors, for those who are attracted by such things. And many other diversions, such as may be seen in any modern amusement arcade.

You may also see souls clamouring at the railings of the abbey from the inside. That is, scrabbling to get out toward these diversions. Indeed, if you so focus your eyes to that particular level of reality, the grounds of the abbey are full of souls striving to get out and into the street and the mountebank show. Whilst there are others who have wearied of the show and seek to pass from the street and through the gateway of the abbey.

Two figures from the Tarot illustrate the aspirations of each of these two sets of souls. Those seeking to get away from the abbey, crowd around and pass through a gate where there stands a representation of the Devil. And those who seek to get off the travelling show and into the still reality of the Abbey grounds, pass through a gateway where stands a representation of the Magician or the Juggler.

Now both these images are part of the same reality, although seen from different sides. The Magician/Devil is Lord of the Revels - and in this lies some very deep teaching.

The Devil here seen is not evil in the everyday sense of moral turpitude and its manifestations and consequences. He is indeed evil, but as a false tempter, luring souls away from the true light of the abbey into what is by comparison a tawdry diversion. Although at another level, this is physical existence itself, and the experience of the human condition - knowing good and evil. The Devil is thus a Lucifer figure, the tempter, the adversary, the serpent, yet at the same time a servant, in his way, of God.

And indeed all that exists, or that is allowed to exist, must be a servant of God. Otherwise it would lose its existence, its fundamental coherence, and dissolve into nothingness. All evil is in essence illusory. Although when bound up into forms within the fairground pageant of the physical universe in human space and time, can be real and horrible and terrible enough for those who for a time are entrapped within it. But from all the experiences, good and bad, pleasant or painful, the soul can learn. There are lessons even in distorted reflections, for much of the imagery and experience within the cavalcade is projected there by the desires of souls. Where else would the complex reality come from? The Master of the Revels puts up and maintains the machines and the fabric, but they are inhabited and used and adapted to their own desires by those who willingly enter this world of artifice.

But at the exit to it all stands the Magician. He knows all the ins and outs of the machinery, the secret of the illusions, and he marks the way out. So also does the figure of the Fool, who wanders throughout the whole cavalcade itself, helping, assisting, even comforting and guiding souls within. Of course this is a figure of great ambivalence. He may appear mad, deluded, or strangely wise, or frightening, or a trickster, or a joker - whatever he wills to aid the souls - and so he seems at odds with much that goes on around him. His complementary image, as seen from the still reality of the abbey is, however, the Hanged Man. This image also appears in the precincts of the abbey, just within the main gate. Either in the form of a man, hung upside down within a framework, or as the Christ crucified.

{The Chancellor, 15.8.93}

24

From what has been said about the images of Devil and Magician you may have discerned two further points about their role. Remember that the entry to incarnation or physical birth is through the coming together in sexual conjunction of two already upon the physical plane. This is indicated by the pair of naked figures chained to the base of the Devil's pedestal. We would not wish this to be interpreted as the idea of sexual intercourse being evil, nor indeed entry into the physical world. This has been a persistent delusion down the ages, particularly in the eyes of certain types of religious dogmatist who confuse the axis of matter and spirit with the axis of evil and good. There is, it has to be said, a certain basis of truth within it, which is what makes the error so persistent in the hearts and minds of men.

The physical material world as it is has come about as a consequence of the Fall. This does not mean to say that it is intrinsically evil, or to be cast into perdition. The winnowing of the husk from the grain on the cosmic threshing floor has yet to come. The physical world is rather a means whereby the human soul and spirit can be redeemed, and indeed made of greater spiritual potential. As a divine theologian has said regarding the Fall, "What happy sin!", for it raises mankind up, despite the more immediate toilsome and painful consequences.

The figure of the Devil is grotesque, not because he is evil, but because he is not spiritual. He is more a figure of Caliban. One hears much talk about the Dweller on the Threshold who stands between the outer and inner worlds. Think also of the appearance of this Dweller to a soul upon the inner who seeks the way without. The soul intent upon incarnation sees it as a mirror image of itself bent on material desires. Thus is the light in the devil's hand held downwards. The figure upon the pedestal is not a great and powerful hierarch of evil, but an image of the incarnating soul itself. And whose purpose, in one sense, is the coming together of its two potential parents beneath, who are chained, albeit by voluntary bonds, although they are moral bonds as well, to the Devil's pedestal. For in normal parental circumstances they are chained to that physical child until it attains maturity. Sometimes beyond.

The Magician, at the other end of the scale of the train of caravans that make up the pageant of earthly life, stands before a table, with elements of his craft or trade upon it. His is a sacerdotal function. He is a figure of the priest before the altar handling the sacraments and the implements of redemption and the tokens of a higher world. He is thus in truth more of a priest than the Tarot figure of the Hierophant or Pope.

You may feel that looking upon the physical world in this way, in the form of a somewhat un-real and gimcrack fair, is hardly a balanced and accurate one, that there is much within the physical world that is of the true and the good. And so there is, but the spiritual gold within it is alloyed with the base metal of falsity, misdirection and corruption. If all were spiritual gold, the caravan would not be a tawdry show, an imitation of reality, but a wondrous show indeed. A spectacle beyond all highest imagination. A true reflection of the courts of the Most High.

So do not be discouraged; we do not seek to disparage the physical world. But remember where we stand. We look upon it from within and from on high, so to speak, in the greater scheme of things. From the tower within this holy place that is not made with hands.

So let us turn from viewing this aspect of the outer world, and look within. For here we see, spread out before us in four square order, many ancient volumes and scrolls. It is what you might now call a library, but is rather a scriptorium, a treasure-house of knowledge wherein is written all the accumulated wisdom of the ages. And not only historical sagas or records, but inner truths and records as well.

Some pertain to civilisations and evolutions of which you have never even heard. Although some gleanings may have escaped or been revealed to the outer world, as certain souls, skilled in imagination, and with a particular spiritual bent or destiny whilst in the outer world, have come, and seen, and read, and imparted some of what they saw in terms of legend, fantasy or fiction.

From here spring the legends of Atlantis, and indeed much of more familiar myth and legend. Much of this is truer than many think. Such heroes, monsters, creatures, really did exist, although in a time and in conditions other than your own. Current historical space and time is in truth but a very small part of the whole expanse of space and time - even as is that part of cosmic space and time that some of us know.

{The Chancellor, 16.8.93}

25

As Our Lord said: "In my Father's house are many mansions". It is little realised that whatever vastness may seem to be revealed by the instruments of modern science, whether in the deeps of outer space or within the inner universe of atoms, it is but an outward show, an appearance, of the true vastness of the mind and heart of the Father of All. And that in that mind and heart there is also awareness of all.

That awareness, if you reflect upon it, is a true vastness. Vastness may seem an argument against the existence of God to those who are temporarily blinded by the veils of matter. Yet each human body consists of myriads of cells and atoms, like a miniature physical universe, and you may be well aware of anything that occurs to a part of it. Reflect then that so may it be with God, who represents the oversoul of the universe and is the spiritual mind that oversees all.

The words Universal Providence are so big in their content that they easily become ciphers. They trip easily off the tongue and may be pushed about on a game board of mental speculation by the mind. But if you pause to ponder them, they may reveal something of their vastness, like peering through the eyepiece of a telescope whilst still being aware that there are fields of the unconquered and the unperceivable, beyond immediate human vision.

With something of this in mind we may turn to the great library within the abbey tower. Recall that we are speaking of magical images, and that all of this library, as indeed all of this abbey, is a magical image. That is, a device within your mind in the outer world whereby you may see or discern a reflection of inner truth, the real world of the spirit.

And it is easy, and indeed a common error, to mistake the imaging for the reality. This is a device that is known as "confusing the planes". All that you see when confined in your minds bounded by conceptions of matter, or body consciousness, is expressed in terms of the Tree of Life in Assiah, the Material World.

What the spiritual or higher worlds really are, you cannot conceive whilst in bodily consciousness, any more than you can simultaneously perceive what is happening in London if you happen to be in Timbuctoo. It is difficult even to imagine it if all your life experience has been in the latter place. You may have visions, intuitions, descriptions, but you see only "as in a glass, darkly" if you cannot actually be there. All has to come through the magic mirror of personality consciousness, which has all the images of its consciousness drawn from perceptions of the outer world.

So you must bear this in mind when you come to examine any of the books or scrolls or panoramic scenes that may be revealed to you within this wondrous library. You may conceive the general ambience of this place as consisting of shelves of books, with monk-like robed assistants ready, discretely to guide you to whatever you seek in knowledge. You may also conceive parts of it rather like a display room of horizontal cabinets in a museum, each covered by a concealing and protective cloth against the light. And if you look beneath the veil that rests over any one, you will see within, a living panorama.

These in fact are living books. If conceived in your constructive imagination as books, then, as you open the page, you would find a coloured picture, so brilliant and real and deep that if you wished you could walk into it. This would prove a very vivid "astral working" in the technical parlance of modern magic. Or you might find a full length portrait of an instructor, who could lecture you or inform you, or lead you to a survey of interior images within the book. At another level you might find pages of abstract numbers, figures or hieroglyphs that, given persistence, the required abstract perception and attunement, could lead you to learn of very abstract cosmic vistas and aspects of the interior machinery of the universe.

{*The Chancellor,* 17.8.93}

In some teachings these have been referred to as the Akashic Records. That is, all that has ever happened since ever time began. That is a step towards an approximation of the truth. Remember that although everything that ever was may be recorded in the minds of individuals who have undergone the experiences, each will recall the event within their own way. For instance the scene of a public execution will have a different record if viewed from the mind of the executioner, or the condemned one, or the prosecutor, or the condemned one's family, or the victims, or their families, of whatever crime has been committed or alleged, or in the onlookers, be they there for personal curiosity, perverted desires, or, as pickpockets or pedlars, for personal gain. In that sense any Akashic Record would need to be a multi-skeined record or vision of various streams of consciousness, themselves multi-layered as is all human consciousness, and subject to various distractions, memories, visions, or passing trivia.

Whilst it cannot be denied that an objective or total record might exist, it would need to be in the mind of God, or some other inconceivably vast intelligence. Indeed in so far as it is said that not a sparrow falls to the Earth without the Father knowing it - this on-going multifarious consciousness of passing experience may well be conceived in the Eternal Mind. But exposed to this, your limited and finite mind would be "sheeted out" with excess of energy. Your conscious mind can deal with one thing only at a time, that is the focus of the Ego. And whilst in some respects the conscious Ego may seem a limiting thing, (and in some circumstances extremely limiting), it is a means of focus, of concentration, for the Spirit.

It is like a magnifying glass, if unfocussed its image is diffuse, it brings a blurring of consciousness of reality. Or if small or misted it can unduly limit consciousness. Or if cracked or distorted may present it in a false, illusory way. But in its proper use it is a focus on reality - even if reality in its wider sense is considerably more broad and encompassing. For what is the true reality? "Aye, there's the rub", as Hamlet said, and this is the reason behind his other remark that "there are more things in heaven and earth Horatio, than are dreamed of in your philosophy." This was no injunction merely to believe in ghosts, as may appear in the deeper circumstances of the play.

Shakespeare is an instance of an ego who had a wider focus than is normal by any common standard, and so remarks that many of his characters make may have much wider implication and application than surface appearance. The same applies to much of Holy Writ, and this is why, in exegesis of it such as the Zohar, the Qabalistic rabbis seem to seize any text out of context to apply it to something that seems entirely other. This kind of thing seems bizarre to a modern, tightly focussed ego, but it is a means of expanding the mind in the direction of higher and wider mystical validity.

And so you may go to any of the displays, or "books" or "scrolls" within this library, which is a "treasure-house of images", many of them moving images. Thus you could, I suppose, in modern terms, see it as a film or a video library, or even of devices in virtual reality. A kind of cosmic amusement arcade! Indeed all things have their equivalents in higher or lower contexts.

You may also see here the novelist, the thinker, the imaginative creators in the outer world at work. It is here they come for information and inspiration. Particularly romantic visionaries. Although not all writers or spinners of fantasies come to this place. Many of them simply derive their writings, pictures, or ideas from the outer world.

Those who come here need a certain key, or pass of entry, as you yourselves have had. They usually have an inner guide or introductor, although they may not necessarily be conscious of one. But the key lies in their own possession, and it is composed of high intention and dedication, that attracts the servers of this place to them, to lead them in the mind's eye, though their own interior vision, to these sources of vision from whence they can derive their inspiration. And from that much else follows. They have themselves to be responsible for how they fashion or craft their vision for the outer world. But very often it will be found that however inadequate the craft or technique, the vision carries sufficient power that the book becomes a wide or long-standing success. And this is because, whatever its external defects, it carries the powerful visions of this place within it.

This is the source of many fairy tales, childrens' stories, romantic fictions, fantasy chronicles, and similar works. For if you were to define this place in Qabalistic terms, it is Yesod, the patterning place of all things, the Machinery of the Universe, the Treasure House of Images. And what is true here will certainly have its resonance in the outer world - in Malkuth, the Kingdom.

{The Chancellor, 18.8.93}

27
You have heard speak of the Lords of Story. This was a group of human spirits very close to your time who incarnated deliberately with this purpose. To sanctify or fructify the group soul, the general consciousness of their times, with the soul nourishment that can be provided by story.

This is a function similar to what is known esoterically as path working, except that for more general use it does not have to be loaded with esoteric symbols. At a basic level there is a health-giving element for the soul simply in the fact of story itself. It is a stringed sequence of significant events, like a pilgrim's journey, or quest. And the very sequentiality of it leads the mind into a linear stream of cause and effect or consequence. And willed direction, or response to providential direction, is a deeply spiritually motivated thing within its own right, even if expressed on what may seem a very trivial level.

Thus even the most basic threadbare plots aesthetically, whether romantic tales of love and marriage, or the derring-do of adventure tales, even of the comic strip, have their place and purpose for souls of a certain level of personality. Genre fiction in this way plays a purpose in the irrigation of the soul, and it is this that maintains a demand for it. You do not do well to look down upon or to decry such fiction. In its way it is in direct descent from the ballad, and the lays of the bards who tapped very similar sources in what have become the myths and legends of the human race in all their detailed diversity.

The rise of narrative fiction, and of narrative poetry before that, can be an interesting area of esoteric research, bearing in mind the sacramental nature of the function of story, beyond any overt instructional or moralising element that might have been superficially introduced. Thus for example there are the gems of literature represented by the Canterbury Tales, although many of the origins of such, as with the plays of Shakespeare, are from a previous common stock.

There is also the great and indeed unique source of story in Holy Scripture - in an overall respect the greatest story of all - and rendered anew by the blind Milton. Homer, the teller of ancient stories that inspire and intrigue to this day, was also held to be blind. In this there is an emphasis on the fact that those deprived of outer sight may be enabled or even impelled to read the inner images more. To spend their time, not in viewing the passing show of the outer world, but the elements of story revealed in the displays and visions here.

The more recent attempt of which I spoke occurred around the beginning of the twentieth century, and in a sense it was also an example of souls of a particular ability and type, responding to a general wave of influence, an ambience in time, or "ray" initiated under God from the inner planes.

Some of these dedicated souls became famous, who put their efforts into narrative poetry or perhaps more importantly into childrens' story. This constellation includes those who are out of fashion today, simply for being accurate expressions of their times and the climate of their day. Some indeed will already have been forgotten.

Masefield, Kipling, Wells, Alfred Noyes, were all contributors to this wave - in the field of narrative verse, novel or short story. Wells above all, although decried for a simplistic view of history and human progress, should be recognised and remembered. He was an initiator of science fiction, which was to become a major force in stimulating the sluggish general consciousness of mankind to awareness of its origin and destiny in the stars. And certainly he played an effective role in the strange situation when the greater tales of Milton or of Dante, and the ancient tales of Greek and Hebrew antiquity, were no longer active in stimulating and inspiring the minds and hearts of men.

{*The Chancellor*, 19.8.93}

28

For that of which we now speak is but another form of magical image. A magical image somewhat in the form of a "linear park", such as certain old railway lines have become, or the immediate surroundings of canals or rivers.

The journey, the quest, is an important form of magical image. In its linear progress it leads the soul from one subjective state to another, threaded like precious stones upon a necklace. Or which are like oases in a desert journey - or magic islands upon a long sea voyage.

Such is the function of story. And in older times it used to be fashioned in verse or rhythmic language to make it more easily memorable. And this also gave it a living pulse, a heart beat as of an organic body or a being in its own right. Much is lost by the neglect of learning such metric narration by heart. It has a profound effect upon the soul and its quality and opportunity for progress. And so too is much lost by the rendering of story into prose - that is, into language unstructured by rhythm. And although these poets such as Masefield, Noyes and others may nowadays be criticised or neglected, nevertheless they have left a treasure-house of images for the soul, that may in later days be more truly appreciated as indeed they were in their own day.

I do not decry more modern literary or artistic goals. They have their value in the evolving consciousness of the times, but in terms of magical imagery, which is the subject of our discourse, these earlier poets had a particular and over-riding importance. And it is one that is usually discernible by contemporary popularity, for there is a wisdom of the soul to be found in the untutored masses, readily and directly expressed, like a thirsty traveller coming upon a pool by the side of the road. They care not for the ornamentation of the cup, nor even if the water be not be of the clearest. Remember the soldier's response to the wares of the battlefield water-bearer, Gunga Din. The important thing is that it is life and comfort-giving. No small things to recall, no matter what the attractions of artistic fashion or intellectual cleverness.

And so with the work of prose. More words need to be written than is the case with the economy of poetic metre, but those who are capable of coming for their inspiration to these founts within the abbey library can take the same power back to the outer world of man, and thus give a vision, a direction, a reassurance to souls otherwise wandering in darkness. It is a strange anomaly that much of this fiction should be derided as "escapist". Escapism yes. But not from reality. Escapism *to* reality, from the bonds and chains of the dimly lit material prison cell.

And in the realm of childrens' story, so was there also an impulse that commenced in the middle years of the nineteenth century. Charles Kingsley was one of the pioneers; a practical and down to Earth man of God who could still light his torch at a vision. And then the growing swell of Kipling, Edith Nesbit and others later as the stream came into flood in the first decade of the new century.

Some had a remit to bridge across to the adult world and mind, to help to render people young again in some respect. For those who can be "as little children" - "theirs is the kingdom of heaven". Examples of these are George MacDonald, Lewis Carroll, and later of course the almost unique Tolkien. One whose inner eye was glued to visions and panoramas unfolding before him as he spent the greater part of his physical incarnation at this inner place of vision. And much that he wrote, although in the vein of fantasy, is a more or less true and accurate record of another species of creature, inhabiting along with man the same cosmic environment, this globe or planet.

(In some respects the term "globe" is a better one, for it does not carry with it limiting associations, such as the scientific and cultural assumptions that surround the term "planet". The planet is part, and a somewhat limited or specialist part, of a globe. The globe being much greater, in terms of inner and outer space and time, than even the most comprehensive material and scientific view of the term planet. - *Interjection from the Philosopher*.)

And extending from such works as those of Tolkien and others we have mentioned, are those more directly spiritual or cosmic panoramas, that some have witnessed in this place and endeavoured to reveal at levels of outer expression and consciousness. Such are the visions, often so-called pantheistic visions, of souls such as Swedenborg, or Jacob Boehme, and many other ecstatic visionaries, each in their way, although sometimes partially blinded by the glory and the wonder that they saw. The visionary lore of the ancient scrolls of the oriental mysteries have also been revealed. And although not all that is received by these means should be regarded as necessarily factual, they nonetheless face the soul in the right direction.

Much the same could be said of our efforts closer to home, in some of the great vistas of *The Cosmic Doctrine*. All material such as this, remote from the values and perspectives of the outer world, is akin to shining objects of a rare and volatile metal. As you bring them from the inner treasure-house to the outer air, they immediately corrode and fade from their pristine glory. However the basic shape remains, in part instructive in itself, but more importantly showing the evidence for an inner structure - the fact that there is another mode of viewing the machinery of the universe than the assumptions and researches of the outer world. And that although material discoveries may themselves seem gleaming and wondrous in their own time and at their own level, when brought to the light and conditions of inner reality, they may be found very collapsible, quaint and corrodible!

Last of all are the deliberately structured paths of spiritual revelation and instruction, which are often the work of angelic hands and imaginations, strange as that may seem. These are the stories that accrue around the essential truths of the Holy Books - and later the legends of the saints. These again, are not mere vulgar or fanciful superstitions, as some modern minds would fancy them to be. The Virgin Birth, the legends of the Madonna, the tales of the child Jesus (some of them incorporated in the Gospels themselves such as Luke), are truths of a profound importance that give great richness and nourishment to the soul. Blasphemy in these matters, so attractive to the somewhat analytical destructive modern mind, is a terrible thing; and one should seriously regard the Biblical injunction and warning in this regard, about the seriousness and consequence of leading any of the lambs of God astray. And in another sense of level too, are the stories contained in the mystical gospel of John. But the exemplary nature of all of this is to be found in the parables of Jesus. Does any man truly believe that because they are fictional or fanciful they are untrue?

{The Chancellor, 20.8.93}

29

The abbey library then is a place of almost infinitely expanding knowledge. You simply have to come here and observe the images as they flow. The required keys of entry are faith, flexibility of mind and clearness of vision, and dedication of the soul to a cause.

This last, not in any particular narrow sense - but in the sense that Tolkien had at heart in reconstructing the myths and legends of the north west of Europe. And that H. G. Wells had in the vision of a united and progressing humanity, its means of progression being by bringing science and reason to the physical plane. Or George Macdonald's more purely mystical aim of describing spiritual beings in terms of a quest of the human soul.

And of course the images of the Tarot derive from here, as do other systems of elucidation of inner worlds. Also too the imaginations that are necessary to formulate theories of science, although they are representations rather than realities, such as the structure of the atom, or of the cell, or of the starry origins of the physical universe. All, in their way, are magical images.

You can return here therefore whenever you like, given the sense of purpose and the dedication. There are other things that you should also see however, before you become engrossed in the by-ways of this labyrinth. We seek no "opium eaters" of cosmic visions. They can be an absorbing, but time and energy consuming spiritual cul-de-sac.

Let us pass then through this hall toward the far side. There beneath a narrow arch is a little door. It appears to be of cedar from Lebanon, strong and aromatic, with five iron nail heads in the form of a calvary cross, in the centre of which there is a small golden device in the form of a chalice. A purple sash hangs beside this door, and if we pull it, a melodious bell is heard to ring within. The door swings open. We enter, and before us is a winding spiral stairway, white stone steps within the grey flint rocks of the outer wall.

We climb upward, and from the narrow windows that we pass we see that we are rising ever higher from the outer world from which we started, although the stone column of the wall around us, and the firm steps upon which we tread, remind us that all is set upon and within that ground. That same ground whereon is the serpentine trail of caravans within the street before the construct of the mighty abbey that rises high into the heavens, four square in cruciform shape upon the body of the Earth.

And now we come to our destination at a new level within the tower. It is a place that has been set aside, prepared and dedicated, not for diversification of knowledge as was the library chamber beneath, but for the one-pointed singular dedication to the One who will meet us here. And it behoves us to recall the remark of Our Lord that it is easier for a camel to pass through the eye of a needle than for a rich man to enter the kingdom of heaven.

This place represents the eye of the needle. Each of our human souls is like a camel. And we have to divest ourselves of all pride of knowledge, even such as we may have gained below, to enter in this place, which might be termed an ante-chamber or the outer court of heaven.

An unconditional surrender is required of the pride of the soul. A giving up of every ounce of excess baggage. And here the mystic is at a greater advantage than the occultist - who of necessity carries much traps and baggage in the performance of his service within the outer world. But he has to learn to lay them down at the entrance to this place. In coming forth in service they may be taken up again. And it may be seen that they are like the crutches and braces that are sometimes seen hanging outside the walls of an earthly shrine reputed for curative miracles.

Here we may leave the intellectual or visionary crutches, the artificial aids that may have served us well below. For those who enter in and upward from this place they will be no longer needed. For those who descend again in service, they will be seen in a different form, as burdens voluntarily borne. Indeed, at the extreme, the instruments of martyrdom. And here again we recall to mind the Tarot image of the Hanged Man, with his reversal of spiritual and material values - at any rate as they are perceived in a fallen world.

{The Chancellor, 21.8.93}

30

Let us pass then into this place, which though in fact it is vast, gives an appearance of smallness and of intimacy, as if it were a small private chapel. In reality and in effect this is what it is for each and every one of us. In comparison the library below gave the impression of being a much larger place than it is. This place, the chapel of the Graal, gives the impression of being much smaller than it really is. In terms of function, the adventuring visions that are to be experienced in the room below have the effect of narrowing down the soul in scope, where it becomes a lone pilgrim in a vast cosmic background. In this chapel, although it has the appearance of a strait and narrow place, the opening out of the soul to which it can lead is vast, extending into the very heart of God, which knows no bounds and encompasses everything.

So we each one of us kneel, in the confines of a small prayer desk, an embroidered cushion beneath our knees, a little book on a ledge before us, and look to the altar in the East.

The altar is a simple structure, raised upon three steps. It is a plain stone block. It has a back cloth of fine velvet hangings, in colour midway between crimson and purple, faded by age and light. Upon the altar is a cloth of fine linen shot with silk, and upon this again there stands a chalice of silver.

A sword lies on the altar before the chalice, its hilt of richly wrought gold and cruciform, and pulled part way from its scabbard. What can be seen of the blade is engraved with images. The scabbard itself is of polished leather set with jewels.

Above the chalice, suspended from the ceiling, is a spear, point downwards, not completely vertically. There is a secret in the actual angle, as it can vary according to circumstance. If and when it passes to a steeper angle, drops of blood, or wine, or living light, may be seen to drop from it into the cup. If the spear should ever be seen fully vertical, or completely horizontal, then great events are impending, either in heaven or upon Earth.

The blade of the spear is of steel, its shaft apparently of wood, but of a tree not seen in Earthly climes. It is burnished to give off glints and gleams of many different colours.

The cup itself is very simple and elegant. It has one single device enclosed in a medallion upon its side. This may appear to you as a descending dove, or perhaps as an equal armed cross. The actual sigil may vary according to need, as we explained when we entered the portals of the abbey, of many of the signs that may be found here.

Be aware of the stone altar itself for it is a holy object in its own right. It too has a similar device or medallion carved upon its front which changes according to need. And it is these foci that can act as an aid to meditation, for those who come here in solitude. (Or perhaps we should say in *apparent* solitude for no-one is alone in this place, indeed if they are ever alone anywhere. Loneliness is a self induced illusion).

There are thus four hallows here - the spear, the cup, the sword (with its scabbard), and the altar stone.

High above them all, where the back wall joins the ceiling, is a great silver plaque of a brooding dove, the emblem of the Holy Spirit.

There are pictures hung upon the side walls, as also to the rear, but these need not concern us now. This is not so much a place of images, but the "potential" of images. And it is not so much a matter of what the images are, whether of the hallows themselves, or of other images that may appear, but what is conveyed through them. They function much more as doorways rather than as things in themselves.

They are certainly real enough, and their reality is in truth more solid than anything you may meet upon Earth. They are *transformative* agents or agencies.

In the outer world you appear to be enmeshed in images. So much so that you who are immersed in them may even think them the one and only reality. In the library below, the treasure-house of images, one is very much an observer of the images that flow. They may give diversion and instruction, but one is not immersed in images as within the physical world.

Here we have a paradox in that the images are not simply for instruction or observation, nor to be immersed or entrapped within, but are windows and doors. Windows and doors to a higher reality, a higher world, that your immediate senses are not too well established to discern. But which when attuned, will give not only a higher kind of vision, but experience, inspiration, "indwelling" of holy things. (I regret that language permits no more adequate description).

One may even be "taken up" in ecstasy. This is not a wild or sexual frenzy as commonly understood, but a standing outside oneself, literally *ex-stasis*. It is an experience and revelation of one's true spiritual and cosmic being, in the courts of heaven. This is where the prophets are snatched in visions, and is figuratively the place to where Elijah rose in his chariot. These are the upper realms also of Jacob's ladder, sometimes touched in poetic vision as with Dante, or perhaps to a lesser extent with Milton. And also in the less epic attempts to describe such scenes: the divine lyrics of St. John of the Cross, or the ascent of St Theresa, or the Lady Julian of Norwich, and of course many others, some known, an even greater number unrecorded, for the witnesses of the Kingdom of Heaven may be greater than you think. Chinks from the brightness of the eternal light may appear in the most unlikeliest of places within the world.

And it is here, humbly waiting upon our knees, that we may be blessed or vouchsafed with inspiration. Although it will not always be so. The wonders of heaven do not always reveal themselves in colourful and dramatic vision. There is also a quietness that may come in upon the soul. It is the rising of the waters of righteousness, of the grace and peace of God, the cleansing baptismal waters from above the firmament.

{*The Chancellor, 22.8.93*}

31
Any mighty visions might be expected to appear in the space over the altar, indeed any mode of revelation or epiphany is possible. Neither the Lord nor his Holy Spirit is limited by his own conventions. However we should not set store by the wondrous or the miraculous. It is a setting aside, for some unusual purpose, of that which has been put together for the normal processes of solar evolution and the cure of souls therein.

What seems normal and conventional is, in any case, as much a wonder as anything which may seem miraculous or transcendental. It is only our own habits of consciousness that cause this distinction. Whoever can see the wondrous in the so-called commonplace is doubly blessed, in the realisation that every manifestation of life, and thus every thing, is unique.

This is the other side of romanticism. Besides being able to see the noumenous *through* the veil of nature, the romantics can see it *in* the veil of nature. The glory of god is seen through his works as well as (in part) face to face - for no-one may see face to face and Unveiled the Ultimate Glory and return to tell the tale. Such is that Love and that Glory that whoever gazes upon it is immediately united with it. This is the polar opposite, if you will, of what is conceived by astronomical scientists as a "black hole". And of this ultimate "Glorious Mass" - the sun, or a star, is the nearest physical plane equivalent. Hence is God sometimes known as the Sun behind the Sun.

Be aware therefore of to Whom you kneel and of what may be possible within this holy place; and do not expect it to be an experience that will not change you. This is not, as the levels below might be, a cosmic picture show. Here the instruction is of another nature.

You have before you, on the tiny shelf of your prayer desk, a little book. It is bound in supple brown leather, with a thin line gold calvary cross upon it. In the upper corner the initials of your name are stamped upon it, or some similar device to indicate that this book belongs entirely to you.

You may sit or kneel and open it up. The pages within are of fine paper, and whatever printing you may find is rich black and red - and possibly with fully illuminated initials as in a preciously inscribed manuscript by a dedicated monk of the Middle Ages.

Whatever is within these pages however has been transcribed by you. It is a record of the communion of your own soul with God.

It is the record of a relationship. Therefore one might regard it as a very intimate book, like unto one perhaps that is shared by lovers. A close record of personal confidences, of little phrases, endearments, notes of places, verses of adoration. For the outer loves of soul between soul is but another form of the love that can be also expressed between the soul and its Creator. "God so loved the world that he gave his only begotten son...or daughter." And that is you. For all are brothers and sisters in Christ. Let no misunderstood theology disabuse you of that fact.

In the sum total of human experience, the closest to the contents of this little book you hold might be regarded as the Books of Wisdom - of the Song of Solomon, of the Psalms and of the holy Proverbs. But all these are heart-felt, intimate, between yourself and your Maker. They are best kept, or left, to yourself therefore. If laid before the gaze of others they might only be misunderstood. Although some great souls have revealed something of their contacts. The Sufi mystics, the transcriber of the Song of Songs, and others such as St John of the Cross and mystics particularly of every age and clime.

To the untuned outer eye and ear they may bring more stumbling blocks than revelation. Just as the sighs or vows of lovers may seem out of place, out of proportion, to the worldly wise. But that is a factor of their intimacy. And of the uniqueness of each soul before God. Each soul, whether human, angelic, elemental or of any other kind. The creativity and power and love of God are boundless, and one and true and whole for each one of His creation, each of its kind. For He is the One true centre, unique to all. No matter how many facets there are in the jewel of creation, no matter how many petals in the mystic rose, He is common to all the myriads and the millions, and yet unique to all, for all see Him from their own particular elevation and angle, their own unique point in space.

{*The Chancellor, 23.8.93*}

32

And you may perhaps find, when you look inside your little book, that very little indeed is written within it. That your conscious contact with, or response to the love and reality of God, has been very little indeed. But fear not. This is not a matter for judgement. The extent of what is written within that book is a matter only for the individual spirit, or soul (that is, the outer expression of the spirit) and God.

The spirit indeed is always with God and has never left God. Thus in another sense the writing within the book will be a record of the link between the spirit and the soul - although I would not wish to encourage anyone to think in solipsistic or psychological terms, of what is not so much an "integration process" as a reconciliation between independent but related beings.

You know the parable of the prodigal son. The book, in another way of speaking, is a record of the conversation that passed between the father and the son upon the latter's return from his wandering to take up his inheritance. And before that, and perhaps nearer to your own condition, the record of the odd intimations of memory, promise, and perhaps regret and remorse, felt by the son, cut off by his own deeds and decisions, when in the farthest distance from the Father's house he ate of the husks that the swine did eat.

It is thus, if you care to put it yet another way, a personal prayer book. But the prayers are a record of the responses of the heart - not the intellectual doctrines or expressions of others.

Sit then, and read your book, or kneel. The posture that you choose is of your own choice and comfort. The Holy Spirit is not limited by such things - even though it may denote a slightly different state or stage of the soul. The Christ knelt in the Garden of Gethsemane. The Disciples at the time were lying and sleeping. Shepherds were watching their flocks by night. Those on the road to Emmaus were walking. And upon the day of Pentecost the disciples were seated about a table.

And as you open your book to read within, you may see on the little lectern before you, a simple candle, which lights up as you commune with the book. And as the candle lights, so the general ambience of light within the room, which has come from a hidden source, begins to lessen. And you find that the chapel is now lit by your small candle alone. And also what was plainly seen upon the altar are now, in the dim religious light, more in the nature of dim but evocative shapes. "For now we see as in a glass, darkly....."

I have brought you now, in the sphere of images, mystical or magical, as far as I can. To attempt to go further would be an intrusion upon the sacred and sanctified intimacy of the soul with God. To be an unwanted guest, an intruder in the bridal chamber.

For One may come to you in the silence, drawn by the attunement of your own heart - which is as clear of imagery in its simplicity and aspiration as is the candle flame. One bearing bread and wine, as he came to our forefather Abraham, after the slaughter of the Kings of Edom, whose kingdoms lie in the pools of illusion around the Dead Sea.

So if you lack an image for concentration, or the book before your eyes seems empty, think upon this archetype of priesthood. Even Melchizedek, whose very name means priest (Zadok) and king (Malekh), and who is King of Salem - or King of Peace.

This is a place to which you can return at any time, whenever you will, and wherever you may be, for it is a place of the heart. And whenever and wherever you may be, you may come to this place instantly if only the heart is prepared, and the mind cease its clamouring, its defences, its justifications. For as has wisely been said, "The Mind is Slayer of the Real".

In another sense it is like the band of devils who possessed a man and who said their name was Legion. It was they who passed, by the word of Our Lord, into the Gadarene swine, who then plunged down the slopes to their destruction in the sea. I do not mean by this that the mind is by any means evil, anymore than the images within consciousness, that may cloak the ideas and intentions of the mind, are evil. That would be to condemn all consciousness, certainly all lower consciousness. But the mind is, or should be, like the image-making faculty, a wondrous tool. The tools of every trade and science of man are there to be used in their right place and their right time. Not for destruction or self-mutilation.

They are to be left at the temple or the chapel door. Yet when you pass within, through the eye of the needle, having laid down your treasures to pass through that strait and narrow gate, then they will be restored to you, in images and thoughts that pertain to a higher world. But first must come the silence and the stillness. The act of faith and the acceptance of love. Then shall the true treasures of the mind and the inner eye and ear be revealed.

The voice and the vision that comes in the silence, is something that comes between the soul and its maker. The figure of the double triangle represents this path of reality and realisation. It could also be rendered three dimensionally in the form of cones. And the discipline and figures of projective geometry may also be providers of helpful symbols to a rapacious mind. But the truth and confirmation of the path is in its treading. The mere contemplation of the map, although a valid and useful preparation perhaps, is no substitute for the reality.

May peace be with you. May peace come unto you. As a living reality. The Limitless Light of the Love of God. Amen.

{*The Chancellor, 24.8.93*}

33
{*The Soldier takes over*}
Time we moved on. It's up to me to show you the rest. To take you up to the top of the tower. It's not that I'm the most senior here. We're all equals really. Although it sometimes doesn't feel like it. The other two have been around in Earth conditions for a long time. So it is a bit like working with older colleagues in a bank or in a company.

I mean I expect you would have thought that the lawyer, the one you call the Chancellor, would have been running things, with me as a kind of junior partner. And the worthy ancient Greek as a kind of paterfamilias, the grand old man in the board room. A managing director, chairman of the board, and general shop floor manager kind of thing. But as I say, all are equal. Because I'm using a personality, (or magical image), that is fairly recent to your times - (although eighty years is pushing it a bit) - it falls to me as often as not to make the initial contact.

It happened with you, just as it did with your friend Dion Fortune, back in the twenties. In full trance that was. And went on for a number of years too.

When you get a good contact it's funny how one thing leads to another. You might be surprised to learn that synchronicities, or what we used to call happy coincidences, or serendipities, come as a delight or pleasant surprise to us as well as to you. We don't exactly run the world you know. There are plenty of others in the background. It's just that we three are in the front line trenches, so to speak. And with me as the one that goes first over the wire. But as I say, this is because I can generally make the contact more easily, because of the lesser time gap between my magical personality and the one you're using now.

And it's much the same with my function on the journey we're embarked upon today. The Chancellor is very much a middle man, a kind of sheet anchor, captain of the team, I suppose, and he's well qualified to be. With a magical body that comes from an age of much greater faith in the noumenous, and one that was very much in the centre of things in the court of Henry VIII, he can plug into and bring through forces and contacts that can be pretty rare these days. You can pick up a pretty solid faith, or spiritual nourishment (it's a bit like spiritual body building) just to be near him, or have him talk to you.

The Philosopher, the Greek, can seem pretty remote, which is on account of having a long time gap to span. Although he's helped by the ongoing reputation through the ages of the personality he uses, which is a natural focus. And that's another instance of the powers and forces of magical imagery.

Its the same with the Chancellor too. You can see that general interest in these historical figures and their times is like a long tunnel, or spiralling vortex, something like an old gramophone horn, leading back to them. In fact that's not a bad image - if a slightly bizarre one. If you think that at the other end of the horn from which your ear is pressed there is an ancient sound box, with needle resting on a turning disc or cylinder that gives forth with the talk or the entertainment. Not that any of us three are wax records! But in terms of the difference in reality between what we really are, and how we may seem to you, there is a difference that's not far from that order.

But never mind the mechanics, the *modus operandi*. There's no point in trying to pull the butterfly to pieces to see how it flies. You can bet your boots it won't fly so well after that! So take things at face value and they will work well enough. And thinking about it, there's a world of difference in how you see a butterfly and how a butterfly sees you. Even though you are on the same plane of physical existence!

Anyhow you know now, to a little extent, why it is that the Chancellor takes up his natural place in the chapel. And why the Philosopher is at home as master of all the peepshows in the library room. And why I'm taking you up and out onto the watch tower of this abbey. I have a closer concern, or special involvement, in what is happening in the outer world right now. Though the outer world as it appears to you and as it appears to me, or any other of the company of heaven, may very well somewhat differ!

However, let us reverently leave the chapel, and we will pass to another doorway leading to a winding stair. It is much the same size as the last but not quite so well appointed or reverently cherished. In fact it looks pretty short of paint, and not a little scratched and battered. Anyway, we ring a handbell that stands beneath, and as it opens, up we go.

When we reach the top of these winding stairs what do we see? First of all we are conscious of a blustering wind, strong enough almost to lean against. Yes, we are in the open air, and if you look around you will see the land of Logres as it appears to an inside view.

{The Soldier, 25.8.93}

34

It is probably not as you had expected it. In fact I'm sure it's not as you expected it. And it may take a minute to form your vision and to get used to the wind so that you don't notice it. Then you may see that everything around is in a kind of purple pink mist. Almost like a fog. A kind of dusky pink all round in the sky, but darker shapes, in blues or purples, closer to the horizon. And maybe indicating shapes, some moving, in the same dark colours.

And now you should be able to see quite a pronounced form in the mist. It is like a great round hill, some way in the distance. But perspective is a bit confusing up here. It doesn't work in quite the way you're used to. The medieval painters rendered it better. Things tend to take up a size according to their importance. And what is a bit disconcerting is that the importance is not just what may be intrinsic to them, or in the eyes of God you might say, but their importance to the eye of the beholder.

Much the same kind of thing happens in the outer world as a matter of fact, only you don't notice it. The conceptions of the eye have become fixed upon certain conventions of commonsense and seventeenth century optics, so you think you are seeing that way. But if you think about it, things do loom larger or smaller according to the emotional charge you put upon them. A young man's girl friend for instance looms very large in his horizon of vision. In fact can be quite obsessive so as to take up the whole field of vision - and you can't get much bigger than that. Perhaps field of conception rather than field of perception might be the better term. Conceptions lie somewhat behind perceptions, in a manner of speaking, perceptions being rather like spectacles, perched upon the nose.

Anyhow, take it from me that we are looking generally westward, and a bit southward. And in that direction there is a dark blue/purple shape in the pink mist. You might think it was just a few miles away in Earth terms. It has a sort of light around it, as if it glows, and somewhat more so at the top. When you focus your attention upon it, it is quite impressive. A great purple, breast-like hill, that is certainly charged with some great power. But that is all you can see of it, dimly in the strange pink mist.

But when you look at it you also get a feeling of primeval power. It has been there a long time. And yet it is not a power that is fully defined in terms of anciency, because it has a future feel in it as well. I am sorry about trying to explain all this, but words are such clumsy things when you are trying to talk about what's going on on the inner. Words in the main were shaped in response to outer perspectives.

The "feel" of the hill in front of you is one of a power and presence in and out of time. It has a span larger than human mortal existence, but mankind's consciousness can tune in to it. It carries past and future in it, yet is centred, rooted in the material earth. So it is not some abstract or idealistic or mystical hill of vision. It may have a bit of that in it, or induce people to that kind of higher vision, but in itself it is very material, of Malkuth as the modern Qabalist would say. And what we are seeing at the moment is just its power and force on the etheric level - on what are sometimes called the higher aethers. You know about solid, liquid and gas; well each plane has seven sub-planes, according to the book, so what you are looking at now is this holy hill, as it appears on those levels only - beyond solid, liquid and gas.

{The Soldier, 26.8.93}

35

It is when you are on this level that you can get some idea of the kind of powerhouse that this kind of thing can be. Because although it may just seem to be a great shape in a strange kind of mist, you can feel it radiating, if that's the right word. You could perhaps call it a kind of magnetic field, but it's not so cold and abstract as that. This is more like the feel of a living being. As if you put your head alongside the flank of a cow, and were conscious of the warmth and the smell and the great power and bulk of the animal beside you.

Even from a distance you get that kind of feeling. And you can sense, or feel, rather than see, some kind of active life going on within it.

The whole of the surface of the Earth is like this. It has these points upon it. On this level almost like a great round Christmas pudding of the old fashioned kind, hot and steaming and bubbling, with these kind of pustules (if that's the right word) about its surface. Kind of potential volcanoes, able or wanting to vent off inner pressures.

And as I say that, you can see the dim shape in the mist before us suddenly give off a great display of light, rather like an aurora borealis, which then subsides. You might also be aware of a kind of humming, buzzing sound emanating from it, not just general to it as a whole, but going off in bands or channels along the surface of the earth, like the noise you hear near some high power cables.

I am sorry if this description is none too intelligible, but if we have this trouble explaining something off the physical plane of appearances, yet so close to it as the etheric matrix, spare a thought to the difficulties we face when we get further out into the more spiritual aethers. That's where the Greek Master comes in with his specialities, although they are all clothed in abstractions or highly abstract symbols. A kind of cosmic algebra or multi-dimensional trigonometry. But here we are a bit closer to what you are commonly used to on the physical plane, as it's called, although most of your reactions to it are far from physical. Hence the power of magical images.

So let us take our attempt to gaze on this reality a stage or two backwards, and deal in magical imagery. And lo, you will see the mist clear, and at first a kind of ordnance survey map of the counties of Southern England appear before your eyes, quickly to take on actual, idealised features in miniature, rather than the printed or painted conventional symbols on a map. And then you will see that we have been gazing upon a small green hill in the distance, that is familiar to you as Glastonbury Tor.

You can focus as you prefer upon the abstract map or upon the more realistic model. Both are in the realm of magical images, representations that is, of an existent reality. In this case the existent reality that you can know, and move and tread upon by journeying across the terrain, the green fields and roads of England, and the flora, the fauna, and web of human life that surrounds them. Not only in the present I might say, but also of the past, which is present, at a subtle layer, like an inner archaeology.

A magical image can tap into that too, which makes it a sort of tuning device for tapping in to vision and to power. This is modified to a certain extent by the intellectual and clairvoyant equipment of whoever is doing the tuning. The problem is that lots of people have rather inadequate old radio sets in this regard - so things come out somewhat garbled, with lots of background interference, but with enough coming through to make it pretty plain there is something at the other end.

You can now perhaps understand how a magical image can represent a reality that is not of the outer world. If it stands for nothing, it is idle fantasy, and there is plenty of that about. It is part of the psychological make-up of every human being. It allows for personal internal amusement, reflection on outer events, desired inner events, and general intelligent interchange, even at an elementary or sub-intellectual level. However, if there is something, an inner reality, that can resonate with that image, then the image is by definition magical. It makes real connections.

But while this is a great gift and power, duly developed, you will realise that one has to be a little careful as to just what one is calling up, deliberately or by way of chance, with one's mental radio. Not all is sweetness and light, and even in the higher aethers there can be some unpleasant creatures and characters around. Not so much fallen angels perhaps, who are generally rather too grand to concern themselves with mortals, but certain types of being that might be likened to scavenging pond life. Though most of the mischief is at your own level.

So one of the reasons for esoteric training is so that, by virtue of your purified intention, when you venture into the "unseen" by way of magical images, you automatically make contact with that which is helpful, and beneficial to yourself and the greater well-being of the world. And this is because esoteric training, (which has been somewhat refined over the years), is largely, and most importantly, a training in the orientation of the spiritual will, apart from any matter of techniques.

Spiritual will and the direction of inner intention is bound up with faith and belief, which makes it the most crucial element of any esoteric training. Otherwise you risk opening up all kinds of Pandora's Box. There is quite enough of this about with ordinary natural psychics, and a natural psychic of abnormal sensitivity is usually a pathology rather than a high and natural occurrence. Insensitivity is a healthy, useful armour, when considered in proportion.

You would not for instance want to be in a condition where you had no skin. The natural psychic is in the condition of one who is very thin skinned. You can imagine the problems when such a one, or one who is verging that way, enrols for psychic development classes, for without due precautions they could be influenced or manipulated by any passing influence upon the inner planes.

That is why an esoteric training in the Western Mystery system differs from a psychic development circle. Not that the spiritualist movement has been devoid of useful work and action, and this because, human beings and human nature are, on balance, on the side of the good, the sane, and the sensible. This has meant that the worst possibilities of abuse or psychic accident are reduced or kept under control.

The matter of spiritual intention comes into the spiritualist movement too of course, although it is differently oriented from the aspirations of the average occultist. It is concerned less with cosmic philosophy and abstract generalities and more with humanity, human feelings, and the closeness of the family. All these are ties of affection and mutual responsibility and are to be encouraged.

There has been a rather distressing erosion of these values in your own time, but it is a passing phase - and attracts more attention at times than it really deserves. You share the principles of family and loyalty with much of the animal kingdom and there is a great general flywheel effect of the wheel of nature that keeps things on the right track. (This is another aspect of the Tarot image of the Wheel of Fortune). It is unlikely that the cycle of human generation and general family care will come off its axis. If it did, then that's the end of humanity on Earth and I don't think we are anywhere near that.

However, too much interference with the powers behind the atom and the building blocks of genes and chromosomes, and who knows what might come?

We get into deep waters here. Principalities and Powers behind the nations are bad enough, but some of the greater malevolent angels left over from the pit, and swarming between the celestial spheres in their own brand of inter-stellar space, are something yet again. They can be quite capable of entering and interfering with the best laid plans of men and of angels, and that is one of the consequences of living, or being spiritually centred, in a fallen universe.

But these are not of a kind that you are likely to come into conscious contact with. They would have rather less regard for you than you would have for a fly, unless it bit you. And then of course there might be reactions. But you feel their general effects all right. In disease, famine, pestilence, and wars. The four horsemen of the apocalypse are by no means inaccurate representations of them, or at any rate of their effects. One cannot recommend however, summoning up this kind of magical image, even if you should think of yourself as some kind of esoteric Don Quixote. Align yourselves with the forces of light and you will receive your due and appropriate guidance and instruction.

And that is also why another of the objects of higher esoteric training is to learn to do what you are told. This is not a matter of abrogation of personal initiative or spiritual will. Humility, chastity and obedience, are the time honoured formula of the religious orders of the church - who are perhaps the best equipped to meet face to face with "spiritual wickedness in high places".

Looking at the spectacle of the church in some of its manifestations in the world, this may not seem very convincing, or indeed very hopeful. But you see only the outskirts, the out-riders, the camp followers so to speak of the great army, mighty with banners. The heavenly host of Michael is perhaps the nearest useful image. And if one wants to be blunt about it, one genuine mystic is probably worth a large handful of occultists - even good ones! Not that there are too many of either kind about - or as many as we would like to see, to help the human race along.

{*The Soldier, 28.8.93*}

36
We have been talking about Glastonbury, and its quality as a spiritual power point that is capable of acting as a beacon on the etheric level. This means that it slides in under the level of the mind and conscious mental processes. Many theories about the place have been constructed from the fancies and the speculations of those who have been pulled there at the etheric level. In terms of the human aura we are talking of a pull that is at a solar plexus, or sub-solar plexus level. This means that irrational or sub-rational things can be said or done that nonetheless have a higher validity. There is a kind of cyclic law involved in this wherein planes link up - 1st to 7th, 2nd to 6th, 3rd to 4th and so on.

You experienced something of this yesterday, in that you unexpectedly found yourself there. Well it was unexpected for you perhaps, but had seemed a pretty obvious consequence to me, from my slightly elevated vantage point. You had not planned or expected to go there, but you found almost as a matter of inevitability, or natural consequence, that time and place and circumstance turned out so that it seemed natural to go to Glastonbury.

I know there are elements about the place you do not care much for. That's understandable. Sub-intellectually it is like a jammy dustbin that attracts all kinds of psychic wasps and flies, brethren of the psychically insectivorous mode. But that is part of what I have been describing and implicit in the images I was using, the great purple, pink mass, just like a fruity sugar cake. Perhaps a more appropriate and salubrious image might have been a flower. You have been seeing enough of them in the last few days, like those in the garden at Lytes Carey that broke upon your consciousness in a burst of bright golds and yellows - attracting all those bees and other nectar gathering insects. That's Glastonbury too.

And so it is not surprising to find "signs following", or subliminal linkage. These things tend to go together and are all part of the same ambience or process, like the plane linking I mentioned earlier.

It is a mistake to try to analyse parts out as "spiritual" or "psychological" and so on - that is simply intellectualising it. That metal sun-burst you bought was a part of it all too, reflecting back to when you first started acting in an esoterically independent manner, after your basic training had been put in, in the founding of Helios Book Service, and all that subsequently has sprung from it. All this was in terms of natural growth, like the flowers, and all responding to the Sun, and with further resonance to an old initiatory mantram.

And so also, by way of bonus so to speak, was your coming upon the newly published book *The Avalonians*. The first perhaps, apart from her biography, that comes out quite so baldly with the detail of contacts your friend and colleague Dion Fortune made with us at Glastonbury, and to which you have now switched on to consciously at last.

All this is part of Glastonbury. It is what attracted Dion Fortune here, and what impelled her to have her bones laid to rest here. And whatever you may read in the record of *The Avalonians* will show the effect it has had upon others spiritually oriented and sensitive to this power source.

Each reacts in different ways. Sometimes not entirely wisely. Sometimes in ways that appear, particularly to the outer world, as foolish. But in these matters it is an un-wise man that calls anyone else a fool. There are often reasons within reasons, and often somewhat beyond the reach of reason.

It can be important for instance, for some purposes of those upon the inner side, to get some action performed by someone on the physical plane - no matter how trivial or inconsequential that it may seem. It can be as a kind of earthing. Sticking a wire into the ground from an electrical apparatus may seem pretty inconsequential and stupid, just like sticking an aerial up into the air, until you have some inkling of the technology that requires and justifies it. Psychical technology is much the same. And part of all this is the science, and the art and technique, of handling magical images.

You will also be aware of the location from which we have been apparently viewing the tump, the power source of Glastonbury. It is as if we viewed it from London, for this is another national power point.

Again, as you can see in the book, Dion Fortune realised this, for not only did she state it specifically, but set up a physical location for her group in each place. And she emphasises it again, (in an indirect and lyrical, but because of that, a very magical way), in her description of the journey between them, down the Great West Road. And of course the old great trunk roads, going back through time, are also very much a part of the power lines that coincide upon the inner and the outer, between the etheric sub-planes, and the actual convolutions of the physical track.

So when we have been gazing out upon the inner side of Glastonbury it has been as if we were sited in London. And this can lead us, in turn, onto another series of important magical images, for London is thick with them.

{The Soldier, 29.8.93}

37

And particularly rich in magical images is the place we are at in London, for the site is another great power house, that acts as a psychic magnet and as a spinner of magical images. It is in origin the White Mount, upon which the four-square, four turreted White Tower of the Tower of London is built, and which was refurbished by Sir Christopher Wren in his time. It is the legendary site where the head of Bran, the great old Celtic god, was buried and was said to repel invaders. Bran was pre-Celtic in origin really, for the Celts built an image on a power source that was already there.

King Arthur was supposed to have dug the head up, feeling himself capable of keeping invaders at bay, but that substitution is not quite what it seems. It shows another level of magical imagery as we move up a substratum in the magical consciousness of the race. This is what you might regard as an overlay on what we have so far described, which is the basic ground level of the etheric sub-planes, only one step removed from the physical plane itself. The overlaid images are in what is commonly called astral matter, and lie in the mythical or dream symbolism of those who have identified themselves with particular stretches of the land itself and its etheric counterpart.

You may see here, and in what flows from it, the importance and consequence in feudal times and before, of the identification of the king or the lord with the land. And also of the dependence of the various sub-lords and ladies and various ranks of society upon the lord as upon the land. The lord was the land, and all this is not quite so primitive, inconsequential or irrational as might appear to the segmented and somewhat rootless modern mind.

At the Arthurian level, you could say that the head of Arthur was substituted for that of Bran, and if that is the case then the heart of Arthur might be said to be at Glastonbury. That sums up and illustrates in one way, the different ambience and role played by the centres of London and Glastonbury. That is if we assume Arthur to be the lord of the realm of what later became known as Logres.

There is a great deal that is confused in the symbolism of the tales as they have come down, fragmented by the conscious minds of men, particularly as those conscious minds themselves became increasingly more independent, more fragmented. Thus more like a disturbed and disordered mosaic, as opposed to a wall painting or a fresco that had survived intact.

In origin the king, the defender of the realm, is also the maimed king of the Grail legends. And he has taken the place of the sleeping giant Albion, who rests at a deeper level. And all the other Arthurian characters, or certainly the major ones, (for some of the minor ones have been later conscious fabrications), are movements in the great complex of magical images that is the soul of the land.

This is almost at an elemental level. Like fertile loam that gives food and conditions of growth to the flora and fauna of nature, and by extension sustains all humankind upon the same tract of land too. It also has an effect upon it. And although we are dealing now with individual and human spirits, separate sparks from the divine fire, nonetheless by their being embedded into a common gel, so to speak, with personalities and physical bodies of a particular human genus, tribal and racial stock, so they are affected by, and become, at any rate for the extent of their mortal lives, co-dependent upon a part of the land. And in the past the bodies they inhabit have been sustained in large part by the fruit and produce of the land upon which they dwell, until their bodies return to its dust.

Part of the internationalism, the broader cast of mind of modern man, comes about as a result of a diet that comes in its physical origin from a different place on the Earth from which the body itself dwells. There is quite a deep linkage here between where the food and other necessities of life come from, and the conscious assumptions of human kind. The expansion of trade has brought about an expansion of mind that is ingested into the tissues. It is this rather than, at a more superficial level, the rapid dispersal of news through the modern media. This is certainly important but marks a more mental/emotional conscious response, rather than the emotional/etheric unconscious stratum of the well-being and maintenance of the physical body.

The older linkages go deeper, and it is these that are at the roots of nationalism, and local and tribal loyalties, which come to the fore when communal danger is threatened. This can also be exploited by those who have a feel for it and a particular axe to grind. You see it in civil wars, particularly of an ethnic kind, which is why the surest cause of trouble for the future well-being of humanity is the deliberate engrafting of one race or culture inside another, or upon another's ancient territory.

On a massive scale, problems may seem to be overcome. An amputation once suffered has, by definition, no minor problems to follow it, no matter what the pain or guilt involved at the time. But other situations become as running sores, that superate for generations, or may break out unexpectedly in seemingly placid times and circumstances. This is because there remain lines of natural cleavage in the cultures of humankind.

And when you have an intermixture of races or cultures, particularly on artificial or superficially expedient lines, it is like a similar situation on a biological or botanic level. It is possible for a graft or an implant to grow, and become a part of the general whole. But there is also the natural immune system, that normally serves the whole by ejecting foreign organisms. Either this has to be ameliorated or contained or it will become like the avenging Furies, the underground underworld revenging powers, working at their own level of function and justice, which may well not be the same as perceived by the civilised mind.

In this you have examples in the dilemma and pursuit of Orestes, torn between duties to kill his mother in the cause of justice or to honour her under the call of filial duty. As a result he was caught in conflict between Apollo and the Furies, a dispute only settled in the end by the wisdom of Pallas Athene. In such circumstances all parties have to be satisfied or justified, which calls for superhuman wisdom. And in this kind of dilemma lie most of the conflicts of the human race - and of the other beings who have a stake in how the cake of the world is divided at its many levels. That is, those angelic beings, amongst others, referred to by St Paul as Principalities and Powers. So-called Lords of this World, and of other worlds also, or who so aspire to be.

But that is another story. It is enough that we address ourselves to doing our best to cultivate our own plot of land and seeking a deeper meaning to the phrase that charity (the most fundamentally important of all human virtues) begins at home. Express love in your own small corner, and much else may then follow.

{The Soldier, 30.8.93}

38

But what we are leading up to? What has all this to do with standing upon the watchtower and looking forth upon the world as it appears from the inner side? It leads on to another type of magical image - one that is related to the external world and to events that may occur historically within it.

This species of magical image is broadly two-fold. There are images of persons and images of places. But remember that in all cases they are images. Remember what has been told to you about "the Masters". What they are "you cannot realise and it is a waste of time to try to do so." You just do not have the required organs of perception.

But they can be made known to you via the images that you build in your imagination. That is the meeting ground of objective and subjective as far as all these dynamics are concerned. This does not mean that they are any the less real, any more than the images that flicker upon your television screen, or that are built in your minds from the sounds that come through the radio, represent anything less real. They may be no more than images evoked in your mind but they represent realities. There are realities behind them, beyond them. They are like banknotes, cheques, letters of credit that are backed up by real wealth and assets.

So there are actual realities behind the images that come to you, which you are inspired or instructed to visualise. And note that I say "that come to you". For work of this nature and level requires inner direction. It would be folly indeed for any of you, in the lack of clear sight that besets you on the physical plane, to try to tinker with things at this level, as a result of your own political or even moral persuasion. You might as well go down to the local power station with spanner and screwdriver and try to divert the power lines to your own personal preference and satisfaction. Even if you got past the barricades, with your limited vision and understanding and lack of proper equipment, you would be unlikely to achieve anything, and lucky to survive the adventure unscathed if you did.

We are talking here of a properly contacted and functioning, well trained esoteric group. There are not a great many of these around, although perhaps more contacted individuals than you might think - linked interiorly by ways that you, and they, might not suspect. That is to say, the inner guardians of the nation, the land and the race, whose true and proper function is to handle these energies, will have their contacts with particular chosen sensitives and intuitives. These may seem to be doing very little to the outside world, but they are in effect points upon a circuit board designed by and maintained from the inner.

In a broad sense this may be discerned in "public opinion". This is often seemingly conservative or even reactionary, although it is capable, as in the recent rise in ecological awareness, of being very progressive and on occasion even revolutionary. It is this body of "conscience", held in the minds and the hearts of the many, but with particular significant power points, to which politicians of every rank and kind, even upon the international stage, seek to justify themselves.

Even the most despotic, the most callous in use of violence or terror, seek to justify themselves before this bar. And well they might, for it is the outer representative and manifestation of an inner bar of justice, that all wielders of earthly power will be accountable to, when they pass off this mortal coil upon which they have sought to impinge their views and ways. And that will be a judgment seat that is not readily fooled, conciliated or impressed by methods of media manipulation, public relations policy, or image management.

There will also be those upon the material plane who are directly responsive to inspirations or initiatives from the inner side. These are the writers, the thinkers, sometimes also the front line activists, driven on by patriotic, political or moral fervour. Although many of these may be unwittingly responsive to artificial elementals - or currents and eddies within the emotional atmosphere. This affects particularly the impatient young, some of whom may harden into narrow-visioned bigots like fruit that has withered and hardened on the bough. Although occasionally one, at the fanatical and visionary stage, becomes a martyr or national hero.

{*The Soldier, 31.8.91*}

39

We were saying there are two modes of magical image that concern us on the observation tower. One that appears as people and another that appears as places. What is the difference, we may ask, between what is observed up here and the moving pictures to be seen in the library?

The difference is that up here there is a greater element of immediacy. In the library you may be looking pretty far into space and time, or even fantasy that is symbolically underpinned. But here you are looking out into a current objectivity that concerns your own life and times in physical terms in the outer world.

It may not always seem like that, especially when you come, in the library, upon ancient or historical elements, or flashes of a future that may have been envisioned or mapped out, here or in some other plane or time. But whatever you see up here will have a bearing on what is happening in the physical present, in a location in space and time.

Looking out from here you will see England, and the many Isles of Albion. And spreading out from them, as if we were the centre, immediately neighbouring lands.

These you may find to be not quite the same as if you looked at a modern atlas. They have a layered effect, according to what level you are looking at. It is somewhat like a contour map in culture and time. In one perspective it may seem that the basin of the Northern Sea is predominant, with the countries about its border showing up more plainly than the lands elsewhere. This is the Scandinavian connection, and depends greatly upon ancient rulership. You may recall that King Cnut was king not only of England but also of Denmark, Norway and Sweden too. Those links still remain, however tenuous they may seem to a contemporary eye. They are like strong fibres within the leaf of a plant.

The same principle goes for the lands upon the mainland of Europe, from Calais down through Normandy, Maine, Aquitaine, and Anjou in modern day France, down as far as the Spanish peninsula and the borders of ancient Navarre and Aragon. - for when Norman kings were on the throne this land came under their rulership.

Then at a more extended level there is that of the British Empire, latterly called the Commonwealth. This still retains more obvious and conscious links despite a natural reaction in the current mind against the concept of colonial empire. But there remain, despite modern cavillings of conscience, deeper ties, and that may be no bad thing. Indeed, whether they be bad or good, they exist nonetheless.

The multiracial element of modern England is one consequence of this, unheard of, undreamed of, before the last World War. Before the so-called collapse of empire. Yet this is one result of the connections thus made. The roots of this, of karma if you like, you may find in Captain Hawkin's slaving trade, and the trading and later political links that grew from that.

And so you find a complicated web grows up, with threads both weak and strong, although any apparent weakness is usually a matter of perspective, for you will find all threads very strong if you personally come up against them. Thus the Roman connections may seem remote, a concern of antiquarians, classicists or schoolboys, until you come up against the consciousness, restimulated by your attention, of the magical image of a Roman centurion tied to a particular place. Then you will find it is a question of apparently meeting flesh and blood people, who come at you out of the mists of time. Thus it will appear, as you investigate this area both magically and consciously, how links exist that were built up by exploration and trade. And also, and above all, by links of blood - either of kinship, marriage, interbreeding, or the other kind of blood bond, even of sacrifice and slaughter, defence and conquest.

There will also be links created by powerful confrontation even upon an intellectual or emotional level, (above all, an emotional level}. And indeed on any level where the participants are enacting, in their own roles of personality, the clash or interface of the spiritual will of peoples, of nations, of families and tribes, or of Principalities and Powers.

In this you may have the links that are very strong, despite surface antagonisms, between these islands and Belgium and France. Before ever Norman united them, they hung together as the Gallic Empire under Victorinus and the Tetrici, that split off under Postumus at the time of the Emperor Gallienus. And so were they well ruled and established and maintained as an entity, upholding the principle of civilisation against barbarian invaders, until such time as the Roman Empire was reunited under Aurelian.

Later you will find links much closer in time from your present observation point. Of the bloody sacrifices on the Somme and the trenches of the Western front, extended latterly to more indiscriminate slaughter, on both sides.

This is this result of ancient cleavage trying to knit together, and may result in a Europe of the future. United Europes come and go, it is ever the swing of some great pendulum set swinging long before our time. We simply at a human level strive to adjust to its consequences. These are times and tides beyond the wit and control of any man. This is really archangel country - disbelieve in such airy-fairy concepts as modern man might.

So all of this is being opened up to you when you ascend the observation tower. It is thus not an area in which to indulge one's curiosity, or even sense of service, lightly. Things are much more comfortable in the library/scriptorium. What you see and feel up here is immediately impressed upon your consciousness. You experience it rather than observe it. Although there is an element of experience in the visions below, it is vicarious and not direct. And although there you may have the cohesion of a unified story line; here the links of causation, and the beginning, middle and end of a constructive story are never readily apparent.

Here there is an extension of life experience, there you have an extension of wisdom. Knowledge comes into both. But a different kind of knowledge. Here it is that of the navigator; there that of the map-maker, the scribe. Both have their value, each their place, and I would not recommend a qualitative judgment between the two. They are, like all in the tower, modes of service, and no-one should judge another's servant. For we all serve, each in our way, the same Master and masters. And here too we may gain some sense of that much misunderstood term of "Hierarchy".

{The Soldier, 1.9.93}

40

You will tend therefore to meet with the type of images associated with the observation tower under some kind of inner direction, whether or not that inner direction is consciously realised.

It may sometimes come in conjunction with a visit to an actual location, when such images might be confused with "place memories". Place memories certainly do exist, particularly where momentous or highly emotional events have occurred at a location, be it by murder or battle, or from long brooding in despair, sorrow or imprisonment. Although of course not all memories of place need be tragic or depressing. And while, by the nature of things, prolonged intensity of joy is not often the lot in human affairs, devotion, dedication to a place, or certain ideals connected with a place, may not uncommonly be discerned. This is particularly the case with organised and disciplined prayer, as in buildings of religious contemplative orders. There can also be a more secular "magnetic well-being", so to speak, associated with a garden long and lovingly tended. Or again with the ambience of learning in the precincts of an ancient college. Seats of government may also contain it, where good order and high ideals have, on balance, gained the ascendancy over self-seeking or bureaucracy.

Hospitals and prisons, barrack blocks also have a magnetic atmosphere surrounding and associated with them. Hospitals, despite their association with sickness may not be so bad as might be expected. They have an underlying idealism engendered by those who work in them. Prisons of course can be pretty grim, and barracks give, on the whole, little inspiration, apart from, in certain quarters, a gallant and comradely *esprit de corps* which can be beneficial or uplifting.

However the images I have in mind are those encountered generally by those more sensitised, usually by some course of esoteric training. Although this is not an essential prerequisite, for the sensitive and imaginative can all be reasonably easily contacted and impressed upon this level.

The figures of autonomous or semi-autonomous magical images are generally of historical characters, and those about whom there has grown some kind of charismatic ambience. This may not necessarily be a very accurate reflection upon the actual life or personality of the figure involved. The more famous are invested with all kinds of larger qualities. The reality was generally considerably less obviously significant, but by the nature of things, ideas are woven in for which the person provides a convenient pattern, hook, or role model for the projection of ideals and emotions.

These figures are therefore synonymous, pretty well, with those to be found in a popular approach to history, whether that be in school books intended for the very young, or in the fancies of historical novelists and their readers.

We can choose a few names at random, by way of example, from British history: Queen Elizabeth I, Mary Queen of Scots, King Richard the Lionheart, Sir Francis Drake, Sir Walter Ralegh. Indeed there are certain popular poets of recent times, of which we have spoken, whose works contain almost a systematic roll call of these figures. For instance Alfred Noyes' *Tales of the Mermaid Tavern* contain all the above, besides literary figures such as Ben Jonson, Christopher Marlowe, Francis Bacon and William Shakespeare.

Some of these figures were built up to mythopoeic proportions within their own times. For instance Elizabeth I, as Astraea, Gloriana, the Virgin Queen, embodied certain important religious, cultural and political ideals. Important not only for her own time, but as a channel or watershed for ideals, aspirations and codes of conduct for later generations.

Mary Queen of Scots also. A great romantic figure, and one with claims to a martyr's crown, despite, or indeed because of her romantic vulnerability as an idealistic, sometimes impractical and passionate woman. She embodies, or takes into her ambience, all the emotions and aspirations engendered in the Stuart cause, which embraces a number of ideas and ideals, from Scottish independence to restoration of the Roman Catholic faith.

Richard the Lionheart too, although by no means an ideal monarch in the historical record or the flesh, provides a popular image for all ideals associated with the Crusades. Of giving up one's life and living and for a higher spiritual or international cause. There was of course self-seeking and intolerance in the mounting of the Crusades - and we hardly advocate the benefits of holy wars - yet in and amongst all of this, and brought to the fore in the heightened circumstances of conflict, are the supra-personal qualities; the hall-marks of the martyr and the saint. Exemplars of human conduct who place a spiritual ideal before the material expedient.

{The Soldier, 2.9.93}

41
You will also meet others who are not necessarily figures of the rich and famous but representatives of their times. The Roman centurion for example, the Templar knight, the London sweep, the Elizabethan cabin boy. These are almost like angelic messengers, bringing through a particular contact at a particular time. They may embody a multidimensional message by their presence as often as not. Rather as an image of a Tarot card can bring through or represent a many faceted communication.

They strike an emotional or responsive chord within you. And any verbal message they bring may indeed be the smallest part of what is communicated, and can often be simply a means of attaining and holding your conscious attention. Although any words expressed, often in a simple phrase, can also have their own vitality, generally more than most people realise. And there may also be a higher element which is brought through intuitively, besides the directly spiritual.

It is rather like getting to know an actual person, even it may seem quite superficially. You make a contact upon many simultaneous levels, not all of which may be apparent to you consciously at the time. But you know you have met someone, or something other, another spark from the divine fire.

So with these personal magical images. They do not operate simply on an astro-mental level. They are no mere conventional pictures held in the imagination. They are contacts. That is the most significant and appropriate word. Just as an electrical terminal can be a contact with a source of power. Get to know and relate to these contacts. Act as if they were real. Take them at face value, and much will be gained.

Save your sceptical analysis until a later time. And valuable though that may be, do not let it be dominated by the intellectual content of verbal interchange, nor highly critical of any seeming anachronisms, even though they seem bizarre.

When we make contact with a personal incarnate consciousness, including your own, we are dependent upon the concepts, images and ideas floating within a subliminal pool contained in the recipient's brain cells, which are readily available, at a touch of stimulation, to the conscious mind. And much of this may be floating debris, flotsam and jetsam picked up from reading, conversations, forgotten impressions from life or culled from pictures or books. The mind at this level is like a colossal magnet, or a vacuum cleaner. Without sense of purpose or direction, it is a maelstrom of impressions and images, conceptions, prejudices, childish or romantic imaginings, upon which we have to rely to formulate a message and maintain our contact.

Thus we have a difficult but by no means impossible task, for there are elements in the mind that cause or enable coherence. This is similar to the way iron filings will form into a pattern if vibrated or shaken in the presence of a magnet. You may sometimes be aware of that shaking activity when we need to stir up the contents of your subliminal mind a little, so that it can react and conform to the appropriate "magnetic" pattern that we are bringing within your range of consciousness.

This can be quite disturbing to those brought into contact with levels of field, in terms of power, that they might not normally encounter. Hence the practice of careful graded training in the Mystery schools, and the need for some care to be taken in the running of public or semi-public "workshops". We do not seek to overpower anybody. We are not an inner plane "mafia".

{The Soldier, 3.9.93}

42
{The Philosopher takes over}

The Soldier has been speaking to you about the magical images of persons that may be met in association with certain places. I wish now to say something about the importance of places. That is, either in a physical location to which you may go, or in visionary terms via the powers of the watch-tower or those of the library.

Whichever avenue you may choose, as far as you in incarnation are concerned, the end results are much the same. The experiences, or the difference between them, would be a good deal more perceptible if you did not have your consciousness anchored in a physical body. For in that case you could be considerably blown about, magnetically attracted, even to some extent earthbound by too close an involvement with the forces of the watch tower.

This is because on the watch tower one comes into a more direct and immediate relationship with the Earth sphere, the outer aspects of the planetary globe, which has its own turbulent forces. Imagine geomagnetic forces like a churning maelstrom, which to an attenuated form of consciousness are as palpable as wind or water tides are to you on the physical. In this respect the Earth globe is like a great beast, for conscious living entity it is, although without a highly developed rational consciousness. It has the equivalent of pounding heartbeat through veins and arteries and the power of breathing in rhythmic cycles. The science of sun-spots, solar wind, gravitational and magnetic effects is as close as you can come to describing this process accurately in outer terms. In terms of inner experience it can be similar to being a little too close to a volcano, earthquake or other spectacular geophysical phenomena.

The type of visionary faculties used in the library are a less direct approach. "Crystal screens" might be the best word to describe the mode of contact, for they rely on a species of earth memory (or indirectly of other spheres) that is encapsulated in a certain resonance of crystal faces. These are partly natural and partly artificially constructed. The holding of the records tends to be natural but the means of access to them the work of human minds.

(Why the works of human intelligence should be considered artificial, and not part of the natural order is, on consideration, a little strange. The reason is an oblique acknowledgement of the difference resulting from the direct possession of a divine spark. All forms and forces of nature are fashioned by beings of another order, who are as equally spiritual in origin as ourselves. But their creations, most of what is called the natural world, are "creations of the created" and are of a different order to the creations we make ourselves. Our own exploit what is already to be found in the creations of the others - the "earlier" swarms. {We talk of cosmic rather than terrestrial time}. Just as they in their turn made adaptations to, or built more complex constructions of that which had been created before. We are all brothers and sisters, co-workers, in the same cosmic task, voluntary co-operatives of sub-creative artisans in the building of the City of God.)

The "library" form of vision is akin to looking at an electronic display screen in the course of investigation or research, as opposed to going out and doing actual field work. This differentiation holds quite well in your own plane of consciousness too, whether you go out and abroad physically in search of direct magical experience of people and places, or whether you confine yourself to the quietness of meditation and inward vision in your own place set apart.

There is however a meeting point of these two modes of activity. You may visit a place and there pick up the necessary etheric link, even unconsciously, which is then available for use in your own more private place at a convenient time later. This is rather in the nature of a geologist going out to a location to collect samples to investigate in his own private laboratory. It is neither needful nor convenient for him to carry his scientific apparatus to the site. Similarly, ritual or other performances to aid vision or for the direction of forces are seldom necessary or a practical advantage at a specific site. But the contact made by such a visit, the simple physical presence of your own body there, provides sufficient link for later use.

The possession of a small object or artefact from the site can also be effective, or even a picture of it. This is best drawn or painted, but a photograph will do, especially if you make your own drawing or painting from it. All these methods form an effective talismanic link. To the skilled operative upon the physical plane neither method need be essential, although this requires the conscious co-operation of experienced co-workers upon the inner planes.

{The Philosopher, 4.9.93}

43

You have yourself experienced something of the pull of places in your own visits to Hellas. This is the name I prefer for the ancient hallowed land that is now called Greece, in much the same way and for the same reasons that we often refer to these islands as Albion or Logres. It gives a greater resonance to ancient holy and sacred things than modern designations. The common names of nation states are but the product of the modern age, and the powers of the land go back a good way further than that. In terms of human experience every land is many layered, and for the building of magical images and effective working with them, you need to be able to respond to the ambience of the appropriate level.

Thus is the study of history important to the occultist, not in the study of multitudinous detail but in an appreciation of broad trends in the rise and fall of dynasties and epochs and to try to arrive at the feel of an epoch. This is as likely to be done by a knowledge of the literature, should it survive, and preferably in the original tongue - although that is a counsel of perfection. Also acquaintance with its works of art and artefacts, and preferably seeing them in actuality and handling them where possible, visiting actual places as they stand now, with eyes and inner perceptions attuned to their historical foundations.

Myth and legend also play a part, including more modern and popular tales. In his own land and clime William Tell is as important as Hephaistos; as are the angels of Mons to the army with banners of St Michael.

Handling quite common artefacts can be as helpful a means of attunement as viewing at a distance more precious and therefore inaccessible treasures. In this coins can be effective, or cheaper artefacts such as lamps, bowls, ornaments, bottles, even glass or clay shards from them, or fragments of tile or stone. There is a rationale, an inner sense of talismanic action and significance, behind the instinct of the souvenir hunter. Not that we would wish to see historic monuments torn to pieces by collectors.

The custodians of such sites try to meet this need by sale of manufactured imitations. These can have a certain value. At least they have a link in conception and have been stored, displayed and sold at the appropriate place. And as the medieval church discovered, where relics had ceased to exist, it could be profitable to invent them.

Here we have the operation of an interesting law. Through reverence from those who really believe, or have been induced to believe, a genuine resonance, or inner etheric patina, can be induced upon a particular object, even though its provenance be false. This is none other than a truly effective operation of talismanic magic: to induce within an object, by concentrated emotive, mental and spiritual attention, magnetic qualities and power that it hitherto did not possess.

Thus although venerated relics may subsequently be proven less venerable or ancient than was supposed, they can still retain a special significance and power. This can, it is true, be diminished by consequent scepticism, and erosion of faith and belief, but to those who still believe in some degree, the power will still be there.

One particular instance of this is the Holy Shroud of Turin. Now believed to be of medieval origin, although of the Holy Land, and probably containing the impress and the blood of a crucified crusader rather than the Corpus Christi. But think what years of veneration have done to empower that shroud, powerful enough in itself in any case through martyrdom, stored and in the custody of contemplative orders, with their concentrated reverence that surpasses in effect even the intensity of mass popular belief.

For belief is an important element in the geography of the inner planes. And although there is much to be said for scientific objectivity - which by definition is devoid of all subjectivity - even in the outer world belief retains its power and is largely a dictator of events. Hence the importance of public opinion, which modern manipulators of power ignore at their peril.

There is, whether we like it or not, a very subjective element in the whole conspectus of human life. Hence the importance of right, or healthy belief. That is, belief which accords with "the waters above the firmament" in ancient biblical terms. For the course of life in "the waters below" is not particularly well structured, it is a voyage upon a turbulent sea. The attempt to attain an order of civilised life pertains to a higher order of being. It is a memory of heaven worlds, and not a natural consequence of the lower worlds below - the inferior waters.

{*The Philosopher,* 5.9.93}

44

This is at root why the concept and the reality of place is important. For a place will invariably be a construct, a human construct that is based upon spiritual lines. That is, upon a spiritual blue-print with values beyond this Earth, inklings of a golden age of spiritual being, of the life immortal.

It may well be that human constructions have their original foundation, the reasons for their siting, coincident upon an element of nature, such as a high hill, a spring, a chasm - all these you have at the oracle of Delphi. But the building and the purpose and the dedication associated with such a place is a consecration, a raising of a portion of the Earth to a spiritual attunement that would otherwise not be within its nature. And where such dedication, such attunement, is aligned with, or conferred upon, or apparently springs from, under-earth or underworld forces, then the force and significance is great indeed. For the highest has a meeting place with the lowest, cosmically speaking, and a mighty vortex spanning all the planes can be set up.

So it was with Delphi. The underworld chthonic powers of the dragon, Ladon of the Hesperides, brought under the dedication and the power of the sun god Apollo. With the consequence of having perhaps the greatest oracular centre and shrine of the ancient world, and one that is still visited and revered to this day.

It embodies truth and value for the discerning, it is a more prosaic curiosity for the rest, but it was ever thus. So does one have a complete range of interest, from the spiritually informed to the curious and inquisitive and mundane. You find much the same span of interest in the very modern species of vortex called the Tarot.

And in ancient time the tribes of Israel were led by pillar of cloud by day and a pillar of fire by night to Mount Zion. Here the rumbling, roaring flashing volcanic powers acted as a focus for the invocation and the manifestation, in terms of human consciousness, of the Most High. This has produced an ever widening vortex of spiritual consciousness that has encompassed the globe, for it is the common basis for the faith of Christian, Muslim and Jew.

So much for religious vortices. One could go on. The examples are numerous, from Jerusalem to Glastonbury, for every country has its sacred centres, and their powers and their potency, (not the same thing), will be as individual as the race and the circumstances that conceived them.

Human habitation itself centres about geophysical features. The rising of towns often about a crossing of a river, where land way meets water way, with ultimate access to inner lands and outer seas, and to lands beyond that. This meeting of elements, of the trackways, is the forming of a vortex, manifesting as a trading post, soon to be fenced around and walled in, to become a defined cosmic system. Within that perimeter, that Ring-Pass-Not in the language of *The Cosmic Doctrine*, the increasingly complex interplay of life can begin. The formulation of laws, civil interaction, the process of civilisation, are all the outer expression of the inner city, the City of God in the Highest, even though the shadow may be a poor representative of the pristine and spiritual reality.

But over and over again, that form, that image, is built. Only to fall as often as not, and then perhaps to rise again, for all such constructions are upon a shifting foundation. The only solid land is in the heavens. What solidity you appear to have on earth is like the shifting sea of the sands of the desert.

However, it is the task and purpose of man spiritually and physically to irrigate that desert, to make it bloom, albeit just for a time in human terms.

This panorama of plants coming to bloom and dying off, either by natural process or overcome by the disturbance of superior forces, is a magical image of the history of civilisations. Even though barbarian outbursts and forays may overturn a superior civilisation, so these in their turn realise, undergo and express the civilising process in their turn. Thus we have the spiritual flowers continuing to bloom in the wilderness.

That which is seen upon the outer plane as fair cities, centres of law, of justice, of the flowering of arts and sciences, is like the growth of buildings of religious worship expressed in stone within. From this you may discern the reason for our emphasis upon the abbey church, or temple in its broadest sense, as a comprehensive magical image. For such a place is a complex of shrines or dedicated chapels within an overall focussing of common spiritual purpose.

And the links between cities, the centres of human expression and civilisation, become important also. These are the trade routes, by land and sea and latterly by air, lines of power expressed by humanity and extending across the globe. The great web or network of civilisation is like the net about the sacred stone that in ancient Greece marked the centre of the universe, the *ombilicos*. Even though in a fallen world its expression may be far from the ideal, ever subject to corruption, the ultimate purpose of human life and expression is redemption. The raising of that which is fallen. And this restitution, honoured and precious and celebrated with joy, is as the finding of the lost sheep, or the return of the prodigal son.

{The Philosopher, 6.9.93}

45

These land ways, sea ways, and air ways, together with the great centres of human civilisation and congregation that they interconnect, are as important as what have come to be known as ley-lines. That is, they are inter-connecting ways within the etheric, which indeed are numerous, and of different kinds. In the search and popular interest in ancient tracks and power lines it is an odd quirk of human nature that the important outer ways and centres should have been ignored.

The subject of course is a vast one, even upon the outer plane, and comprises no less than an historical geography, in urban, political and economic terms, of the human race. And within this there is an element of the importance of commodities and where and when they are to be found. The significance of great natural resources, be it of copper, iron, gold, wheat, maize, rice, cotton, has its roots in their creation and implantation, their original species and form, through the work of pre-human spiritual orders ("swarms" or "creative hierarchies"), that laid the conditions within the overall Divine Plan that is currently being worked out, as best as it may, by humanity, (the "human swarm" or "human creative hierarchy").

Thus the great complex of "outer" science, of outer happenings, of the natural and the human order, are as important for study as is esoteric science. For they are expressions of forces that have their origin upon the inward and the spiritual planes. The whole thing, the whole matrix, is a seamless robe, and it is a strange anomaly that in present time there should have arisen a division between the two.

This is a chasm in current human culture that is only temporary, although in this sense we speak of a longer time scale than that of the individual mortal life-span - the incarnationary unit of measure. So it is particularly difficult for you, and others of the generations immediately before and after you, to have to cope with such a split in consciousness, a generally accepted world view at the time you were born, and which will still be there at the time when you die.

This temporary split however is a necessary one. It is a by-product of the developing individuality of human spiritual expression. To see oneself more clearly it is necessary for a time to have the ability to step outside of oneself - even into unreality. To take a split-off, cut-off, fragmented and limited view - the better to advance and come to full self-realisation. I speak of the human race as a whole, not of individuals, although of course the forest is made up individual trees.

So in practical terms the immediate task you have is one of discernment and differentiation - discrimination if you will (traditionally the first qualities and virtues of a training for the Mysteries) - so that you can then re-unite the separated branches. Those whose gaze is entirely upon the inner planes, (although their perception is not without value), are indeed as fragmented, as isolated, as out on a limb in their approach, as the most benighted of materialists. It is important that the esoteric student of the present and the future should realise the indwelling nature of the spiritual within the physical. This includes the spiritual origin of its presence in various forms, and the reason for its coming into human consciousness in the working out on Earth of the Divine Plan.

A failure to do this is merely a kind of regression to the past. The forming of a kind of psychic blister upon the flesh of human actuality - a de-sensitising. Whatever happens upon the earth has its psychic and its spiritual counterparts. The physical plane is the plane of effects. If you limit your attention solely to the physical you limit your vision, and your effectiveness, such as it is, to the plane of effects. You are as in a game of blind man's buff, floundering around, ignorant of real causes - which are upon the planes of causation.

On the other hand, to limit your focus of attention to the inner worlds entirely, without regard to their physical interconnection, is to wander in a mist of possibilities. This is ineffectuality after another manner. It is necessary to see connections. And whilst this may not be easy, it is the way and pattern for initiation, and the development of true adepti in the science and art of magic.

You will gather from this that magic is a responsible and important discipline within the conspectus of human destinies and abilities. It is no mere playground of self-deception for the weak, the ignorant and the foolish. There is a reality behind the imaginings of real magic that is every bit as powerful and objective as whatever or whoever you may encounter upon the physical plane.

This element of "whoever" is doubly important too. Limited as you are in your vision, by incarnation, (or incarceration as some might see it), in the flesh, you are hardly in a position to work unaided. Yet your situation is such, (worldlings with a vision or inward link to the realms of immortality), that you are uniquely placed to help the Divine Plan forward. This relies on intelligent and willing co-operation with those upon the inner planes who can see more clearly over the broader span of evolutionary needs. And so together, effective action within the world can be undertaken.

This does not necessarily result in a life of great outer powers or activity. There are some, rare souls, who play a major part as men and women of outer power and responsibility in the world, allied to inner contact and realisation. But more often it is a question of an attunement of consciousness to certain inner dynamics that have, as their mode of expression, types of action that in the terms of the outer world might seem inconsequential or ineffectual.

This is one reason for ritual. It is also an element in the visiting of places and making inner connections. It is a process of making the ways that you tread through life into a truly magical journey or quest.

This is symbolically expressed in another mode when the magus makes his circumambulation of the temple. It is an enactment, a pacing out, a conforming to, an "earthing", of inner principles.

To do this without the inner connections is indeed mere day-dreaming, fantasy and children's play. To do it with the inter-connections, the co-operation of dedicated workers upon the inner planes is to provide an effective means of expression for the Hierarchy, whose apex is no less than with the Most High God, and whose companions are the angels who, with you, seek to do his bidding.

{The Philosopher, 7.9.93}

46

By the contact and internal co-operation with inner plane helpers, you may be led to ways of service that would not be possible by any other means. Connections can be made, small, seemingly inconsequential or coincidental, that nevertheless form an essential part in operations of the brotherhood of light. You may only seldom glimpse their significance or magnitude but these links are fundamental in importance because they are "earthing".

In this work you needs must have much faith, and this we try to establish by these contacts to which you, in your fulness as human beings in the world of matter, can respond. And so faith, over the years, gives way to experience and knowledge. A knowledge of something of what we are and what we try to do, and the means whereby we try to do it.

If this were ineffective or delusory it is hardly likely that you would continue to cooperate with it. It is no idle solitary occupation that feeds upon illusions or self-satisfaction. Indeed you are tested, often quite severely, on some parts of the way.

You form part of a brotherhood, a sisterhood, that is as yet invisible to you. A gleaming net of starlight that shines like a web in the morning dew, crystal reflecting mirrors of the dawning light of the day star.

You yourselves are, did you but realise it, reflecting and recording instruments of this star shine. For as spiritual beings you have the links, the inward antennae, to capture and respond to the resonating message of the stars. This message, this network of communication, of help and succour, is ever about you, like the waves of the far more material and gross waves of sound and radio.

You live in a cacophany of earthly generated noise, upon the physical and electro-magnetic levels. The radiating network of the star waves is equally real, equally accessible did you but fashion the right equipment and accurately tune it. That equipment is within your own mind and soul. Did you but know it you are walking receivers, indeed I might go so far as to say it is the reason for your whole existence. Yet there are so many non-functioning or malfunctioning examples of apparatus that non-functioning often seems to be the norm. Yet if all human spiritual transceivers were properly and truly functioning then the face of the world as you know it would be transfigured.

Perhaps this is too much to ask, even too much to envision in the present state of human and planetary evolution. It is a slow march forward, back to lost perfection, although remember that time and evil alike are transitory illusions. They have no place in the cosmic scheme. The place they occupy is only in the false creations, (false sub-creations strictly speaking) of some rebellious spirits.

Some of these might indeed seem "mighty" in human terms, as you have become used to conceiving them in your current limitations, but this perception of comparative size, of vastness, of overbearing magnitude is also an illusion. They are illusions of twisted perceptions in a hall of distorting mirrors.

Your opposition, our opposition, such as it is, comprises a band of tricksters, masters (or aspirants to mastership) of illusion; deceivers, beguilers, the real value of whose blandishments and seductions, even their threats, is hollow empty air. And were it so realised the better it would be even for them, for they are trapped in their own self-deception, their own delusions, within their kingdoms of unbalanced force.

The gift of free will does not entail by necessity the expression of perverse will, the pushing of freedom to the limits of disobedience and anarchy - to a fragmented and fractured net. And yet you have the illusion of a universe, that may seem as "a tale full of sound and fury, told by an idiot, signifying nothing," but believe me this perception is far from the shining network of reality that encompasses you.

The Incarnate Lord is depicted as a fisher, as he bid his leading disciples to be fishers of men. Be aware of that silver net that is trawled from the heavens within your element, the inferior waters beneath the firmament. This is the meaning in spiritual terms of that great story, itself also a parable, of the Christ bidding the fishers to cast their nets at his bidding the other side. They did his spiritual bidding, although in earthly terms of common sense and experience it well seemed futile, and were rewarded with a mighty catch. That mighty catch is later seen in the history of the world as the power of Christendom.

So be aware of that silver net. It is also a stairway, a star way, an extended version of Jacob's Ladder. By it you may climb. By merely holding on to it, you may become aware of vibrations within it from afar off, even to the highest, and to remote and spiritual regions you dream not of. Perfect civilisations, expressions in perfect matter of the divine will and grace. Worlds that may seem impossible to your occluded senses.

For this net is also one of harmony. Like a great harp, whose every interval is attuned to a cosmic harmony. It is a visual image of the harmony of the spheres, the paeans of praise of the worshipping angels - the Seraphim, the Cherubim. It is indeed an angelic network of light, to which human spirits in Earth can become gradually attuned.

There is also an inferior network, that to spiritual vision seems gross. It is like a tarry network of rope, flung repeatedly into the air by a gross, darkly splendid but besmirched and begrimed Caliban-like figure. The inferior Adam you might call him although he goes by other, sometimes more grandiose names. Standing upon his rock of Earth in a dark and silent wilderness, he repeatedly throws his rough spun and woven net into the air, only to have it fall about him in entanglements.

He has the instincts and the aims of a hunter of butterflies using an equipment out of proportion to his aims. He seeks to bring down heaven to Earth, to be in command of it. And crude though this magical image may seem that I have constructed for you, the action and reality is seen in the aspirations to render a physical perfection on Earth by means of material technology. And though such ways and means in some degree may ameliorate human suffering, I have only to point to the state of the world and how the best intended and conceived science and technology serves only to make the world a worse as well as a better place. It serves the strong, exploits the weak, and justice is unknown to it, save as it is modified by the higher intentions, the ultimate conscience of women and men. But the true technology, even though I present it to you in terms of magical imagery, is the work of the net - the stellar and spiritual net.

{The Philosopher, 8.9.93}

47

By reference to, by visualising this starry net, you will realise that the space between the stars, and within the system of the Sun, the planets, is no empty vacuum, no dark void. It only seems so on the outermost level, to eyes, ears and inner senses that are spiritually dark, and further darkened by evil counsel. But by visualising the network in its bright and silver gossamer flexibility and strength you will begin to attune your minds and your inner perceptions to the mighty possibilities beyond. These are actualities and realities in the spiritual realm, but possibilities for you, and potential for the re-blossoming of the Earth with the flowers sown from the star seed.

For these are trackways upon which power and thought can flow. And shakings of the net within the higher realms may be discerned in the sympathetic resonance in the lower, in the levels of the net that are closest to your own perception. Therefore, although the initiative, the tremblings in the veil of the spiritual will of the Most High, emanate from a realm of Cherubim and Seraphim in terms and modes of glorious life about which you can barely wonder, the resonating of the net, magically attuned to your consciousness within the level of your immediate perceptions, allows you to register and to react to, and in some measure to understand, the happenings of the higher worlds - where "words" are "deeds".

I thus present to you in visual terms things that can hardly be conceived in their unadorned reality. It is much the same with your efforts to comprehend the nature of the sub-atomic or even the atomic worlds that make up physical nature.

Here, the current mode of investigation is not by direct perception, but by numerical readings from complex instruments. To interpret meaning from the high mathematical abstractions of mathematics you need to build pictures in the imagination. Yet none of these are strictly accurate. All are resonances, representations, childish drawings upon the wall of human comprehension. But they serve a purpose, as a basis for discussion, interchange, understanding. And what hope has the most brilliant mind if it discovers the inmost secrets of the universe but cannot communicate what has been found?

That is the ultimate negation of spirituality, the isolation of the ultimate hell. So, like the mechanism of a working clock, you must have the tolerance of slight inaccuracy, of error, lest the system seize up altogether, tight bound through lack of tolerance that allows its parts to move. In one sense this is the realm of permitted evil. Although that is a far thing from the positive evil of spiritual fragmentation, the ultimate loosening, where good things fall apart in anarchy and chaos.

The cosmic net has been constructed in intellectual terms in ancient times. In some crudity it is the actions of the gods of ancient myth, but more accurately the doctrines of Pythagoras, and latterly Plotinus. And the cool bare intellectual outline of this clearest of thinkers has been embroidered upon by Christian visionaries such as Dante, and in the speculations of the Jewish Qabalists and other like minded adepti of the Orient.

Those with a mystical consciousness of reality, which they were willing and able, sometimes with great courage and daring, to try to express in visual terms. Although to try to describe the reality of the higher worlds within the terms of the lower is rather like trying to make a mighty painting, say Leonardo's Last Supper, using the palette of a muddy puddle.

And so there have been various interpretive constructions, closer to your own time. Of Boehme, of Swedenborg, of Blavatsky and of Steiner. All by their very nature, crudities - and I mean no disrespect when I say such things. I intend no cavilling criticism. The task by its very nature must yield an inadequate result. They are but fractions of a mosaic. Dim distorting representations of a fair and wondrous reality that will, however, have served their purpose if they but turn the eyes of the human race into more or less the right direction. Descartes too and Pascal, in their ways, have sensed the divine vision. But in various ways all such visions are open to misinterpretation, even by their instigators, to say nothing of their followers, or those who journey afterwards in the intellectual ashes of their fiery comet trails.

The original vision was of the spirit. But it cools. The living spark will turn to ash. Although very often a deep and banked up heat and glow remains, that can be fanned to flame by a discerning spirit who follows, with sympathy, after. One who reads their works with intelligence and tolerance, and with their own spiritual eye at least partly open.

And so I have endeavoured myself, in the tradition of which you form a living part, to paint something of the glory of the inner universe, up to the most high, in what has been called *The Cosmic Doctrine*. It has its faults, its inaccuracies, the same as all the other attempts to light a candle in the sun, to capture the moon in a pail. But we continue to try. That is the essence of the human condition. And perhaps we may be able to improve upon, to modify, to explain a little further, something of the intentions that were meant. To clarify, to polish up the darkened mirror a little bit. To reveal the true glory beyond and inspire the incarnate soul to seek it.

{*The Philosopher,* 9.9.93}

48
{*The Chancellor resumes*}

We have now given you at least an outline of the powers and visions that are a function of the tower. You now have some understanding of the types of service that are open to you by the use of magical images of various types. Any further instruction of this nature is one of detail, of explicit experience. I would now have you continue our perambulation about the abbey, for there are further things to see and explain upon the ground level as well.

You will be aware, immediately before us, and to our left, the chapel that we saw from above. That is, the chapel of the devout and newly dead souls. Although "newly" is a very relative term if we take account of it in Earth years. The amount of "time" a soul may spend in this type and level of contemplation is of little moment in earthly terms, and is the cause of some apparent discrepancy in accounts of this stage. It may be months in earthly time, or it may be very many years. Let us enter in.

A golden curtain on rings of ivory is all that separates us from the souls in the chapel within, and so we reverently pass through it and quietly kneel at places that seem left vacant for us.

There is a great peace and quietness within. A certain quality of the atmosphere that seems to invest the air with a golden light. You may also see above the altar, that is richly decked in cloth of red and white, a deeper golden haze. Beyond it, marking a place within the wall where the Host is reserved, there is an equal armed silver cross of diamond light, softly gleaming. It is at the level of the heart of a figure of the Master, Jesus, that builds over the altar in the golden light. The golden haze might have been regarded elsewhere as the gathering clouds of incense smoke, but there is no discernible thurible here. The clouds of golden glory emanate from the prayers and thoughts of all who are kneeling within. They are thoughts and feelings of penitence. This comes from them like a deep purple emanation, rolling towards the altar, and when it reaches the foot of the altar it turns to a golden light and ascends. It is within this cloud of transformed penitence and aspiration that the figure of the Incarnate One appears.

We may, for the good of our souls, as well as an act of reverence and service, add to those prayers. This anticipates also an immediate task that awaits you after physical death. Let your thoughts dwell on the circumstances, the acts of your life, in the outer world. Here you may experience a detachment from them. But it is not a detachment of analysis and cold abstraction. This is not a judgement hall, it is a place of intimate assessment, review and acceptance of that which IS, offering it for use in service. And no matter how blank or black the actions that arise before you, your dwelling upon them in the spirit of this place will draw good from them, as their pain, their error, or sorrow is transformed into the golden light of acceptance and forgiveness. Into the redemptive power, through the heart of God, of blessing.

This is the place therefore for the exercise that is often recommended to esoteric students who seek to prepare themselves for service, that of the Evening Review. A time at the close of each day, when the events of that day are unrolled before the mind's eye, in inner vision. It is frequently taught that this unrolling of the carpet of experience in space and time should run backwards. This can be helpful in a psychological manner, it helps to break up conglomerates of action or thought by a reversal of perspective. What however is more important is the tone or manner in which you perform this exercise. And it is to encourage and amend this that we have revealed to you this image of the Chapel of Redemption, of the Holy Presence, within the abbey.

If you see yourselves entering here, you may become aware of being in the company of other souls, of every age and clime. Of the newly dead, and of those who have passed from the burden of the mortal flesh for some time. I see one of Cromwell's time even now. One who feels he has sinned much in the execution of religious duty and excess of enthusiasm in the civil wars. But concern yourself not with the detail of others who are here. Simply be aware that you are not alone. Part of a company of others far removed from you perhaps in temperament or in time, but with whom you are united in the common cause of your redemptive purpose here.

This awareness of others is a natural remedy against spiritual exclusiveness, and such may be the problem with that Cromwellian soldier, whose presence came so strongly upon us. He may have sinned greatly, and in ways that he bitterly regrets, seeing himself as a deluded hypocrite perhaps, and so filled with remorse. Thus he has much pain to release, but the end of that will come as and when he becomes more aware of the presence of others. We are not alone in the midst even of our iniquity, however grievous it may appear to be. Indeed then we are never less alone, within this fallen world. And we help to bear one anothers' burdens. This is another aspect, or element, of the sacred, the holy net, of which the Philosopher was speaking.

It is possible that our presence and our realisation may have helped the Cromwellian soldier. Some shaft of our concern may have responded to an outreaching chord within his soul. But we are not here as missionaries or as helpers - that is a role that may be performed by angelic presences. These may be discerned simply as delicate shapes in the light above the heads of those who are assembled here, the presence of the Holy Guardian Angels and their lesser known helpers.

Our main concern here is that of ourselves and our own account before our Maker. Let the events, the actions of your life, roll before you, not unduly condemning yourself, or passing judgement; for that is, as often as not, simply an intellectual interference. There is only one judge, one judgement that is here. And that is the Sacred Heart of the figure that stands before you in light over the altar. Whose presence upon earth is encapsulated in the bread and wine of the sacred host, the sacrament.

I recommend therefore that you come here each day. Each evening perhaps when you lie down to rest. And let the experience do the teaching. It has a resonance, a relationship to the chapel within the tower, but this chapel is dedicated to the on-going experience and daily round of initiates, and those who are seekers in the giving of service, and the help you may receive here is attuned to those needs.

{*The Chancellor,* 10.9.93}

49

And now, quietly and with due acknowledgement to the power behind the altar, we depart from this place. Let us reflect for a moment upon its reality. In its form as described it is a form of magical image. An image upon which your attention and imagination can engage so as to attune your mind, and your greater consciousness, to the necessary self reflective condition for the power of redemption to do its work. Thus it contains the function of what we may call a "composition of mood" as well as a "composition of place". It turns your mind to a form of after-death condition.

That condition is sometimes called "The Judgement Hall of Osiris", which in itself has gained a certain popularity in esoteric circles largely through its ancient Egyptian pictorial element. It is depicted on the great Papyrus of Ani, displayed at the British Museum and frequently reproduced elsewhere, where the soul of the dead, or of the initiate, is shown approaching the scales of assessment and divine justice, there to be weighed against the feather of Maat, before being either admitted to the heaven worlds or thrown as unworthy to the crocodile. It is not of course the soul itself that is consigned to the pit of destruction - unless entirely evil, an unlikely condition, for there is good in all - but rather the unredeemed, spiritually unreal aspects of the personality in terms of the good.

As with all ancient Egyptian religious painting, there is a purity of line and quality of simplicity that makes it easily memorable, as befits any Book of the Dead, of which there are numerous examples, as guides for those newly bereft of their physical bodies to find their way in the immediately inner world. Such range from the sophisticated mantra of the Tibetan Buddhists to the less cerebral formulations of the shamans or medicine men of what we are pleased to call primitive tribes, (primal might be a better word, men of the beginnings, without the pejorative implication).

No matter how "advanced" in civilisation we might be, or so regard ourselves, we have our basic humanity in common. And as is sometimes forgotten in esoteric training for service in the Mysteries, no matter how high our assumed or functioning grade, we none of us ever leave the 1st Degree. We build upon foundations. We do not leave the common ground behind. Sometimes a painful lesson has to be experienced or imparted before we fully realise this.

It is the same with the condition of the newly departed from the outer terrestrial life. Many are those, from evangelists of a fundamental kind to esoteric theorists with all the wisdom of their own speculation grafted upon their studies, who are prepared to say with tones of certainty just what it is that happens.

Dying to the world, departing from the imperatives of the flesh, and all the astro-mental moulding that has gone with it, is however a very personal matter. In a sense it is an ultimate psychoanalysis or psychotherapy. Your etheric-physical body is to some extent like a jelly mould, fashioned in part by heredity, up-bringing and environment, the climate of your times, subsequent and early experience, all or any of which may resonate with experiences of another life, here or in other spheres, or with a lesson to be learned, a spiritual task to be done. And the soul within conforms to this mould, even for some time after it has been broken.

In a sense however, this useful image of a crystalline mould is not entirely accurate. You might also recall the image of a plant that is grown in a fibre pot, in which the roots, which at first have found sustenance within, have then found constriction, to the point where they are growing, closely bound within themselves inside, and then into and through the pot. This is frequently the condition of old age, or of aging, when the soul has outgrown its vehicle and is ready for death.

Not that the newly discarnate soul is always immediately in a state of mind to break the mould. Indeed this may prove to be a very gentle and gradual process, wherein the being dreams of life that is past in a kind of idealised way. This is the kind of afterworld evidence you find in the testimony of certain spirits of the newly-dead, in what have been called the Summer-worlds of the spiritualists. However, the tradition is not confined to them, it is the popular conception of the heavens of ancient or modern pagan antiquity, of the happy hunting grounds of the Amerindians, the Valhalla of the Vikings, the *huris* of Islamic heaven worlds, or even the more abstract idealisations of the harps and clouds and crowns of simpler Christians.

This however is not eternity, it is simply a passing stage, a place of transit, while the soul recovers it real being, its centre of gravity, to slough off much of the accumulated baggage, the burdens it no longer needs.

Now what we have led you to do, in taking you into this chapel, is to help you to make a start in this dissolution process, and in the most healthful, direct and helpful manner possible. That is, to review your past life as you go, presenting it as an offering, be it good or bad in your transitory eyes, to the all forgiving, all empowering fount of your creation. And by these means, when your turn comes to die, you may find the dissolution process not, as sometimes occurs, the painful cracking of a rigid mould. Nor the overlong confinement in constricting conditions of delusion or self-indulgent dreams.

{The Chancellor, 11.9.93}

50

The image I would give to you of the condition of souls in the "summer worlds" is a swarm of gnats dancing in a cloud on a summer's evening, within a patch of warm air that surrounds them. But as they dance they consume, as it were, the patch of warm air upon which they feed until none is left, and then they die - they truly die. That is the condition of souls in the summerland state. They are dancing within, and feeding upon a cloud of images and emotions of their own emanation. But when those images, that emotional emanation fades, so their heaven world becomes fainter and fainter until they naturally pass on to the next stage of the dying process.

This is a state of being beyond that of the thought forms - the magical images if you like - although, in the condition we have been describing, the soul is unconsciously and involuntarily embedded in the magical image, not consciously producing it in a controlled and willed act of magical transference.

It is not that imagination or visualisation ceases in the higher state, otherwise how would I, or my colleagues, communicate with you? It is rather that the imagination ceases to be bound in the mould into which it was induced by the circumstances, habits of mind and thought patterns of the previously completed incarnation.

And the patterns of that incarnation are in a sense rather like a sloughed off snake skin. This, given the right instruction, technique and purpose, can be re-inflated or re-animated. But although this is one means of making communication with your world, at any rate to a degree, the main purpose lies not in that direction, for communication with those of the earth plane is not, I have to say, a common mode of existence or duty upon the planes of causation.

But those memories of earth life, or the pattern or potential revivification of them, continue to exist as part of the capability of the spiritual being. They are of the nature of what have been called "tracks in space". This is rather more than a type of memory. Another image of it could be called an imprint or impression upon the potentiality of the spirit. So when it desires to manifest in a higher type of world, or in other spiritual conditions far removed from earthly incarnation, it can indeed do so by means of revivifying these images of past lives upon the levels of form. It is like a bank of experience, that can be revivified in appropriate circumstances.

Such circumstances it is difficult to provide in very meaningful terms to your levels of earthbound conception, but something of the truth of it is contained in the long sustained belief in the Christian world of the resurrection of the dead. Thus the personality has the potentiality of life within the highest heaven, the paradisal worlds, as they may be remotely conceived by you. The former personality is a means of interchange and communication at the appropriate level, but washed clean of much of its imperfections.

This process is depicted in ancient myth and in more modern esoteric imagery by the washer of clothes by the ford. And by the biblical injunction, at the time when Moses was introducing the tribes of Israel to the presence of the Most High, that they prepare themselves by washing their clothes clean.

This washing, this cleansing process, is just such as has been presented to you by the presence of the souls within the chapel that we have just left, and which I have recommended for your use. For this is a means of washing your clothes, preparing your heavenly raiment, even while you still wear it. And what is done now, as you go, will not have to be done later. Indeed it can be performed more effectively now. Not more effectively in terms of the end result, I should say, for the cleanliness of perfection is the only final and acceptable state for passing further onward, but in terms of greater ease and effectiveness for you. As in worldly washing, stains are easier to remove when they are new!

And the practice that you perform now, whilst inhabiting the earthly garment, will have an effect within it, and help to form it into a more fulfilled and effective body for future use through all eternity. For all such earthly "clothes of skin" to use a Biblical phrase, have a different quality. Some may indeed be tenuous. A life that has been filled with little but ill-doing, the bulk of which needs to be sloughed off, may leave a somewhat attenuated wraith. This is one meaning of the injunction that the strong may be weak, and the weak strong in terms of the Kingdom of Heaven as compared with the Kingdom of this world. The straight and upright soul, even if of seeming little consequence whilst incarnate in the world, may yet have a stronger, more vivid, more effectual body of expression to take as potential into the higher worlds than the powerful despot whose principles, deeds and condition of soul are unacceptable to heaven - which is to say are unreal, formed of illusions, when viewed in cosmic terms.

And it is thus, you may also realise, why souls return for more incarnationary experience - even though it may seem, with conditions in parts of the earthly world as they are, that no spirit would wish to incarnate within them. Yet obviously there is ever a great impress of souls bent on reincarnation.

This is not necessarily because they are of the nature of earth-bound, hungry ghosts, the ranks of the unredeemed, devil driven in their lowliness, candidates for eternal perdition, seeking the lusts of the flesh, or the exercise of power in the lowliest of ways. Rather are they souls driven to seek more effective "resurrection bodies" to take with them from the sphere of Earth for their future cosmic citizenship within the realms of heavenly space, far beyond the world we know.

{The Chancellor, 12.9.93}

51

But we pass on now from this chapel of mortal repentance and earthly regeneration, past chapels of whose purpose you need not yet know, for as in any physical cathedral or abbey, there are private chantries or chapels for specific purposes. Within these the specialised work of saints and masters goes on for specific intercession and vocations. Very often this is for the amelioration of some specific problem within the world, channelling spiritual force and balancing and healing powers with angelic and elemental assistance, as directed by a higher power, for we have those set over us in guidance and instruction just as we, the masters, are set over you. This is not in any sense of master and servant, but in grades or degrees of service.

We seek to help and guide you in order that you may help and guide others. The sole criterion for admission to each level is a little wider power, knowledge and vision than is ordinary at the previous level. Plus, of course, a desire to serve that comes genuinely from the heart - for there is a false or pretended form of service that seeks only to interfere or to control. Thus we never order. We simply guide those who are willing to listen or who wish to be guided. Sometimes we may warn them if their ways go too close to danger or there is a lapse in the quality of service. In which case, if the guidance is rejected, it is possible that contact may be cut off for a while, but always are we ready and waiting for that soul's return.

And where there is a continued willingness to serve, perhaps after a painful lesson has been learned, or an attractive by-path explored and found to be wanting, a diversion from the true and direct path, there are no barriers raised or maintained by us. The hierarchy is an association of free souls, themselves the expression of free spirits, and no-one is compelled to go against their spiritual will.

Membership of it is however a process of education, and a training of the spirit and the soul (the spirit being trained through the experiences of the soul) into the ways of service. It is therefore not necessarily a direct way to the light eternal. It is certainly a valid and sure way there, but it is one that entwines and encompasses many avenues and areas of experience, just as the Serpent of Wisdom climbs the Tree of Life through many spheres and interconnecting branches, as compared to the mystic, who takes the direct and strait and narrow way, directly up the Middle Pillar - the pillar of life consciousness.

The chapels that I take you past are very much the province of the mystics, and the way that mystics render service, for the mystic's direct approach of the soul to God is by no means a selfish path, or one that ignores the plight of creation or the world. It is indeed a very demanding path and one that comprises in intensity of experience what in the occultist is *extent* of experience.

Both have equal range and diversity in potential. And what the mystic faces and is drawn toward, the occultist would find hard to bear. Just as the mystic viewing the occult path would find it, less intensive perhaps (although it has its share of strains and pressures) but strange and seemingly lacking in direction in its wandering. This in part is why the serpent, as image, has a somewhat ambivalent role in mystical teachings.

The path of the serpent is one of knowledge of what may indeed prove to be serpentine ways, the turnings within the labyrinth of multifarious creation in all its levels and even distortions. The mystic shoots up in the power and force of love, in a different dimension. And I may say it takes considerable force to blast off vertically in this fashion - even though helped and raised in part by the ministering wings of angels. That is the testing experience of the mystic, and it can be in the directness and speed of ascent, like the experience of a deep sea diver too quickly raised and suffering problems from the difference in pressure.

You have heard the phrase "God is pressure". Despite its somewhat shallow mechanistic image for something that is multidimensional in life and love, it has its point. One might call it a pressure of light. At its most intense it is brighter than the sun and with the real force of a thousand thousand lasers, which acting in concert will be a force indeed. This puts a nuclear explosion somewhat in the shade, for nuclear fusion is only the potential force of one of the greater Suns, or sons of God, in whom less complex spirits live and move and have their being. The power of God in essence is of the order of a supra-supernova - of light and life and love.

The occultist by contrast winds up the mountain by a winding track, and certainly gains the summit of the Mount of Vision in the end, but his rate of progress, despite its toils, effects a gradual acclimatisation as the spiritual heights are ascended. And there are those upon the path to the summit who, like myself, are there to assist and guide you.

But just as you may be tempted to misjudge the mystic as one who has no outward worldly effect, and to be self or God obsessed, so is the mystic often misguided enough, in obsession with the love of God (which is a holy obsession) to misunderstand and sometimes misjudge the aims and pursuits of the occultist. The over-riding rule of course is to judge not another's servant.

So saying we pass to an area of the abbey, beyond and behind the high altar, which is very much the province of the occultist.

{*The Chancellor, 13.9.93*}

52
Here we come to a series of plaques upon the walls, and there are inscribed stones beneath our feet, whilst leading down, under the high altar itself, there is a narrow stair that is protected from our entry by a grating and leads down into a crypt where lie the bones of the illustrious dead.

In an abbey or cathedral within the world this would contain the earthly remains of men and women, somewhat out of the ordinary, who were associated with the building or who were of the local community and tract of land served by the presence of the abbey. In great national cathedrals or abbeys, as at St Pauls or Westminster, there are laid the bones of national heroes, kings and queens, and men and women of distinction.

However the abbey in which we tread today is a general pattern for all earthly abbeys, and any such figures may be envisioned to have their presence here. It is a centre, a focus, for the power of the ancestors. Those who have gone before in the stewardship of the earth and the land and the civilisation thereon. The expression through human consciousness of the earth forces, and their meeting and commingling with those of the angelic orders. This, in a wider, cosmic sense, is the very purpose of humankind: to be a meeting point and bridge between the worlds.

That is, between the creations of God, (the holy angels and the higher worlds), and the creations of the created, (the elemental worlds that are embodied in the etheric globe of the earth, and which includes the animal realms). So now you see the importance of the human role and destiny, and the grave consequence of its being twisted and deformed, weakened by rebellious intelligence and interference by the spirits you know of as the fallen angels.

Great suffering is caused by this weakened and twisted bridge. And it is the task of the brotherhood, the hierarchy of masters, adepts, saints, all of the human race upon the inner planes, and those whom they can contact upon the Earth while in incarnate consciousness, to mend that bridge. To make straight the way, repair, build, renew, until the glorious road from highest heaven to the elemental centres of the Earth is renewed, and all entrapped and fallen spirits released. Things are to be made as they were and as they should have been. This is the meaning behind images and phrases such as "restore the plan to Earth" or "bring the New Jerusalem to Earth".

This is not simply a glorious prize, a conferring of blessing from a delayed and recalcitrant heaven, it is an act of redemption, of restoration. For the Holy City, the Heavenly Jerusalem, should have been here in all its glory from the beginning and throughout all time.

Although had there been no fall, and a destruction of the Holy City and the driving of its inmates into exile, time would not exist as you know it. Time is a merciful blessing of heaven, a means whereby a cosmic fallen state can be saved from eternal perdition, fallen and disintegrated into the abyss, and be restored as part of the heavenly kingdom. And then the true, the one and only true king, will be returned, restored to his domain.

That king is he who sits on the Throne of the Most High, and Who has foreshadowed his return by the prophets and by his Crown Prince (the Messiah), who is another aspect of himself, the Eternal Godhead, as manifested upon the Earth. The Incarnation was but a foreshadowing, a promise and covenant that the day of redemption, of the Second Coming will indeed arrive. And that will mark the end of the world, not in terms of tribulation, save for the fully committed and unregenerate evil ones bent on their own power or destruction, who would rather rule in hell than serve in heaven, as Milton's vision put it. It will be a transformation and restoration to glory. The whole Earth and all that therein is, raised to the bosom of God. The prodigal returned, restored. The lost sheep found.

As has already been told you, the Book of Revelations is an accurate portrayal of that which will come, although to fallen and unclear human eyes, the understanding of it may yet be dark. Indeed it may have served so far to darken counsel rather than to enlighten. However, it is there purposely and of necessity at the end of the sacred book of your race, and merits your attention. You waste no time by study of the Bible or in contemplation of its seemingly simple stories. They are mystical/magical images that, taken to your heart in the faith and belief of child-like acceptance, will be as gems that will burst forth in comprehension, understanding and realisation at a later day. That is, when spiritual reality begins to dawn upon you as you approach the heavenly kingdom - or as the heavenly kingdom approaches you.

You do well to be prepared for that day, as does all mankind, by the taking to heart of these holy stories and images, in all their apparent simplicity and naivety. It is only childish pride in those who make a premature judgement upon them! The theology of the third form! Yet even for wilfully ignorant children such as these there remains the Kingdom of heaven.

{The Chancellor, 14.9.93}

53

We do not descend into the crypt of this place, for all that is necessary for us to see and encounter will arise to us. It is in a certain sense a polar equivalent of the topmost point of the abbey tower, for these steps lead down to its subterranean chamber at its base, passing under the High Altar. And whatever the national call or need maybe, as sighted by the watchers on the tower, it will be met by a stirring within the vaults. The ancestors will be aware.

This is the inner and very real power behind such recurrent and popular legends as the hero's return. Be this King Arthur, Merlin or Sir Francis Drake. And of course ultimately the return, the coming again, of the Christ. Although in all these cases it is not so much a coming again as a re-appearance, for they have never, none of them, really left the Earth. Their essence remains on the higher aethers of the physical plane as a source that can be, and is, re-activated again. King Arthur, Drake, and other heroes and heroines remain upon the etheric and continue to have a leavening influence, although it is also a matter of their being called.

Of course in the last days all will break through in full glory, but that is another matter, and in terms of time somewhat far ahead. We deal now with the bridge building efforts of the way inbetween and the course of human history.

In this there is encapsulated the power of evocation, and the need for it. "Ask and ye shall receive. Seek and ye shall find. Knock, and it shall be opened." The call and need must come from those who are incarnate upon the physical plane. There can be no question of the heavens' interference.

From this you may gather the importance, in time of war or national crisis, of the impulse and initiative to have National Days of Prayer. There is far more to this than an empty formalism, or an out-dated and superstitious ritualism. At the time of their implementation, in the late world war, in time of peril for the nation, they were indeed a rallying point for morale and the courage of the nation, and they worked in many subtle and secret ways, despite the intellectual cynicism of their critics.

Such criticism assumed that they were void of any power or significance. This of course is a fruit of the shallowness of the intellectual unbeliever, and the stony ground of their mystical awareness, devoid of growth but for perhaps a few ill fed and malformed wispy stalks of social aspiration. Their view of mystical reality is as void as, indeed is a reflection of, the barrenness within their own heads.

The other, apparently more spiritual and pious contention, was that such a day of prayer, or the intention behind it, was but a throw-back to ancient tribal gods - and that the concern of religious aspirants should be on a wider scale, concerned with all humanity and the whole Earth.

This is a universalism that has its truth, but it is a truth that has its basis out of time. It is a concern and reality only of the last days. In the toilsome path of humanity until that date the human family is divided, into class, creed, nation, tribe, family as indeed individual. And no immediate good is to be gained by appealing to a premature and unreal universalism.

Heaven will not return to Earth until a closer match is made between that which is below and that which is on high. And until that day we have to deal with the interplay of fragmentations. We work with a mosaic. Learn to love your family, and you may learn something of true citizenship. Learn to love your locality, your community and you may learn to love your country. Learn to love your nation, and be true to it, and you may learn to love the world in all its diversity of expression.

The story of the Tower of Babel is one of the Fall, and as a consequence of it the nations were divided and there came a confusion of tongues. This may be a thing to be deplored. But the way back to the pristine state is not the learning of Esperanto and a rebuilding of a communal tower. That is a false goal, of the Old Adam, of the inferior net, as has already been explained.

The way ahead is for full expression as a spiritualised individual within the family, within the community, within the nation, and only by that means achieving a new universal kingdom.

There are many false steps on the way, and one of these has been the concept of Empire. But it is one that has more reality than that of ideal dreams of a world state. A world state has got to be a family of nations. Just as a nation has to be a family of creeds, communities and "tribes" - be they cultural or familial. And as families are, they have to be based on a mutual acceptance, a cohesion in diversity of individuals - tied by blood.

And remember that in the higher sense there are ties by land and by blood that have their roots in all qualities and aspects of human relationship, and cannot be ignored. They are not grown out of, abandoned, left behind. They are the earthly links in the heritage of every individual.

Therefore you may see that we have something of a tangle, in that many elements of all this have been misapplied. The vision has become faulty, and the well-intentioned and even natural has been led astray. Just as a gardener may train a rose to climb in a right or a wrong direction, so is the level of a real cosmic conflict concerning Earth to be found in the inner realms, where angelic and other forces seek to train the rambling rose of human progress into right or wrong direction.

The evil minded anti-human spirits seek to cause it to enmesh itself in ever greater entanglements or labyrinths of thorns, rather than the heavenly intention of seeing it spread in flowing beauty and profusion over an expanded network of the world - an aspect of the net. But can you imagine the difference between a rambling rose climbing up the fixed and steady universal stellar net that leads to the heavens; as compared to one that is looking for support in the unstructured, throwing up and falling down of the rough rope net of the inferior Adam? This is more likely to end as a bramble bush, interspersed with nettles and strangled with bind weed.

And so, in many respects, does this present an image of human history - at any rate in its detail. In a wider context, a more distant perspective perhaps, some sense of over-riding achievement or purpose may be discerned. The good will in the end have its way. But the way inbetween is barbed, twisted and toilsome.

{The Chancellor, 15.9.93}

54

The powers of the ancestors are power points upon the etheric web of the nation that have been seeded there by great lives. They have gathered about them a vortex of aspiration and power that is fed by like-mindedness, and distinguished by natural cleavages in the emotional body of the nation. There are indeed two sides to this, one we that we might call voluntary and the other involuntary.

As centres of power, reservoirs of force, emotional and indeed spiritual reserves, they are the property of no one individual, or small body of individuals, but they are fed by the aspirations of individuals. This is particularly so when individual aspiration is directed, for the power of individuals' aspirations works by a process of multiplication rather than by addition as more come into agreement at the same time. This is a factor in practical magic and there comes a point where intelligent structuring and direction is needed to make the most of what might otherwise be an amorphous mass. However, even so, an unformed mass can have a considerable degree of power as may be demonstrated in the weight of public opinion, and the corrosive effect of public ridicule. It can cause governments or public men to fall; an outraged public opinion can effect changes of public policy in a governing power.

This is not entirely a matter or votes, for fear of the ballot box is a very occasional worry in the application of government, and even less so in undemocratically governed nations. As has been somewhat cynically observed, if voting really changed things it would be abolished. Well it has had most of the sting drawn from it by the collective will of those who live by political aspiration and will to power, whatever the direction of their politics. And more real power exists from day to day in those who are able to channel public opinion, to transform currents into vortices of obsession or concern.

These may last for a longer or a shorter time, just as the small spirals and eddies in a running stream are generally short-lived unless there is a more or less permanent form of obstruction to the force flow, a conformation of pebbles or a caught branch. So it is with the emotional state of the nation, and in smaller units of people. Indeed even the individual can be described, at a particular level, like this.

There will be times however, when the mass of public opinion or emotion rises of its own accord apparently. That is, not manipulated by the tools of information of incarnate men, the Lords of Misinformation one might call them. Then one is talking less in terms of the imagery of eddies in a stream but of the heaving tides of a sea. These too have their major currents and eddies, as one may observe in the breaking of the sea upon rocks and upon the wrecks they have caused.

This is the result of powers beyond the wit or will of incarnate men, no matter what their apparent temporal power. Upon the surface of the real sea of human emotions will they float like sticks. Such major movements are caused by great movements in powers beyond the Earth, from mighty spiritual powers. They might even be construed as the shock waves of angelic powers in battle.

Once more we can only speak in terms of incarnate human understanding, of what have been somewhat baldly termed Principalities and Powers, although some passages in Milton of the war in heaven come near to imaginal truth. Their externalisation in Earthly terms is seen in the trials and conflicts of tribes, races and nations. But this is by no means their only concern. Human beings, even states and nations, are as pawns in their wider game, not even major pieces.

These are the ongoing reverberations of that which has been called the fall of the Tower of Babel, or of the Lightning Struck Tower, whose masonry, and its inhabitants and builders, are still in a process of fall. In terms of the imagery of the Tarot card, put your faith in the backdrop of the pattern of the heavens, which is sometimes depicted as a Tree of Life in the sky. This is the true net behind the falling masonry.

That masonry in itself represents a falling to the Earth of the inferior net of the Inferior Adam, cast there, as the tower was first builded, at the behest of inferior and lying spirits. It may be that they can appear superior in majesty and power to individual human spirits, but as we have earlier implied, this is a fruit of illusion in terms of the realities of heaven. The small cherished and protected flowers in a garden have a brighter cosmic future than the seemingly rampant weeds.

In a fallen world, the natural ground tends to favour the more luxuriant growth of weeds. But have no fear. The Divine Gardener plans and oversees all, with his band of dedicated servants, of whom we of the hierarchy form a part.

The archetypal forces of a nation are represented by seed ideas, focussed by magical images of famous women and men. These are examplars of a particular quality of character and direction of aspiration, which is unconsciously fed and also drawn upon by individuals of the nation. This is a feature of patriotic sentiment and patriotic teaching, which certainly should not be decried, on the same grounds that we have spoken of some illusions of religious universalism.

These powers and forces are such that you should not seek to manipulate them upon your own authority or initiative. Such attempts do exist, by a magical process that is no less powerful for its being uninstructed and uninformed. This is a process which leads to violently expressed forms of vortices, the narrow drive of spite, envy and fanaticism that fuels a terrorist movement, and which on a broader front can launch civil war.

There may be certain injustices to be resolved, but whoever unleashes the dogs of war, has raised from the ground a pack of ravening wolves, or hounds of hell, whose control is beyond the powers of those who called them forth, whose masters are the keepers of the cosmic hounds, the outriders of the Horsemen of the Apocalypse. If you seek to be invokers - we advise and beseech you - for your own good if for none other - be not invokers of hell.

So what you should do in this regard is to be conducted under guidance. This will be most naturally given to you by response to that which appears before you when you are led in these ways These are the ways of the Hierarchy, whose ways and means are those of the King of Salem, the King of Peace.

{The Chancellor, 16.9.93}

55
Under guidance therefore do you go, in the Mysteries, when you come upon the spirits of the Ancestors. These are the guardian angels of the race, for they partake more of the angelic than of the human spirit that gave rise to them. Not that the seeding initiating spirit is unconnected with the magical body, the rejuvenated personality, that you see. It is a species of resurrection body, but not one that is used by the originating spirit as a means or mode of personal expression. The soul itself has gone to rest, has passed through the judgement hall, the period of penitential cleansing.

And so when you come upon that which appears to you as the spirit of Elizabeth I or Mary Queen of Scots, or of Drake, you are not partaking in the operation of a spiritualist séance. These are not the spirits of the departed as commonly understood. They are more perhaps in the nature of wax-works, or automata - or holograms, to use an image of modern technology. They are representations of power - indeed ensouled magical images.

They are not put there or imaginably constructed by you. They have an objective existence upon the inner planes, and they may be used by those who are invested with sufficient authority, and who have the power and ability to do so. Much of their motive power comes from the stored emotional response to the ideas embodied in the particular archetype they represented as individuals when in incarnation. This can also be fed, or drawn off from by you, whenever you contact such a being.

In normal circumstances they are put before you with a purpose by those who have a responsibility to do so. They are brought before your field of attention, to be, in a sense, restimulated within your aura, thereby imparting a certain energy to the image, and also a corresponding energy to you. An exchange of energy takes place, an energy that may last and be drawn from for some time.

In other words it has the effect of dedicating a certain part of your aura to the works and the powers of that particular racial archetype and its needed work in the world today. This may be by realisation as much as by physical action, for as when St Paul spoke of "the flesh", it is more than the physical body and its actions that he intended. It includes the thoughts and desires that are focussed within it upon the plane of Earth.

And so you see you also have the basis of a teaching here upon the nature of the aura, and of the means whereby energy may be exchanged between the planes. This is a part of that which was intended in the transmission and transcription of *The Cosmic Doctrine*, which was also in effect a current demonstration of it, but which in the transcription and transmission became expressed with too much abstraction, so that often little is realised as to what it means. This we may hopefully remedy, and if necessary, if there be errors of fact or comprehension, correct.

This is all part of the science and art of magic, which is the transmission of inner energies that they may be effectively expressed upon another plane. In this, images play a major part. All is not abstraction - particularly upon the planes of Earth, within the "world of the flesh" in St Paul's terms.

You need to work with images. You also have to understand them, and their internal mechanics, their *modus operandi*. This is the Yesodic experience of the Vision of the Machinery of the Universe. With this must go its understanding, if the spiritual experience of Malkuth, the Knowledge and Conversation of the Holy Guardian Angel, is to have any effectiveness. It is one thing to learn to know what is needed, by conversation with the Angel, it is another to put it into effect by a knowledge of the appropriate Machinery of the Universe. And without that, what hope have you of dealing with powers of higher spheres?

It will not be by mere good intention or abstract thought. And although I concede that that is at least a preparation of the ground, it is not initiation. For that we seek and expect active workers in the Hierarchy. Hewers of wood and drawers of water in terms of the astral plane. This means the working with and selection of images, and investing them with or drawing off their power. Hence our intention to show you the required skills, first of the axe and bucket of hewer of wood and drawer of water, from which in time you may learn to wield and administer the sword of the Adeptus Major and chalice of the Grail.

Then you may approach the veil and the portal of the real and inner mysteries, of which those within the world are but a shadow and a crudely reflected representation.

{*The Chancellor,* 17.9.93}

56

You may see arise before you then, dynamics of the racial consciousness that are represented by this part of the abbey, and that are behind the high altar and reaching down into the crypt. The term "racial unconscious" is a species of nomenclature that inclines towards a psychological conception of the realities involved, which, as you know, has its limitations. But it is perhaps a more familiar and useful way in to this complex subject for men and women of the outer world in modern times, when talk of "magical images" may seem bizarre, even though the older term is, in the last analysis, the more accurate.

"Racial unconscious" is however perhaps a less misleading term than "personal unconscious" because it does imply a certain level of objectivity. And objective these forces are, even though you cannot weigh or measure them with a physical balance. Their conception and their existence derives from beings that lived and occurrences that happened upon the physical plane. And their influence, or the influences they represent and encapsulate, can have a very powerful effect, through human agencies, upon the physical plane. They contribute to general inner influences, and thence to outer cultural conditioning. Contemporary culture also contains the residue or after glow of the experience and conditioning of previous generations by these and other interior forces, there being always an element of drag upon the physical and lower planes.

The only subjective element enters in precisely as it does with observation in the physical world. When witnessing an event, however "objective" upon the physical plane, the experience comes through the gates of the observer's personal perception. This can indeed increase in level or intensity to become active participation.

Participation extends from the intellectual registering or noting of events, through emotional reactions to them, to possible physical involvement, involving the sense of touch. That is, via the nerves within the skin that radiate through the entire body, not just those that are centred in the head - of sight, hearing, taste and smell.

There are also, it should be said, subtler psychic senses that may become involved, the chakras of gonads, solar plexus, heart and throat besides those of the head. These at their own level are also registers of objective events, whether by direct reaction to what occurs on their own plane, or by sympathetic response to what is happening physically.

Should there be a record, an impression in the memory as a result of these experiences, (whether by direct effort, unexpectedness or vividness up to the levels of clinical shock), then there is an impingement upon the aura. The auric field contains these impressions stamped upon it - to put it in a visual way - and this may have a greater or lesser effect upon subsequent "subjective" behaviour. It is often in this that we find the roots of prejudice (opinions deeply held or considered axiomatic) apart from idiosyncracies of character that may sometimes amount to erosion or damage of the personality vehicle.

It is the review of this personality vehicle that takes place after physical death, or which can be begun before it. This, to use a crude analogy, is a hammering out of the dents, or cutting out the bruises of a fruit before it is consumed. It is a form of psycho-analysis in a certain sense although one hesitates to use a term that is so variously defined.

In the more limited magical sense, of confrontation with objective magical images that have been conceived and constructed in the past, one's reaction to them, (or perhaps a better term might be inter-action with them), should be in the nature of a deliberate and personal controlled commitment. However, as in all matters of magical dynamics, there can be an overloading. That is, a less controlled, less conscious reaction, magically speaking.

This might be likened, in terms of radio, to an overwhelmingly powerful signal coming in, swamping all, either through the receiver being too close to the source of transmission, or because the receiver itself, for whatever reason, is abnormally sensitive. Often there can be a combination of the two. This is the cause of fanaticism of a political nature, leading to outbursts upon the physical plane of unbalanced force. This can be by explosion, bullet, brick bat, verbal abuse or riot; even, in extreme cases, civil war. These dynamics come very much more to the fore in times of national crisis, or when states or nations become formally at war. Much of this, and of the consequences and modus operandi, you can find in the weekly wartime letters of Dion Fortune.

The balanced and magical way is altogether less dramatic, yet can be a powerful experience when it occurs. We might best cite this by examples.

{The Chancellor, 18.9.93}

57

One instance has passed into popular culture by way of comic song, and that, I may say, is no ineffective method of affecting the group mind, and even the group soul, of a race, or even a wider culture. A prime example of esoteric teaching being injected into the popular mind in a similar way is the Tarot, and to a lesser extent the ordinary playing cards upon which they ride, as an esoteric knight upon an elemental steed. This in turn is rather like the Tarot image of the Winged Victory in her chariot - as depicted on one of the Trumps. You have of course heard in Qabalistic terms of the Work of the Chariot, and this forms a practical example of its interpretation into western esoteric terms. Purist Jewish Qabalists may not much like it but this is the heritage of the Hebrew mystical genius as esoterically received and understood by Gentile post-Renaissance culture.

The song I have in mind is "With her head tucked underneath her arm she walks the Bloody Tower", and refers to the already famous and popular tradition of the haunting of the Tower of London by Anne Boleyn, the second wife of Henry VIII.

Now this popular conception of an earth-bound spirit has little or nothing to do with the actual soul of this poor benighted queen, a young woman who was plucked forth, it would seem by destiny, to play her role upon the world stage of her time. The cause with which she became involved, in its effects and ramifications, was truly an international affair, and no mere national convulsion.

It was certainly that too - but much more was sparked off by this amorous intrigue. Anne Boleyn became the vehicle for greater than merely human forces. She became the elected one by whom the force of the Protestant cause should enter, and become incorporated in, the aura of the nation.

Henry himself, trained originally for the priesthood, left to his own devices and natural respect for ancient traditions, would not have initiated such a revolution. He had after all received the encomium of Defender of the Faith because of his public stand against Luther and the ferment of new religious ideas within the German states. The history of Protestantism is not a discourse into which we can embark, the canvas being so complex and so large. But it is an historical study that I can commend to you, for instructive and fascinating lessons in the behaviour and the power structures of group souls and minds, and of the influx of ideas and influences from the inner planes.

It is by no means the only example of course. There are other great movements, tides in the affairs of men, that will repay study. Such as the Renaissance, with the delayed impact of the culture and ideas of the ancient pagan world upon a ripened medieval Christian culture. Or the arising of the scientific method - around which of course one has the appearance of another charismatic figure, in the form of Lord Bacon.

The strands within all this are many and deep and varied and very often they are at the instigation of what I can only describe, (although the terms are somewhat distorted by modern cant), as extra-terrestrial forces. One sees the influx of such inner forces whenever events, (and above all, popular representations of them), blow up beyond their expected or proper size. In other words, seem wildly out of proportion. This is seen when the force surrounds one particular charismatic figure, who represents the spiritual seed for it - or the speck of grit around which there forms the pearl within the oyster.

One sees this effect in particular with Francis Bacon, whose memory has been invested with many claims, which characteristically are often held with very high emotion. Thus you see the placing of internal constructions upon diverse circumstances and events. This is much the same mechanism as when a victim of paranoia interprets all things seen within the environment as a complex plot. This is really the structuring of his own repressed obsession, that uses his imagination like a puppet master his puppet, bending all facts or events, however accidental or insignificant, in support of his thesis.

Thus has Bacon, according to various minds, been accorded the writing of all the works of Shakespeare, (besides those manifestly his own); been head of a Rosicrucian order; been son and heir of the Virgin Queen; as well as being a harbinger of the scientific revolution.

In Anne Boleyn we have a less overtly prominent figure, but one upon whose head, (and in one sense that is why in the popular mind she continues to carry it), lies the direction of flow of the religious history of this country. She is in this respect rather like a rock within the path of an oncoming stream, that diverts the flow largely into another channel. The rock itself has no intention of being such a crucial factor in the direction of the stream and the irrigation of the land about. Indeed such considerations would be quite beyond its capability - which is simply confined to being a stone, solid, weighty, true to its own nature. But the mightier, more significant question is, who put the stone there? Was it by design or accident? And who configured or foresaw or adapted the lie of the land for the potential course of the stream?

{The Chancellor, 19.9.93}

58

This is a question of human destiny, and the interaction of personal human destinies, in which is comprised in essence: the development of consciousness, experience of the lower worlds, and abstraction of those qualities for the growth and instruction of the spirit in the ways of creation. And all this within the interaction of movements in the affairs of men which are the consequence of larger, greater beings - angels at the level of Virtues, Mights, Principalities and Powers, who have an effect not only on the destiny of nations but in mass movements and ideas and their expression in the history of mankind.

As far as the individual soul is concerned this is like being a molecule of water that is violently agitated by the passage of a great liner. There is not much that the individual can do except react to circumstances, and that only by interior realisation, for personal action in the world is unlikely to have any effect upon the course of events that are set in motion on a higher plane and have a mass effect. Thus even individual will can be overloaded by the force of events, despite seeming to be a cause of them.

For example, the assassin whose bullet struck down the Archduke in Sarajevo in 1914 had little personal say in the matter. Had he any personal choice it was one that was exercised some considerable time before, as to whether or not to become involved in a political organisation of a particular kind. Having embarked upon his course, he was drawn ever nearer to the vortex of events, until such time as he had no more personal will in the matter than a molecule of water being sucked down the plug hole of an emptying bath. And had it not been he who fired the fatal shot it would have been done by another, being the pretext that led to a sequence of other pre-prepared events on a mightier level than personal assassination.

Much the same could be said of the amatory affair between King Henry VIII of England and Anne Boleyn. There was a time when either could have withdrawn from it, and avoided certain personal consequences. Yet in one way or another the general trend of circumstance was bound to happen, once the forces were set in motion and had gathered a momentum.

Thus you may gain a certain insight into the matter of divination. There are times when things can not be precisely predicted, for they exist on a more abstract level as general possibilities, probabilities or trends. As they come nearer to the formation of a vortex however, so they may gather an inevitability about them that is a compound of destiny and circumstance. The destiny is the general will and effect of mightier beings beyond the human level, the circumstance more within the immediate control of the humans involved.

Then there are souls or spirits of destiny, incarnating for a particular reason. Of these you have Anne Boleyn's daughter, who was destined to be queen even before she entered her mother's womb. And the later cult of Gloriana, and the semi-deifying of the personality involved was a recognition by those about her that she was greater than them in a certain sense - that she had been placed there as an agent of a higher power, and encapsulated within herself the sovereignty of the nation. She was, in this respect, an initiate, an appointed one of higher angelic powers concerned with the destiny of nations.

To a certain degree this is an element that has set royalty apart, and has been the root cause of the principle of aristocracy. The spiritual causes lie in a concourse of spirits upon the subtler levels of the inner planes whose destiny it is to be incarnated at these particular levels of social expression, often buffeted by great affairs of state that emanate from a higher angelic level.

This coming to birth and to power is linked to elements of land as well as to elements of blood. The rulership, or sovereignty, comes through a certain pattern of blood lines, and is associated with particular tracts and patterns of land. These are exterior expressions of interior powers and realities. Royalty, and those who become involved in it by marriage or close association, is a state, a quality, that is set apart in the normal governance of human affairs.

None should feel envious of this role. Simple observation of history should be proof enough of this, for a ruler's life is not a happy one. It involves far seeing, beyond the lot of most of human conditions and requirements, which is one reason why a king, by tradition, can never be blind. He must have the powers of sight. Thus one way to depose a king, short of regicide, was deliberately to blind him, a form of functional death or assassination.

It is a mark of modern times that this principle of sovereignty has been widened, broadened away from a sacred clan. Along with democratic principles, this is in line with other human developments such as the rise of science and the liberalisation of religious and social attitudes. It may be a matter of opinion as to whether current rulership is at all superior to anything that pertained before.

{The Chancellor, 20.9.93}

59

Now let us describe the experience of an encounter with such an historical figure. Imagine that Anne Boleyn is with me. This is an eidolon, a real figure, with all the hallmarks of a fully fledged magical image. It is a form seemingly of solid flesh and blood, that you could describe from your inner vision. But apart from that it seems to have no movement, it is rather like an exceedingly well rendered wax work. But there is more to it than this, for you may experience something of the great charge of emotion that is about it. This is a combination of what you might describe as an overwhelming sadness, together with regret, and some preoccupation with execution, which in her case was with a sword in her private apartments rather than with an axe on Tower Hill. There is also consciousness of the involvement and fate of her closest kin and friends, and reflection upon the way that events turned out. A sad and tragic figure then, as one might have met her shortly before her execution. Dignified, and reconciled to her fate, and largely in the condition of souls within the Chapel of Penitance of the after-death condition that we have visited.

Indeed this condition is a close description of the state of being or of mind that is perceptible with this figure, and of other figures like it. It pertains to a summing up, an assessment of the past life, as viewed or experienced in the Judgement Hall of Osiris. That is to say, the after-death condition when the true self is assessing and absorbing the experiences of the immediately past life.

Yet while this is an essentially private matter in the case of the individual soul, in the case of these national magical images, the process, or something of what appears to be the process, can be discovered from outside. The figure thus resembles a magnet, in that it has a strong field about it, or an aura of its own.

The analogy of the magnet is indeed more appropriate if one thinks in terms not of a solid bar magnet, but of a coil. Of what is in effect an electro-magnet, when an electric current passing through the coil induces a magnetic field around the coil. The stronger the current, the more powerful and extensive the magnetic field. Indeed this process is very similar indeed to the formation of the human aura, with the spine as the equivalent of a soft iron core through the centre.

When the life current stops, the aura ceases. However, the inner core will have become magnetised by the life experience. Thus it can be the nucleus for other higher experiences elsewhere, with other rods. Or perhaps to form the core for other coils in subsequent earthly lives. But let us not push the analogy too far.

What we have in the case of the figure that I have just shown you, is the coil - which is the figure of Anne Boleyn, through which a current may be passed, which creates a configured emotional field, which induces the configuring of a similar field within yourself, (your own coil), experienced in terms of particular images and associated emotions.

That which passed through, that which was induced in terms of "life current" and "emotional field" was not the imprisoned soul or spirit of Anne Boleyn. That individual soul and spirit has passed on, and it would be sin, even if it were possible, for you to recall it.

But the figure and its potential evocative power is made up from what at a particular level are "tracks in space" or "memory grooves", impressed upon the recording aethers, caused in the first instance from the life and emotions of the tragic queen, whose individual soul was enmeshed in these high and far reaching matters of culture and state.

Thus you may see how a figure can act as a centre of power, or of inspiration. It need not be discerned as clearly as you have seen it, for its effect can work on a formless or unconscious level, manifesting as blind feeling impulses, or devotion to a cause, which if it were configured and personalised, might then take on the lineaments of the figure of Anne Boleyn.

Such a figure, and the charge that emanates from it, can also be tapped by the historical novelist. It is thus to some extent similar to the recordings in terms of moving pictures on screens or in books that are to be found in the great library. But these figures of the ancestors from the crypt have more life, more vitality than that. They might be said to be a halfway house, in experiential terms of the observer, between the images in the library or scriptorium, and the immediate experiences to be had upon the top of the observation tower.

{The Chancellor, 21.9.93}

60

The writer or novelist who works with this type of figure as an immediate source of creative inspiration is going to be a more vivid, or "creative" writer than the one who does not, particularly if there is the ability to draw upon personal autobiographical material vividly also. One might cite Dickens, Kipling or Wells, although it occurs a great deal in whole or in part, with other writers also. That is, the ability to construct such an apparently living eidolon out of their own immediate past lives. In this case they are breathing their own life force into a figure to make it "magnetic", or to emotionally glow. In this way they may even be working out or coming to terms with tracts of experience that were difficult for them to cope with at the time.

In more prosaic terms one has the phenomenon of the imaginative persistence and force of "embarrassing moments", minor misunderstandings often occasioned by lack of maturity or gaps in social awareness in one way or another. There you have a certain instance of the way "life" can be blown into an ediolon. A current is set to move in the coils of fixed memory, that brings to life the emotive magnetic field. This, if very much alive, makes its presence felt to whoever is within that field and who has an emotional body and connected intellect that can respond. In other words it will have induced within it a similar electric current and magnetic field, in the simple scientific analogy of the induction of currents and fields between coils.

But let us return to the question of who is passing the current through the coil of the magical image, or eidolon, of Anne Boleyn, or of other potent historical figures. The question we might well ask being: who is the master of the wax-work show within the crypt?

And here we come upon a department of the hierarchy of inner plane workers who are perhaps little known about. These are the appointed guardians of the race or of the racial consciousness. They are never personally known, for their work is done through the intermediary use of images such as the one we have seen. This work is deep in what might be called, in other terms, the subconscious depths or collective unconscious of the racial mind. They make available via appropriate channels whatever is required for balance and progress in the world outside. That is, in the ongoing consciousness of the race that is currently embodied in individuals living external lives of expression in the physical world.

They have their equivalent at other levels of the tower. In the rather shadowy and unobtrusive monk-like figures who design and maintain and control the images to be observed in the library or scriptorium. And at a higher level, with those who are like hidden acolytes or anchorites within the chapel, the intelligent and controlling source of mystical vision, mediators in a sense between the soul of the aspirant within the chapel and the objective heavenly powers.

Whilst upon the summit of the observation tower there are also hidden workers - not so much located there, although that is their centre of focus of reference. They have their consciousness stretched, in a way you may find difficult to understand, over polar points in wide tracts of territory. But just as you with your imaginative faculty can stretch conceptions over a wide distance, as when you contemplate a map or extensive panorama, a camera obscura for example, so it is with the workers of this type, except that their experience is more vivid. They are more identified with their observations and perceptions, and thus they too are, in a way, conductors and inducers of potential experience. The closest analogy here, again borrowing from elementary science, is the transmission of radio waves, when they are borne within a modulating carrier wave.

In this sense they are more like great elemental or sub-angelic creatures in terms of consciousness. The way you might conceive them is as overshadowing great winged figures - or lesser sized winged messengers, cup bearers of power or information - but they are essentially human spirits in their origin. The human race has wider ramifications and possibilities than you might believe from observation based only on physical conditions of human manifestation and expression.

And so we have mapped out and set before you, for your consideration, four levels of servants of the hierarchy. Those of the basement or of the crypt; those of the scriptorium or library; those of the chapel; and those of the observatory.

Not that in real terms there is a great difference between the beings so mentioned. They simply use different means or media of communication with you and for you. And who, you may ask, are we? The "masters" who stand before you and teach you.

Well we are not mere eidolons such as you see of Anne Boleyn or other historical and charismatic figures but the "bodies" we use, the means of communication, are similar. We are using, each in our way, historical personae, but not in the more objective and artificial way that the masters of the racial group soul and mind utilise the eidolons.

Our connection with our images is a more intimate one than that. They are more personally indwelt by ourselves. The force within is our own, which leads to a more intimate, personal and potentially subtle and intelligent contact, as compared with a character from history ensouled with more objective group concerns and emotions. At the same time our power is comparatively weaker in terms of direct effectiveness within the world.

Some of the eidolons we have been describing would be capable of igniting the consciousness of large numbers of the human race, which has a consequent domino effect as momentum is gained, individuals inducing like thoughts and emotions into others within their immediate environment. Here you have the roots of patriotism, whether it be the ground swell of emotion in the crowds who witness a coronation, royal wedding or state funeral, or in more prosaic movements within the mass mind, often manipulated by the physical plane media, who are themselves sub-stations in the transmission and stimulation of this kind of force. Again think in terms of electricity and induced magnetism in respect to life forces and emotive fields, and you may find the connections instructive.

We, however, rely upon and come through a much smaller band of select disciples. Those who have devoted themselves to sensitising their inner perceptions and then, under direction, to tuning consciousness towards our own chosen vehicles of communication across the planes.

{*The Chancellor, 22.9.93*}

61

You will see that in speaking of these things we have extended your awareness to a higher level of realisation, to that which lies beyond and behind the various magical images we have been describing. That is, to the level of spiritual beings who may indwell, build or manipulate them, as a means of communication with you and other spirits who indwell physical bodies in the external world.

And to have realised this world is an important step in conscious realisation for you. It means you are no longer likely to be superstitiously dominated by whatever images you may meet upon the level of imaginative forms. At first this may not appear so directly helpful in terms of instruction, because this world, to your limited "form" perceptions, is a relatively formless one.

This does not mean that forms do not exist upon the plane upon which we live and move and have our being, but simply that they are not discernible by you – any more than you can discern the forms of atoms or the worlds of remote space. You do not directly see these latter because they are remote in terms of physical size or distance. You do not directly see us because we are remote in terms of "level". You could perhaps call it in quasi-scientific terms a different rate of vibration. Our existence, or the mode of its fabric, is tuned to a different wavelength and frequency within the great globe of consciousness. That great globe that consists of interconnecting globes, one within the other, that go to form the universe.

We are obliged to communicate with you in forms that you can comprehend. And by reason of your focus of consciousness, that is, the forms of the physical plane, and words that you, (the human race, or your particular linguistic part of it), have chosen to designate things. Words are a form of symbol, yet also with a concrete form existence of their own. That is, they are a flow of expelled breath which, by the conformation of the mouth and larynx, causes a particular pattern of vortices and eddies within the air that can impinge upon the appropriate sensory apparatus of others about you.

It is also possible, by a further ingenious convention, the magnitude of which nowadays tends to be taken for granted, to render representations of these controlled explosions of sound into visual forms. Thus rendering words intelligible to the eye, and capable of transmission into the future and at a distance.

The invention of writing, next to the formulation of verbal speech, was therefore perhaps the greatest "enabling" event within the history of mankind in the story of civilisations upon Earth. For it rendered possible the keeping of records (a doubtful blessing you may sometimes be tempted to think) and the transmission of knowledge and wisdom and physical experience from one mind to another upon the physical plane. By these means a circuit had been completed, between hand of scribe, and eye of reader, thus effecting a transfer of idea or encapsulated experience from one to the other, a mind to mind contact across barriers of space and time.

From this in time developed processes of replication, the printing press, and in your own day electronic means of transmission, storage and replication, the words and letters stored in terms of binary number systems upon the behaviour patterns of silicon chips. It is just as well perhaps that silicon is one of the most common elements in the make-up of the physical world. A useful piece of forethought by the Lords of Form at the chemical creation of the worlds.

Now the main means of communication of human conscious understanding is by means of the sense of sight, the receptor of light, in terms of words presented on a screen or transferred onto sheets of paper. Remember that the world of sound is, on its own, a blind world. In terms of greater consciousness and awareness almost a dead world by comparison to the world of forms revealed by light.

And these words are formed by letters. And the intelligence that was behind, and which went into these letter forms, into the orthography of the written word, is of the level and nature of the inhabitants within the "formless" worlds. That is to say, of the instructing spirits who watch over the human race in its struggle for self-expression within the physical world.

This in turn is a reason for the traditional schools of mysticism over the ages that have used the forms of letters as a medium for meditation. It is an attempt to get into a level of communication with the intelligences behind form, by recourse to a use of the elements that they have formulated to describe form.

In this respect shapes of figures and letters can take on another mode of communication than their usual utilisation. I commend this study to you - including the square form of grid that is used by electronic devices to formulate these letters and numbers - which have induced a certain subtle change in their modern presentation and design.

In the western world the standard of the alphabet was taken from a Roman column, and later modified in the Renaissance with the formation of various italic scripts, and the designs of type founders of the new technology of printing, which marked an expansion in human expression and self consciousness. Now we have a similar sea-change taking place, and you would do well to take note of its ramifications.

{The Chancellor, 23.9.93}

62

The abstract terms of the symbolism of the Tree of Life is, in its way, another example of the expression of the level of mentation and communication that is behind the forms of letters and numbers. And by letters and numbers we also include the syllabic forms that for the most part predate the simple alphabets, such as Egyptian hieroglyphs and Chinese ideograms. Also of course the I Ching and other symbol systems, from the Tarot, which is at the most "concrete" end in terms of pictorial images, particularly in the Trumps, to the more abstract prick figures of geomancy, astrological signs, and the more restricted and private realms of magical sigils and alphabets - all are part of this level of intercommunication.

So you see we are moving toward a common language or means of communication that relies not on images of things that you perceive as forms within the world, but as deliberately formed purposive images that have no such direct representation, except perhaps in the derivations of their beginnings. Thus this is a mode of communication closer in its associations and forms to those of us on the inner world than to those of you who are still conditioned by the outer.

They are thus a further stepping stone, up from the magical image, toward an inner mode of consciousness. At its ultimate they are Pythagorean modes of understanding, dependant upon geometric principles and the theory of vibrations. That is to say - Harmonics. This is encapsulated in certain forms of architecture as also in various forms of sacerdotal art, of which the most widely known is the ancient Egyptian forms of gods. Ancient Assyrian forms are by no means devoid of it either, for that civilisation too was also intent on the abstract formulation of the patterns of the stars.

Some of the artistic forms that embody means of higher communication have been deliberately placed in buildings, with varying degrees of effectiveness and understanding. There are also unconscious uses of the material, put into designs by those who were wiser than they knew, either because of their own unrealised depth of inner wisdom or through intuitive contact with schools of wisdom upon the inner planes. There are as many orders of masons and divine architects on the inner planes as there are on the outer, and craft guilds of this nature have their inner as well as their outer membership.

Indeed the esoteric societies and fraternities in their true sense are craft guilds - comprised of artisans, journeymen or master craftsmen - and many awkward apprentices too - whose mode of technology is the building and use of magical images. This is what distinguishes the occultist from the mystic, in broad but fundamental terms. The occultist is predominantly a worker in forms. The mystic goes straight to the formless. The mystic's technology, if one can speak of it in those terms, is of the nature of dynamics. If one might say so without impiety, the aerodynamics of the power and flow of the breath of the Holy Spirit - the rushing wind that no man knows where it listeth. The mystic, in other terms, is like a wind-surf sailor, standing on his frail plank of faith over the deep and tempestuous sea of the divine consciousness. Yet if he falls he has no fear, for he only returns to the arms of his maker.

The occultist on the other hand is a builder of sturdier personal craft, whilst those who form the active workers within the great religions are those who go to sea in great liners, of which the first example was perhaps the Ark. Yet so ornate and luxurious in form are some of these that their passengers become hardly aware of the sea, or the elements that signify God, unless the sea and the tempests become really rough, when minds and hearts become more aware of the nature of the medium upon which they float.

In terms of the Tree of Life you may conceive the higher worlds of those who seek to communicate with you to be in Tiphareth. Yourselves, enmeshed in your concrete consciousness, are focussed in Malkuth. The medium of images through which we communicate is based in Yesod, with the polar dynamics of all such formulations represented by the positive and negative side pillars of Netzach and Hod.

Now when we come to deal with abstract figures and forms of communication, you may see this level raised somewhat, from Yesod itself, to the crossing of the Paths between Tiphareth and Yesod and between Netzach and Hod. In terms of the tradition in which you work, this transverse path is associated with the Lightning Struck Tower, which signifies the illumination of images, and the destruction of those which are too concretely formed. It also the Path of the Hebrew letter Peh, the Mouth, indicative of communication as well as the taking in of food. The upwardly pointing path is associated with the bow, the bow of aspiration of the Centaurs, as also the great means of abstract communication, if ever there was one, the rainbow in the sky, the emblem of God's first great covenant with man. It is itself formed of light, and its refraction through the myriads of tiny crystal spheres of water, that in another sense represent all the spirits created by God. There is fruit for much inspiration in the contemplation of this image - as indeed of much "simple stuff" that is taken for granted in the Bible, which is no mere book of fairy stories for childish minds, but a powerhouse and treasure-house of wisdom. Indeed a rewarding bran tub for whoever is child-like enough to put their seeking hand of faith within.

{The Chancellor, 24.9.93}

63

What we have explained to you is essentially a simple scheme in its essence. Namely a world, or focus of consciousness, of incarnate spirits such as yourselves; and another world of discarnate spirits such as ourselves; mutually striving to communicate across a chasm - and this may be conceived as a pool or lake of reflecting water, or a mirror, or even a crystal ball - in other words a focus for "agreed" or communicating images.

That is, what you imagine to be there; we imagine to be there, and from that confluence of thought and intention a type of vortex is formed. This is different from the ordinary forms of vortex that result purely from natural causes or from unaided work upon one side of the abyss or the other. A different quality is imparted into what might be called an "agreed vortex" that is formed by inner and outer plane co-operation.

It gives an image that is to a certain extent "ensouled", or gives the impression of so being. It is still largely fed by positive and negative side pillar forces, that constitute material objectivity at their own level, but these are modified, controlled to an extent, indwelt to some degree, by energy and attention contributed by those from above and below.

Thus although the resultant teaching often contains a great deal of complexity, the mode of communication is very simple. It is no different in principle from your communication with anyone in the outer world. The basic principles of speech for instance are simple. You make movements in the air with your larynx and these are received by the ear drum of the recipient. And although beyond this simple and very workable principle there lies considerable complexity in terms of physiology, psychology, and sonics, you do not allow such considerations to confuse the directness and clarity of intercommunication. And just as on the physical plane the criteria of effective communication are enunciating the sounds clearly, on the one part, and listening attentively on the other - so in communication between the planes the prime requirements are the clear building of images, and the stilled receptive mind in attunement to these images.

An image acts as a carrier wave for various ideas, words or intuitions that come across to you. These do not come direct but are reconstructed in the receiving structures of your own mind. The analogy of radio is an almost exact one. The broadcasters at their radio station are not standing upon their roof and shouting. They are inside communicating ordinarily and quietly into a microphone, a device that turns their speech into electronic impulses that are then broadcast across the ether to be received by your own personal radio, upon whose loudspeaker or headphones you rely to convert the electronic impulses back into speech again. All you have to do is get your tuning right. Fail to do that and you drift off from what is being relayed, into distortion, into silence, or even into another communication.

The way that you get and stay tuned is by building the required image, and then letting your mind hold it whilst receptive. This is really not different from the process of meditation, except that in the circumstances of which we are talking, there is a communicator, as real as you are, (possibly more so) at the other end. That you cannot feel, touch, see, hear him physically does not mean that he, or she, (or it), does not exist. If you had as much faith in the images of your mind as you do in the images of your television, you would find understanding and communication with the inner planes a great deal easier. This of course is a matter of faith. But faith that can be buttressed with experience, that leads to knowledge and ultimately to the clear conviction of certainty.

So build your images clearly. Let not intellectual doubts, (or theories), cloud your receptivity. And you may be surprised at what a wonderful receiving apparatus you hold within your head, between your ears and behind your eyes, and it is not located there without good reason.

We speak particularly of the pineal gland, which is like the crystal in one of the early radio receiving sets. All you need to do is have faith in it, and tune it to what you need, with some of the sense of wonder that you may have done as a child with your first experience of one of these apparatuses. Your attention concentrated by head phones, all you needed was the patience to attune the crystal.

{The Chancellor, 25.9.93}

64

It is by the tuning of the image making faculty that you are enabled to move around within this abbey, and beyond that to related states, by using imagery beyond the circumscribing pattern of the abbey building.

Dynamics of place are relevant to this part of the abbey, for it is from images of the ancestors that one is often naturally led to an associated place. "Composition of place" is a term that is familiar to you in the technical process of creating a unified mood in an occult lodge or similar meeting. In this technique an imaginary place is described, be it temple in the desert, cave by the sea shore, stone circle or sacred mound that is envisaged by all. Very often these are abstract images, not related to any specific place upon the physical plane, although of course you will be familiar with exceptions to this rule, particularly with regard to sacred centres or famous holy sites such as Glastonbury.

In this latter connection the initiative has come from the inner planes. An inner power point has been developed from a natural up-welling of spiritual force, or where spiritual force can be naturally blended with the up-coming forces from the Earth's interior (its "inner" interior perhaps we should say). There are similar sites the world over, such as Delphi or Carnac in Brittany, and in this respect they are contacted on the world wide etheric grid that has been revealed to you upon the observation tower.

Here however, this quiet point behind the High Altar represents the unobtrusive meeting point between the concerned and dedicated citizen and the guardians of the nation. Such concerned and dedicated citizens may not be occultists in the technical sense, although they will be gifted with a reasonably free and active imagination, and a reverence for the past, together with a real concern for the spiritual well being of their country. And the mode of contact will be unconscious and intuitive rather than any consciously magical technique of working through the evocation of images.

The way we can work through the historical sensitivity of people is similar to communicating through puppets. You will observe how easily for example a group of children will respond and talk to Mr Punch at a fairground stall. Or indeed how an adult audience can be induced to react to actors on a stage. Characters in a book can come very much alive, and as in the case of Dickens, through characters, draw conscious attention to various concerns, be it the condition of prisons, the welfare of the poor, corruption in public life or the horrors of war.

And at this place within the abbey, you may, if you have knowledge, observe, converse or interact with the figures that have been evoked. For the most part they will be familiar from history - although those lesser known or previously unknown to you may also be involved. The purpose is to lead your concern and your consciousness in a certain direction, so that you may become aware of certain forces within the racial soul or mind, certain ideas and aspirations, often seeming lost causes, that require at least some concern and acknowledgement, so that they do not erupt in unbalanced ways. Or on the other hand, so that they may feed good or neglected qualities into the racial conscience and consciousness via your own incarnate awareness.

Some of these characters from the past will have natural talismanic connections with physical places throughout the land, with which they were associated in earthly life and which you might need to follow up. This gives, you will see, an added dimension to the preservation and maintenance, and accessibility to the public, of stately homes and other places of historic interest. It may perhaps seem a little strange that the National Trust, or English Heritage, are profoundly occult organisations. However, the esoteric is where you find it, and of course in the last analysis it pervades all.

However, in the application of this work, you need to know what you are doing, at least to an extent, and to work under direction, for there are ramifications and labyrinthine depths to some of these historical matters that are known and understood only by the greater masters and appointed guardians. They who work within the deeps of the racial soul like masked surgeons over a patient.
In this respect your own function is rather like that of a nurse or junior auxiliary who hands the instruments to the operating surgeon or helps to observe the heart beat, or staunch a flow of blood. A somewhat grisly metaphor perhaps but one that is accurate insofar as it relates to the intention behind this work, which is essentially one of dedication and of healing. This is no mere fun trip, or excursion through a theme park, and although certain elements of the romance of history may make it interesting and even entertaining, that is not the main purpose of the exercise.

You may therefore in your work of this nature, when in contact with one of these historical figures, feel that the term "eidolon" is perhaps too abstract for what can seem a very warm and personal human relationship. Although sometimes it can become "all too human", in which case, before glamour or vainglory swamps the operator and the work, it is as well to have this abstract concept to refer back to, as a means of balance and appreciation of what is really going on. For these figures coming through in full power are capable of becoming quite obsessive to those who are sensitive or inexperienced.

You may, for instance, find yourself as participant in what appears to be shared memory, going in consciousness to a particular physical site or location. Or indeed, whilst visiting such a site or location, you may be, sometimes quite unexpectedly, stimulated into awareness of the human figure or figures involved. What you have in effect is a complex of magical images, some human, some of location, which will be acting in various ways, inspirational or talismanic, with your own consciousness, as part of a turbulent structure or vortex.

{The Chancellor, 26.9.93}

65

We pass now to our next point of circumambulation of this abbey that is not built with hands, to further chapels and oratories symbolically situated in the south eastern quarter.

There is first a chapel which has been set aside as a place to show early relics of former sacred buildings built upon this spot. Or so it would be if this were an abbey built upon the physical plane, one that *had* been made with hands. This is not the case with this one however, which if not eternal in the heavens like its spiritual prototype within the heart of God, is of a mode of being inbetween, built from the imaginations of earth bound consciousness that is being schooled or directed toward the ultimate heavenly reality.

You will thus find on view, for your contemplation and reflection, ancient aids to the imagination in this schooling process. This includes early paintings, carvings, frescoes, and fragments of stained glass, depicting what some might mistakenly regard as naive approaches to the Godhead. Figures of angels and saints, and depictions of scenes from the Bible, Old Testament stories of Noah and his ark, the expulsion of Adam and Eve from Eden, the stories of Jacob and Joseph and the foundation of the tribes of Israel, their descent into Egypt and going forth into the wilderness in search of the promised land.

And all the ancient words of wisdom and early revelation are contained in a great, golden clasped leather bound book, that rests upon a lectern in the form of golden eagle that stands toward the south east corner of the great nave that is beyond the walls behind us.

But we who stand apart, amongst the private chapels of the ambulatory, may turn to a niche within the western wall of a chapel that faces to the east, in the south eastern corner of the abbey. Within this niche there sits a wise and holy man, and you may sit yourself at the small stone seat before and beside the niche in which he sits. He is a holy anchorite who has dedicated his existence to the learning and the exposition of the Holy Word. From him you may learn much. Sit before him and listen, with any of the Bible stories in mind, and he will instill you with wisdom. He is as wise as any Qabalistic *meggid* or any angel of the Most High. He inspired the secret and expository wisdom of the Zohar, the symbolism of the Sepher Yetzirah, the Book of Enoch, the ancient and heavenly secrets contained within the measurements of the temple, or of the ark, or of the configuration of the camps of the tribes. He is the expositor of the hidden truth behind the sacred word. A great Qabalist as well as priest and rabbi - wise man and teacher.

And when you have sat at the feet of the teacher of the ancient holy book, turn and direct your eyes towards the East, for you are seated at the west wall that looks eastward toward the altar of the Lady Chapel. And there you will see upon a blue draped altar, embroidered with silver and supported by vases of lilies, a figure of the Virgin and Child. And within the windows of the clear light of this place is depicted the human side of the Incarnation. That is to say the Annunciation, the Presentation within the Temple, the Child teaching the Elders, as also the familiar scenes of the Nativity, and the Flight into Egypt. Emblems of the unexpected and unwanted advent of the holy, and of its rejection and intended persecution - and later its return and fulfilment of the task and destiny of the young child in the Temple.

You may also see, in the northern side of the chapel, internal pictorial windows depicting the early legends of the Virgin, of her immaculate conception, of her dancing as a child before the temple, her spinning and weaving of the scarlet and purple threads - emblematic of the earthly lineaments of the Incarnation. In all that is within this chapel you will find the fulfilment, the realisation, the casting into human terms, of all that is promised and foreshadowed by the spiritual wisdom that is read to you and revealed by the priest and patriarch of the Sacred Book.

You may also enter further into this chapel, to stand at the foot of its altar steps, to watch and to pray, for here is the ambience of the first of the new humanity, the dedicated and redeemed, the Queen of Heaven, the first among equals of all who wear the heavenly crowns, that have offered their lives and earthly expression to the love and will of God, into whose hands they have commended their spirits, and like her, after the dormition for a space, are raised, assumed into heaven, and crowned with the diadem of the power of the spirit, which is the crowning jewelled radiance of the Divine Spark upon the body or bodies of manifestation.

This place therefore gives a glance into heaven. You have only to follow the example of she who is depicted and honoured here. For she stands not only for herself in space and time but, cosmically and in evolutionary terms, for the whole of the human race. At one with and at the same time the bride of Christ - and this implies of the Godhead as a whole. And also, in terms of Earthly incarnation, the Mother of God. She who, by the Divine Grace it must be said, makes the Incarnation, and the saving of all the spirits in Earth, possible. This is the true meaning and fulfilment of the stewardship of mankind upon Earth. And of which any intermediary efforts, laudable as they may be in intention, are but a faint and faltering shadow of the real divine intensity.

So go to the foot of the altar and think on these things. And also give ear and heed to the background, the foundation to all of this that is given to your ear by the heavenly teacher who sits within the wall of her chapel. Remembering that an attribute of Binah, the seat of form and the feminine, is holy and heavenly wisdom, or Understanding. And from this proceeds Love and Action, or expression within the worlds.

And having realised something of this, we may then pass on.

{The Chancellor, 27.9.93}

66

As we proceed down the southernmost aisle of the abbey you will see above your head a series of stained glass windows. The fact that they faced south in a structure of this type upon the physical plane would mean that they were particularly illuminated by the sun in its course through the heavens by day. And you will see here represented scenes in the life of Our Lord, the record of the Incarnation, starting with the Tree of Jesse, immediately after the chapel we have left, which marks the point of the transept.

The transept, be it remarked, is at the equivalent position to the south of the building and of the great nave, that the entrance to the tower is at the north. Similarly the Lady Chapel is at the equivalent position to the Chapel of Penance for the newly dead. There is a symbolism of position in this place as there is in all holy structures of whatever kind. In this particular instance there is a resonance to the mantric prayer of the church to Our Lady, "to pray for us sinners, now, and at the hour of our death."

The old priest, the oracular wise man of the sacred texts also has his equivalent in the Sacristan of the northern side. In terms of officers within the sacred mysteries they perform the function of Messenger and Guardian respectively.

In the southern transept area you will find that the great centrepiece, the emblem of the Tree of Jesse, is at the same time a philosophic indicator. It is a form of the Tree of Life, and also a plan or pattern in terms of human destiny. If you familiarise yourself with the lives of all who are depicted thereon then you have a structure of teaching which will take root within you, considerably deeper than at the intellectual level. It is a form of living encyclopedia, of all the scripture stories organically related.

It resonates also with the more secular holy work of the guardians of the nation, those who work within the forms and forces of the ancestral powers of the race, which is a more localised function, within the crypt. That which we contacted at the furthermost Eastern point in the abbey, at the root of the High Altar, when that altar is approached from beyond or behind its public face. In this sense it represents an esoteric approach to the altar, but it is the great power of the altar itself that holds in place the underworld forms and forces of the earth below, and also empowers the forces within the tower, that rise vertically above it.

So with all this in mind we may proceed westward down the southern aisle, noting the whole array of stained glass depictions of the life of Our Lord. You will find if you stand before them that they take on not only the vibrant colours of light but take on an action of their own. You have before you then a further type of magical image, one that is lent to holy or sacerdotal uses. In effect you might envisage the soul of St Ignatius of Loyola, contemplating these images, wandering up and down this gallery, in the formulation of his Spiritual Exercises. For here you may sit or kneel at the pew ends that give on to the great nave, and turn your eyes and attention to private contemplation of these events in the recorded life of Our Lord. Note too, that on this side of the nave is the Lectern, where is preserved, ever open, the record of the Holy Writ, the written form of the record that is displayed upon the whole southern side of this great abbey.

There is however a barrier part way down the southern aisle, although it is one that you could pass without pause or regard if you so wanted to. It does not have the positive restricting force of the barrier represented by the Sacristan guardian upon the other side. The consequences of ignoring it are however of no light matter, for it represents loss or lack of opportunity, for this particular barrier is one that leads beyond the abbey itself.

In its outer form it is a desk, a hollow desk, whereon is to be found a great book in which you may inscribe your name. And within it, a coffer in which, were this a place of worship within the outer world, you would be invited to place your donation. However, here is no ordinary entry into a visitors' book, no implied request for a financial donation, but to an act of personal commitment and dedication.

{*The Chancellor, 28.9.93*}

67

This is not a place where you should inscribe your name lightly. For first, do you even know who (or whom) you truly are? I phrase the question thus because it has a double meaning within its grammatical structure "Who" is a subject, and "whom" is an object. If you know *whom* you are, and you may be on the way to discovering *who* you are.

To know who you are whilst entrapped within physical form consciousness is by no means easy. And you are unlikely to come to this realisation until you have spent some time within the abbey. And when I speak of time I do not speak in terms of the measure of physical time crudely measured in terms of the Earth's movement in space about the Sun. I speak of a process in consciousness, of a growth in realisation, like that of the Tree of Jesse within yourself.

This is an organic growth that must come of its own volition, and one that may be "fast" or "slow" in comparison with others. Each soul grows at its own rate and, like a plant or a flower or a tree, that is the correct and appointed "time" for it. The journey around the marker for the long haul home may be long or short according to the integral quality of light within the soul, although there is no differentiation in the quality of the pristine light of the spirit to which each will come. The return to the Father, to the heavenly home, will be however at the rate and in the direction that each will come. And "if it be my will that one (or some) shall tarry, what is that to thee?" saith the Lord.

So at the time that you are ready you will inscribe your true name in this place, and you will make the donation that is required of you, and at that time you will know what that will be. But let me tell you at this point that you will be protected from premature donation, and that is a protection and not a restriction. Just as is the flaming sword of the cherub who stands at the Gate of Paradise - for only the perfect can enter in, those whose garments are washed to whiteness and transparency in the Blood of the Lamb.

This is the element of the Divine Grace. For what is it that you can possibly give that is needed for the maintenance of this abbey not made with hands - let alone its heavenly prototype, which is maintained entire by the will and the heart and the purpose of God? The only thing that He needs, or requires, is yourself. Your self as you are in essence, as He created you, but enhanced and glorified within His sight by the journey and trials of the Sons and Daughters of Eve and Adam, who have with their heel bruised the head of the Serpent. And all of these may enter in to the Kingdom of Heaven before the Last Days of the final judgement, when all shall be rolled up as the back cloth at the end of a spectacle or play, upon the tawdry boards of a theatre.

So at such time as you are ready you may present yourself here. It may not be until the Latter Days, or it may be upon the morrow, or it may be after giving service within this place. It all depends upon what you will, or "what thou wilt" in its true, and un-debased sense. At such time you may present yourself here. And at that time you will realise your true name and write it within the book.

And in terms of the magical imagery of this place, which represents a reality far greater than the plane of images, you may see the form of the Sacristan of the North appear at the side of the dedicated soul, who becomes transparent to sight as the spirit begins to shine through the outer garments of form. Then is returned the golden disc that was first delivered at the foot of the tower as a token of entry to the abbey. That disc will also now have the name of the dedicand etched thereon. And the soul, having had this token returned, will place it within the strait and narrow slot of the offertory.

And as it drops from sight, so at the other side will appear a mighty angel. A guide like the one that appeared to Tobias. An angel with healing in its wings. And in a blaze of glory, the soul shall then disappear from this place. The soul in the company of the angelic form you have learned by tradition to call Raphael. And in that brief blaze of glory the Sacristan may appear to your sight as the great angel of annunciation between the planes, even Gabriel. For these two represent a gateway, the true gateway, between the planes, that leads the human soul into and through the angelic worlds.

But such a journey can only be speculation for you at this time, even though some sense of the glory may be reflected within your heart. You will return here when the time is right and ripe for you. Have no fear. Not a second too early nor a second too late, for these matters are governed by cosmic law, and the will and knowledge of the Father of All. In this sense predestination is a spiritual truth.

But like many spiritual truths, twisted and misunderstood when reflected in the minds of incarnate men.

But come with me, aware of the on-going story of the Lord's journey in the sun illumined pictures of the windows above us, as we continue down the final part of this way toward the westernmost end of this southern aisle.

{*The Chancellor, 29.9.93*}

68

At the far southwestern corner of the abbey there is a tiny chapel, its door within the western wall of the abbey sealed off with a curtain. Before we come to this however, there is a memorial, that rises high against the southern wall. It is draped with flags and banners, and as we approach it you will see that it corresponds to what in an abbey upon the outer plane would be an altar of remembrance for the fallen, for those who have given their lives for the country during war, defending it in time of peril. This is true in principle no matter what the outward particular circumstance, for we know that not all wars are defensive or just, and not all who died are heroes, but the principle is there, and on balance the principle is borne out in practice. Those who died were those who served.

We are joined at this place and time by both my colleagues, whom you have met, and we stand in respect and indeed reverence and humility before this place. It has a cup of sacrifice in dark metal, and in bas relief below a lengthy list of names that covers an expanse of wall. The names are too numerous to read at one time of standing, and in any case most are unknown to you. True heroism and true service usually bear a cloak of anonymity. You have standing beside you though, you may have realised, three who represent those who gave up their lives willingly for a principle.

One who was condemned to death on the grounds that his teaching was corrupting the young. Another for alleged disloyalty to state and king. And one who gave his life in battle, who led his men with an unloaded gun, an act which some would say also bordered upon treachery or the treason of the fool. However you will realise that the Fool, as in the Tarot like the Hanged Man, may prove in the full reality of things, neither so great a fool, nor of such inverted values, as might at first appear.

There is also instruction here if you choose to take time to do it. And that is to come to this memorial, and in the proper mood that it induces, review before your inner eye the sequence of the Tarot Trumps within this light, for you will find that all have this dual aspect to teach, which is most apparent in the figures of the Hanged Man and the Fool.

But now we pass in single file, for only one can pass through the curtain of the doorway of the tiny western chapel at a time, as individuals. Once within, we find it is just large enough for us to stand before the altar that takes up its southern wall.

It is a place whose atmosphere envelopes us within a warm embrace of devotion and dedication. For however lonely may appear the way of the sacrificial hero, the bearer of others' burdens, it is never in truth a lonely one. The apparent victim is borne up by the especial love of God and by the wings of angels.

By tradition this corner is the site of an anchorite's cell. One who has dedicated a life of humility to contemplation of the great work that goes on inside the abbey. That work culminates at the high altar and upon this the anchorite ever gazes. Yet at the same time there is a small window and perhaps an ante-chamber open to the outside world where any may come for advice or simple succour.

The altar before us in this chapel is bare, and the light is dim, for the only small and unglazed window is very high above us. It represents Heh, the window of the Qabalistic Tree. And within this place, a fit subject for thought or meditation is the Qabalistic alphabet, for it is the study of the Word of God, who, half in jest, has been accredited with speaking Hebrew. There is, as is often the case, a great truth hidden within the jest. For although these things may seem to be of high abstraction, almost a mystical algebra of the intellect, if you study them in the spirit of reverence of those depicted in the Zohar, who met in the Greater or Lesser Holy Assemblies, much may be given you. The realisations may take form upon the altar before you.

This is also called the Chapel of the Holy Cross, for if you look with care you will see a dark shadow of the wood of the cross, plain and unadorned, within the wall above the altar. You will also see however, in a space to the south of the door by which we entered, a crown of thorns, suspended over a picture. That picture is, on closer inspection, an imprinted veil. And upon that Veil is to be seen, sometimes clearly, sometimes dimly - at other times, it is said, even with great radiance - the countenance of the Incarnate One. The Great Countenance made flesh, the willing servant and sacrifice, and exemplar and saviour for us all.

And by this token this chapel is one of Holy Mysteries. It is a place of esoteric Christianity. I know there are some, and right worthy and noble souls, who maintain that there can be no esoteric Christianity, for Christ died simply and plainly for all. In this we have of course another example of great paradox, for this is often the only way that spiritual truths may be discerned on Earth. Both views are true. Just as it is also true that there can be a false and deluded esoteric Christianity; indeed also a false and deluded worship and exposition of the gospels and the faith.

There are nonetheless to be found, within this place, knowledge and experience that are not the province of the great majority. But woe be unto him who seeks them in a false spirit of spiritual pride or emulation. These mysteries pertain sometimes to the Graal, or to the Holy Lance or to the Veil, and in some respects you will see that there is a link between this place and the chapel within the tower. However, there is a major difference.

The chapel in the tower, as with the chapel of penance at its foot, and the chapel of Our Lady upon the other side of the nave, are entry points for higher knowledge and wisdom of an individual nature.

There is more of a corporate matter about the mysteries within this chapel. They are flesh on universal bones. And the realised and gathered wisdom, not of this world, of groups of illuminati.

Many of these have met with corporate extinction, but as with sacrificed individuals, the truth they have died for lives on, for it is changeless and immortal. Here is the place therefore where may come to you realisations of the Graal Hallows, of the Instruments of the Passion, of the role of the Magdalen, of the Mysteries of the Crucifixion that lead on to the Glorious Resurrection.

But their discovery is a personal one that is open only to your own desire and efforts. It is the vision of the one who seeks, who knocks, that these secrets may be opened. One who seeks to know, to will, to dare - in the most profound and significant sense of those words - and after that to keep silence. For much of these holy mysteries so reveal the holiness within that they cannot be communicated to the outer world. For they may seem to the worldly wise, and even to the pious worldly wise, only words of folly, even blasphemy. Although those who so strive to persecute the utterance of holy truth are guilty of the sin against the Holy Ghost, about whom the best that may be said is "Forgive them, Father, for they know not what they do."

{The Chancellor, 30.9.93}

69

This chapel itself contains much that is hidden and which is under the dark veil of the period immediately after the events upon the Hill of Golgotha. That is the period within the tomb, the Holy Sepulchre. This incorporates the Descent into Hell, so called, although it is and was an action of far wider implication than is summed up in these bare words. It includes the mysteries of the translation of the body, the Corpus Christi, wrapped in its holy veil. Then of the so-called Empty Tomb, although no physical plane place was ever less "empty", believe me, with its angelic guardians awaiting the coming of the women with the oils and spices.

In approaching this place you are very much in the position of these women, who served even after the apparent death of their master. The true Mysteries of the two Maries, and of the Magdalen, are all under the aegis of the owner and donor of the tomb itself - truly "the holyest erthe" in the whole world - Joseph of Arimathea. And from this depend many of the Mysteries later subsumed under those of the Graal, and of the Templars, some of it kept in store for them by esoteric Judaism, being like a casket around a precious hallow.

And so pass out of this place to consider the Mysteries of the Resurrection and the Glorious Ascension. These are depicted as bas-relief sculptures about the font, that stands outside this chapel at the west end of the nave of the abbey. And it is appropriate that these portrayals of a condition that come about after death should be associated with a vessel, a communal vessel, that is associated with the beginnings of life.

When you later return in contemplation here, ascend the three steps upon which the font is based - a minor ascension in itself is this, an equivalent of the three steps commonly depicted at the foot of the cross. Here anoint yourself with the water that you find within. It is a holy water not blessed (or made) with hands, but straight from the fountain of the Paradise Garden. Then through these magical images will come to your inner eye other images of the Mysteries of the Resurrection, as revealed upon the Earth by the appearance of the Risen Lord. From this will follow the Mysteries of the Ascension. This is a latter day extension of Jacob's Ladder - and of the modes of ascension of Ezekiel or Elijah or Enoch. And real experiences these may become for you in the circumstances of the Mysteries of the Font.

Recall too that the font is representative of the River Jordan, the holy river, in the crossing place of which was the site of the Holy Baptism and the Descent of the Dove, and the speaking from the heavens, for those who had ears to hear, of the Voice of the Father: "Behold, my beloved son, in whom I am well pleased". And may this be the destiny of every mortal, of every Divine Spark.

{The Chancellor, 1.10.93}

70

Look now to the great West doors of the abbey. So vast that they soar up, almost reaching the roof it seems. It is here that once a year the great doors are flung open for the entrance of the Paschal candle at Easter, representing the Joy of the Resurrection, and the Eternal Light brought into the earthly and human kingdom. And then that candle, adorned with the five thorns or wounds, the badges of divine covenant, remains within the building all of the rest of the year. A silent witness as to the glory that was, and is yet to come, and which indeed is now, although not revealed.

You may see with your mind's eye the memory of this action that takes place upon the physical plane each year. Of the doors that are normally closed being thrown open, and a great brazier of the fire of the Holy Spirit blazing outside. And then the solemn joyful advance of the new candle of Easter brought into the otherwise darkened church or place of worship.

In this ceremony you will see that the West end becomes at that time an equivalent, a node or polar point, of the High Altar in the East. Indeed at that point the glory of the Eastern altar is no longer apparent to your eyes. Its power and glory, or the power and glory that are associated with it, that normally sit upon it, are here now manifest within the West.

And the blaze at the Western door is visible even to the benighted, darkened and illusion filled eyes of those who are outside the gates, within the travelling fairground of the ephemera of the outer world.

Not, I have to say, that all concerns of the outer world are transitory illusions. It was not for nothing that the Lord incarnated there. And in token of its importance we have the practice of taking flowers and other objects of natural life within the holy place in the abundance shown at harvest time. But the celebration of harvest, the Thanksgiving at the evening of the year at Michaelmas, for the natural victory in the field of nature and the husbandry of the fields, is a different tone and level of celebration to the joys of Easter. There

there is a supernatural element, and a promise too, that all that is good and true, conforming to the creative principles of nature, shall be taken up into the supernatural.

Nothing that is good is destroyed. Nothing that is worthy is rejected from the heavenly harvest. This is the coming, not only of the prodigal son to his father's house, but the coming of the Prince, the return of the King to his rightful domain, dispelling the dirt and the mirk and the shadows, and illuminating and bringing all, not to purgation and destruction, but fulfilment.

Then the whole abbey shall light up, and be as the one that is eternal in the heavens. For they shall be as one. The Four Worlds of the Qabalists shall coalesce as one. And this is foreshadowed in the Easter ceremony at the Western Door, which is where the Kether and Malkuth of the Tree of Life, as laid out upon the plane of the abbey, shall become as one. The one illuminating and conjoined to the other, in the mystical marriage of Creator and Creation, of Divine King and Earthly Bride, foreshadowed in the Queen of the May, to whose astrological sign, of Taurus, is attributed the sphere of Venus.

You will find that many so-called "pagan" or ancient beliefs and customs are revealed in a wider and brighter light in all of this, for they have been silent witnesses through the ages of the glory that was yet to come. Therefore those within the church, or those without who claim to know the will of Jesus or Jehovah and condemn these pagan modes, do but darken counsel in their narrow vision. Their eye may, in certain, and indeed in many cases, be full of light, but it is a light that has dazzled the wider vision.

Be not therefore as these modern Pharisees. All that is created by God is good, and in the dumb beasts of the stall of the nativity is exemplified the witness of nature, for all of nature is the source, provides the pabulum, is the necessary dictionary, of the language of the soul with God, whether that soul be outcast from the heavenly presence, or is turning its eyes, like the prodigal, back towards its heavenly home. But for the prodigal there were lessons to be learned even in the husks of the corn that the swine did eat. And so it is with the many symbolic forms. Wherever consciousness directs its eye, there is evidence, there are guide posts, of the way back to the Creator.

{The Chancellor, 2.10.93}

71
The Mysteries and the imagery of the High Altar, should be familiar to you from the Ordinary of the Mass. Here all is revealed and it is rendered open to all. It conveys an understanding that is fundamental, of the heart and the blood and the breath and the viscera, that is not dependent upon the shallow intellect, even when it is bent upon higher things. Nor indeed is it to any great extent necessarily dependent upon the imagination, although that great ass is always called upon to carry the Ark of the Covenant, or the Saviour entering Jerusalem, his way strewn with palms. It is the creative medium of human nature as expressed within the form worlds, and therefore has its value, its treasures and its resonance, even in shadows and reflections of the great matters of the formless worlds.

The High Altar is likewise the heart of the abbey. The pump through which flows the blood of the spirit, and upon which are impressed the images of form life, as they reflect or strive to enact or reconstitute in lower modes of perception, the great and glorious realities of the formless world, where all is love and light and power, within the surrounding and adoring and thanksgiving rays of the Glory of the Brightness, the halo around the head of the Divine Countenance, formed by the creative Divine Sparks, created by the thought processes and ideas that flow through the mighty chambers of the mind of God. Of this it is not possible, at this stage at any rate, to try to indicate more.

{The Chancellor, 3.10.93}

PART THREE: THE MAGICAL VORTEX

72

Magical images, the approach to which you have been instructed, are forms engendered in the mind's eye that have their foundation in higher worlds, with which they resonate. These higher worlds you are sometimes pleased to call "formless worlds". However, form and force are relative matters.

The forms you visualise, or perceive to be impressed in the mould of matter in the physical world about you, have their immediate cause in the action of forces upon a higher plane. These forces are of another level or mode of manifestation, but one similar to the world of your physical perceptions, in that it embodies the same archetypal qualities. The fundamental or originating qualities are ideas within the mind of God.

These concepts are at any rate sufficient for all practical purposes, working under the limitations of form consciousness as we do.

It is important in all of this to realise the wisdom, the power and the glory at the central loving heart of creation. Otherwise, in seeking to expound the laws and patterns by which such powers and glories are expressed, one is left with what appear to be the cold bare bones of abstraction. This is a risk one faces in any attempt to explain the inner structures of life.

The intellect is like an X-ray, it highlights only the bones. These should not however be reduced to the "dry bones" of the valley of death and dust and corruption - the ultimate and lifeless end of the forces of decay, when even the lower parasitic forms, that feed on whatever was left, are in their turn reduced to dust. This danger is found in all bureaucracies, the so-called organisers of life who come to regard it as a collection of cyphers, of statistical abstracts, until they are more appropriately regarded as organisers of death. One finds it even in the curative arts, of medicine or psychology.

The glories of unique life should not be reduced to bleak abstractions, to the inhumanity of number. Numbers, it should be said, are holy conceptions, but as a basis for life, not for its destruction or its dismissal. These are hellish powers and temptations when you think of it. Truly the sins against the Holy Ghost that "cannot be forgiven".

They cannot be forgiven because they destroy the one who is in need of forgiveness. For "rising above the form life", as it is sometimes regarded, is a distancing from life, a reduction of life, a desiccation of life. And the projection of an image of desiccation onto all that is observed is but a reflection of what is happening within the observing soul, which like Lot's wife, is turned to a pillar of salt. Lot was wiser, in simply doing what he was told, in faith, and not looking back for explanations.

However, this does not mean that explanations should not be sought, for the higher reason is a stepping stone to God and to higher reality, just as, at their own level, are the powers of the image making faculty of the imagination. The mind may be "slayer of the real" if it is improperly used, but the possibility of improper use should not debar us from its rightful application. Indeed it should be a cogent reason to set the ways straight, to erect a firm and reliable Ladder of Jacob within the abstract mind by the use of appropriate images.

After all, the imagination of lower forms can also be turned to improper use, although after a different order. You see examples everywhere in the follies of this world. Souls obsessed with desire for the illusions of the form side of life - be they the erotica of Venus, the riches of Pluto, or the executive powers of Zeus. All are noble powers in their inception, as the god forms indicate, but are easily degraded in the turmoil of the market place.

And so we seek to cast anew something of the teaching that was given before, and rendered and distributed as *The Cosmic Doctrine*. This has much of great worth within it but is in danger of being misunderstood because it presents the bare bones of creation in very abstract terms. We seek therefore to render flesh and blood upon these bones, to set a heart within the rib cage of what may seem to be a skeleton, and thus try to reveal Adam Kadmon in all his glory.

{The Philosopher, 3.10.93}

73

A fundamental error in approach to the principles laid bare in *The Cosmic Doctrine* is to assume that they explain the beginnings of God. Indeed it is possible they may do, in a shadowed and reflected way. However, as with all such systems, (whether conceived by the human mind or rendered so as to be comprehensible to the human mind), it is indeed a laudable and instructive process to seek to understand the highest constructive principles of creation, but we should be cautious of trying to apply those principles to an explanation of the Creator. This is like explaining the psychology of the cook from an analysis of the cake - and, in some respects, from the point of view and level of understanding of one of the currants within it!

Certainly something of the Creator may be discerned from what He has made but the power and the glory and the reality of the Creator are as far from the grasp and capabilities of the human mind as is the world of the human being from that of an earwig - even though they share the same creation.

Yet we have the Hermetic axiom, "as above, so below", and indeed, properly applied, in terms of the lineaments and structure of the creation, much can be learned and understood from these principles, for they apply to the works of sub-creation too, and human kind is one of the Creative Hierarchies. You all have powers of creation whether you like that fact or not.

This brings a high responsibility. But in essence man is of the order of the angels, the mighty choirs of beings (called swarms in *The Cosmic Doctrine*) who helped to form the worlds. These worlds are the globes of evolving form life, whether that life be in terms of the chemistry of the electromagnetic interplay of the atoms and molecules, the formation of plant and animal life and species from the principles of botanic and biological cellular structure, or the civilisations that rise and fall in the history of the planet.

The Cosmic Doctrine strives to derive a universal formula that may be applied to all of this, in particular by looking beyond the interplay of purely physical forces and forms, to see the initiating and the design of structures of life upon a higher plane to expression upon a plane below. And correspondingly what effects conditions upon a lower plane may have upon the deliberations of those that are above. That is to say, the inter-relationship between creators and their creations.

From this something of the nature of God may be derived. But it would be a mistake to try to define or to describe God by recourse to these principles. One might as well try to do it by mathematical formulae. Truly, mathematics, the science and indeed the principle of number, is behind all of creation, and much can be learned by meditation upon these principles. It is truly a work of the abstract mind, and beyond images, which is why it is so incomprehensible to the general run of humankind. Yet it is the basis upon which most of humankind's devices of technology are invented, understood and maintained. And all by a species of mathematical and technical "priesthood" - with their own "rites of initiation".

But mathematics as it is applied in practice relates to only one plane, even though it is capable of much more. Such as the Pythagorean approach to harmonics for example, or the inferences of Projective Geometry. There are in fact many more, known or unknown and yet to await discovery.

The principles that I seek to give are not mathematical - although mathematical principle could be applied to them. They are structures of the form building imagination, magical images, and thus more accessible to the human mind and its principles and habits of mentation. They are however magical images of a certain kind, that induce higher realisations.

That is, by contemplating these images, the imaginative faculty, and the associated life of form in which it is encapsulated, will be induced to resonate upon the same frequency. And thus to produce similar forms, in different terms of expression, within another nature. The analogy of two adjacent electrical coils is here apposite.

Pass a current through coil A in specific patterns of growth and decline, and by means of the changing magnetic field a similar current will be induced in coil B, which will be expressed in another magnetic field, which is an expressed or realised interpretation of the original. Now if we see the inducing coil A as being upon one plane, and the induced coil B as being upon another, we will have a means of communication, of expression, between the planes.

It is by means of these simple analogies (a form of magical imagery) that we seek to instruct in these matters. The applications are for your own work and realisation. But you can see in this example, that not only could it be applied in relatively mundane circumstances, as the influencing of another with ideas or emotions, or impulses to action, but also on a grander metaphysical scale, when it could even be applied to the relation of God to His creation.

This does not mean to imply that God is only an electric coil. Or that the creation is only one too. Or that God and creation are mirror images of each other, plucked from an electrician's shelf. But that imagery can illuminate the mind if the image is not mistaken for the reality.

{The Philosopher, 4.10.93}

74
Similarly the seemingly abstruse principles that were taught by Plotinus and earlier by Plato and Pythagoras, might be thought bare and intellectual if not sympathetically approached and used. In another sense the system of reading and training might be compared either to the number mysticism of such Qabalists as Abraham Abulafia, or to the "negative way" of mystics of the type who wrote

The Cloud of Unknowing. Or to those who chose a mantic way, as the Jesus prayer of Greek or Russian Orthodoxy.

Now all of these methods pare down, you might say, the flesh and blood, the human side of magical imagery. This however does not remove them from greater approach to holy and heavenly truths.

In one sense the emotional warmth, the divine enthusiasm, that can be felt or engendered by more human magical images, can give a truer reflection of the ambience of love of the higher and the heavenly worlds. However they are, in another sense a misrepresentation, by coming down further into the clouds of matter to demonstrate the clear air above. To try to describe the sun-illuminated clear sky above the clouds by recourse to terms that depend upon the experience of the rain soaked, dimmer world below.

Upon the higher levels, the planes of causation, are the shining, God-given, spiritually-created principles to which all the teeming world below conforms. The golden web of created life rests upon the framework of diamond nodes in a silver net of inner principles. And by contemplation of these inner principles light will shine within the outer forms of your consciousness. And so in time there develops what can only be described as "a loving impersonality". That is not a cold, abstract and inhuman thing. It is love whose poles are at a higher wider plane and level - that can embrace all.

(Here the mind went blank. The communicator seemed to have gone away. Then there appeared a couple of patches of golden light, which solidified into a number of coloured spheres moving about each other in a complex motion, and whose beauty and motion had a strong emotional and aesthetic effect.)

All forms that you see relate to the observer. I am placing before your inner eye images of moving coloured light, of spheres that seem to move in a completely random motion, but do so in a stately dance, in which none is ever in danger of collision with another. They are all beautiful, unique, and the forms and colour and the quality of their surfaces strikes an emotional chord within you, of awe, of wonder, of beauty - just as you might experience in response to any lower form, but this is unmixed with the elements of Eros, or those of personal acquisition as of Pluto. This is beauty of movement and form at a high abstract level. It uplifts the lower man, the lower consciousness, it educates the emotions. And this is an example of the way all such forms can and should be approached. They are not bare mathematical equations, dry sticks to be manipulated by the intellect. Visualise these living forms. Do not distance yourself with the glassy eye of the intellect. The nearest that that can come to appreciation of higher things is a recognition, an appreciation of elegance, as in a mathematical proof or move in chess, or of bowls upon a green.

The images that I shall show you however, are capable of very much more than this. They reveal the wonder within. And through a living relationship with those wonders, whilst still within the form world, give you the opportunity for clearer sight and greater service and more intelligent appreciation of the works of the Creator and of his servants than you are likely to find in any other way.

Fear not then the apparent abstraction. As may be seen in certain forms of art, there can be as much force and wonder and beauty revealed in an abstract form as can be portrayed in any realistic representation from the form world. It is simply another way of looking.

In any case, what could be more abstract, and revealing of love and of beauty, than the face of a flower? It is to a flower garden of underlying forces and forms behind the veil of matter, above the clouds of illusion, to which I would introduce you. As your philosopher, friend and guide.

{The Philosopher, 5.10.93}

75

The forms that I show are of course, "forms of the library", or of the scriptorium. Although a better term for the place and the condition would be the Treasure House of Images of Qabalistic tradition. In the wider sense the whole of the "astral" realm of the imaginative faculty and every image that has been formed therein could be so called. Although this would be not so much a treasure house as a stock pile, a "waste pile" even, with very much dross.

An abbey taken as an imagined construct is in a sense a treasure house of chosen images, indicating where various types of image may be found and how you can relate to them. The scriptorium is however a place within that place, a mode of making contact set apart as a special place of teaching. Indeed, in any traditional abbey upon the physical plane, what was the library or the scriptorium for? It was not a place of prayer, or of inner counsel or experience, as other parts of the abbey. It was that part of the building set apart for knowledge. For knowledge is the thread upon which the bead of the present is fixed. And the other beads are representations of previous times, and their inner conditions, as well as those of the future. Thus you will perceive the globes of which I sometimes speak as like those beads upon a thread of the continuum of life force.

They are images of conditions that are none the less real for being formulated upon screens of perception, of inner vision, that I shall put before you. They are manageable counters in an otherwise unmanageable complexity. Were your mind to attempt to comprehend the whole of reality as it is, it would be overwhelmed. A hollow shell cannot contain the ocean. Yet within the capacity of that hollow shell, the drops of water, the specks of sand or grit, the tiny living forms within the water and the sand, are a microcosm of the greater, the almost inconceivably greater that lies beyond. And by virtue of examining what lies within, may be discerned what lies without, for all is built on similar principles. As within, so without, might be your adage.

And this is the process of all human learning, of human knowledge, and its manipulation and growth and application, in any walk of life. Indeed with the development and use in your time of the computer and its image making facility upon a screen of that which is complex, you have a direct comparison of what is available and which goes on within the imaginal treasure hall. It is a means of demonstrating, and of discovering truth. Although of course the final and acid test must come when you try to apply these principles in actual life. That is the proving ground. Do these principles work?

The true and proper mode of action is to take account of both. It is no path to progress to be for ever in the maelstrom of outer experience, realising nothing in the flood of activity, like a pebble on the bed of a stream. Nor is it the way to go to the other pole and be for ever in a state of meditation, poring over principles; for there is only true creation, true understanding, in their application. And the one who becomes obsessed by the manipulation of images never comes to grips with the real. For the real, (which is the purpose of our instruction), is the expression of the interconnections between the planes of action and of realisation.

Make the connections. We can show you the principles, and the shadows and lineaments thrown by the higher life. And this is our area of service. It is to you, placed within the matrix of the material plane, figures within the looking glass world, that can act and serve where we cannot.

{*The Philosopher,* 6.10.93}

76

Fundamental to all of these questions is the principle of the vortex. What is a vortex? It is the means by which anything is done, or achieved, in terms of one plane of activity, when initiated upon another. It occurs when two free spirits unite in co-operative endeavour.

Thus you may at first perceive them, proceeding like points of light in space, each going its own way, undiverted by any outside consideration. Then something comes to impinge upon each one's consciousness, and this causes a change in their track in space. For in an internal entity, complete in itself, such as our point of light, a change in consciousness causes a change in activity at a lower level.

You can conceive of each point of light being a unit of consciousness within a simple surrounding envelope or body. The spark itself is of another order of existence. It is from the purely creative heaven-world, from the aura or the halo of God, from the divine cosmos, the Ain Soph Aur, whatever imagery or nomenclature you choose.

It has, (for the purpose of expression and experience within a created world,) a body, which is formed of a concentration of the essence of the plane through which it passes.

Now we see that the cause of the change of consciousness of the spark was an attunement to a mode of vibration, or spiritual thought processes if you will, of another similar embodied spark. Their resonant responses will be at first a dim awareness, then a kind of strong intuition. Finally this becomes a movement towards each other, as the existence of each other is gradually realised. At the level of their bodies it is expressed by means of a change in direction of their movement through space.

And so we find that the two points of light with which we started, are no longer free moving along their original lines, but conscious of each other, or at any rate of the presence of each other, which is manifested by a pull, a change of direction in their movement. Thus they start to follow a track whereby each is revolving about the other, or rather about a common space.

As they continue to circulate around this circumscribed space so they begin to have an effect upon it, upon the matter of the substance of which it is composed. Because they are circling over and over around the same small area of space, each in their way they are affecting it, enturbulating it, impressing it with their own nature.

As they do so, so are they drawn into an increasing concern with this area of activity which they share in common. So their attention as sparks is not so much directed to each other as to the common cause which has come to unite them. This grows stronger in their intent and concerns the more they gyrate about its circle, the area of turbulence created and conditioned by their two-fold passage around it.

And so you find that something begins to happen with the space itself between them. It is as if you vigorously stirred a liquid upon the physical plane. It begins to form a cone, a hollow cone, or whirlpool, from the vigour and circular motion of your stirring. In other words it forms a vortex. Only the vortex of which we speak is formed by the action of the two sparks.

{The Philosopher, 7.10.93}

77
Thus a self-contained spiral of energy is formed, initiated on one plane and expressed on another. Anything that has been conceptualised at one level by the activity of two collaborating beings remains as a vortex of force, boring down, as it were, by the force of its spinning, from one plane to another.

The force of that spinning is caused by the circular dance of the bodies of the two sparks. The dance of those bodies was caused by the realisation by those sparks of each others' existence. At first dimly perceived and then recognised with increasing clarity.

The spiral vortex so formed is of independent matter upon the plane of impactation, that is to say, of the substance of their two bodies. (This is not entirely the plane of origin, for that is at the level of the will and consciousness of the originating sparks). The spiralling substance forms however a point of great concentration upon the level of the plane further below. Here it appears to come out of nothing, as far as any observing consciousness confined to perception upon that plane is concerned. But as we know, it has its antecedents, its immediate cause and origination upon the higher planes.

This we can summarise in a sequence of events:
a] Awareness of pull at the level of consciousness of the sparks. Also some gravitational pull of bodies, but very minor and not operable without intuitions from the indwelling sparks.

b] Co-operation in conceptualising. Represented diagrammatically by circular motion about each other.

c]. Matter of lower planes enturbulated. Also some other matter drawn in to increase the complexity of enturbulation.

d] Effect, a form is created upon the plane(s) below.

The originating sparks upon their own plane can now go their ways, freed of the form they have created, as individual free moving sparks again. Or, as a co-operating duo, they can create more of these vortices in space, producing forms on the planes below in exactly the same manner, whenever they will to do so.

They can then, by virtue of the increased power of their duality, and their experience of co-operation and the making forms upon a lower plane, co-operate with other sparks that are also acting as dualities. Indeed they can eventually co-operate as conglomerates - although the process of association is more patterned, more structured, more organic, more spiritual, than the term "conglomerate" would suggest.

Remember we are talking about realms of active, intelligent and creative beings. So the harmonics of the laws of co-operation between them are of a great beauty and their inter-relationship a true harmony of forms.

It is these associations of different types and forms of creative being that are intended, when *The Cosmic Doctrine* speaks of complex "atoms" of different facets and number. Certainly there is a higher "geometry", if you like, involved, but we are not speaking in mechanistic terms of different shapes of grit - but of associating choirs of angelic beings.

Thus we speak of things as immeasurably "above" you, as you in turn are "above" the grit within a conglomerate mass of stone and clay. The analogy and the correspondence may hold and be useful to your understanding. But we must not confuse the illustrative form from a lower world with the glowing reality of which it is but a shadow. The types of magical image that we are now using are, in their way and at their own level, simply parables. Parables of abstraction perhaps, but with a certain simplicity and purity that becomes apparent when true and holy things are revealed in their first principles.

{The Philosopher, 8.10.93}

78

These principles can be applied at any level and will be seen to have validity. They should not, however, replace the rich tapestry of life as it is elaborated and experienced upon every plane, within every clime and time, in all or any of the worlds, visible or invisible to mortal eye. But by their simpleness of line, their basic structure of interlocking vectors of dynamics, they may show you how things happen "under the surface", that may not be apparent to you when the events that clothe them are enrobed in their rich complexity.

{The Philosopher, 9.10.93}

79

In what we have been describing you will have noticed a three-fold principle, and this applies no matter how complex the circumstances become, in the various planes and phases of manifestation.

There is first the central principle, the initiating spiritual core so far as the manifest universe is concerned. Around this the bodies of the substance of the various planes develop or cohere, like a shell, by means of the attractive power of this spiritual principle.

That shell or complex of bodies is the second principle involved. The third principle involved is the effect upon the matter of the plane upon which the body (or complex of bodies) moves and interacts.

There is a polar interchange, a stimulus and response mechanism, to put it in its most mechanistic terms. The action and re-action we seek to explain is more in the nature of an intelligent balancing interaction. Think in terms of the figure of Temperance on the Tarot card.

There is a balance in the whole of nature. A balance within the processes of the systems of your own physical body, the heart, lungs, digestion, nerves. Also in your social interactions, with family and friends. In your response to art, to work conditions, people you meet on the street. To represent all that in terms of stimulus-response mechanisms without a realisation of all the gentle subtleties, the nuances involved, would be a travesty indeed of over-simplification.

So in our simple diagrams, our magical images of principles, we are not advocating a bare and blind reductionism, but a means whereby you can discern the root and the main stem of any situation from the foliage, the blossom and the flower. It does not mean we want to defoliate, to rip bare of flowers the beauty and fragrance of your garden of realisations of how things are.

But spiritual principles also have their beauty, and so behind the rich panorama of heavenly and earthly life, there may also be discerned the beautiful simplicity of the spiritual principles upon which they are expressed. The roots if you like, of the Tree of Life, whose roots are in the heavens and whose leaves and fruits in the planes of manifestation.

This is a reflection of a greater Tree that grows in the heavens, in the Paradise Garden. And what you may learn from the experience of manifestation, from life in the branches of the lower Tree, may grant you a glimpse of the Greater Tree, which in one sense represents the brain cells of God, if one may be permitted a somewhat bizarre image. It is however an image not without point or relevance for it is in line with the ancient traditional Qabalistic image of the worlds of manifestation and their emanations being represented by the beard of God - all springing from the Great Countenance. I am simply inviting you to glance at what may be revealed behind the Great Countenance.

Within the microcosm which is man, (as well indeed as of all created creatures who have a spark of divinity) the Divine Spark is as the Greater Countenance. It looks down into the planes of manifestation and forms its bodies of expression there.

That which formed the Divine Spark, is the activity of a Cosmic Atom, (so-called within *The Cosmic Doctrine*). This is a cell within the body of God, and is the heavenly and ultimate meaning of the phrase of "being of One Body with the God-head." This does not merely apply to the exoteric church upon the outer planes, although of course it has its important application there. Our application applies to any divinely inspired grouping of sparks, and their means of expression, upon the planes of form. And it is the structure behind the substance of these associations and activities that is the focus of our study.

For if you look within yourself as you now are, as you now express your spiritual being, what you ultimately are, at root, is your own spark, which is an expression in divine light of the cosmic reality that feeds and fuels it.

Let us try to visualise this in simple pictures:

The Divine Spark has a Cosmic Atom behind it, as its originator.

The pattern of the dance of the Cosmic Atom gives colour and quality to the Spark, as seen from the planes of form, and determines the type of material it attracts for its lower plane bodies.

This is the origin of the concept of the Seven Rays. You could conceive of the different dance of the Cosmic Atom causing a different wavelength or vibration of the light of the Spark, thus giving it a principal mode of expression upon a particular point on the spiritual spectrum. Or indeed, if we were to think in terms of the symbolism of the Creative Word, and of various "keys" or notes upon a spiritual scale, it is the basis of a divine system of harmonics.

The activity of the Divine Spark, its brightness, colour, and movement, in accordance with the stimulus of the Cosmic Atom, attracts matter of the lower planes for its expression.

In terms of current human experience these are the modes of expression you know as intuitional, mental, emotional, imaginative, nervous, physical, etc. Each is capable of being divided into its sub-planes, but here we run into a danger of crystallising into the deadening structures of the mental. It is essential that we keep our images free, free flowing, not crystallised, nor on the other hand, too volatile or vaporous.

You therefore, upon the physical plane within the Globe of Earth, are in essence a Divine Spark, with a coat of many colours as a means of identification and expression. Indeed one might say with seven coats, (even forty nine taking account of all the sub-planes), but here the useful imagery falls down, becomes overloaded.

Another way of representing this would be as a Tree of Life. What did we say about 10 sided atoms in *The Cosmic Doctrine*? It was not so bizarrely ungeometrical was it?

{The Philosopher, 10.10.93}

80

You have now been given enough in realisations to equate much that is given, in telescoped form, in *The Cosmic Doctrine*, with the traditional structures (also rendered in telescoped form - though after another manner) of the Qabalistic Tree of Life.

The Tree of Life, as is apparent even from a cursory glance, is based upon interlinking triangles of force. This is a factor so basic and simple that it tends to be overlooked. But here again we have a correlation with what has been expressed in terms of *The Cosmic Doctrine*: when two beings upon one plane come into polar relationship, as a consequence they produce a form upon a lower plane. Similarly you can perceive that one particular unit of form upon a particular plane is ultimately, or has within it, the creative forces of a duality upon a higher plane.

Now these are all magical images with which we are dealing. It is not our purpose at this point to utilise them for detailed teaching about the higher worlds or the inner planes towering up into the spiritual realms. Once you understand the principles you can put them to use yourselves in meditation and contemplation. But you will see, particularly when you turn your attention to the higher reaches of the composite Tree within the "Four Worlds", that contemplating the Tree in Atziluth brings about a different "feel" to when you contemplate it in Briah, Yetzirah or Assiah. Yet the images or structures are much the same. In fact they are geometrically identical.

But it is this use, this varied use of similar images at various levels that will teach you to be aware of different processes within you, and of different levels of perception and reality.

This should give you an inkling of another function and purpose of magical images - particularly those that are available within the Treasure House of Images, the library or scriptorium of an interior Abbey. Such a structure is an Abbey of Gateways, for every image is a gateway to further comprehension, to wider understanding, to new experience.

You may conceive of such an abbey as a form of the Tree of Life within the Formative World - the world of images. This is a world that is objective in itself, as for example in the images of watchtower or of crypt, which can give access to other objective states.

On the one hand it can lead back to the outer world, beyond the precincts of the abbey, represented by the turbulent and noisy street outside. On the other hand to an objective world within, a mystical world, corresponding to the Tree of Life in Briah and even Atziluth, gained by recourse to various chapels. Indeed it is possible that you may meet, within the purlieus of the abbey, within its aisles or in the nave, individuals of such a mystical ambience that they will generate within you spiritual realisations and capacities for action or perception upon yet higher planes.

All is a matter of rate of vibration, of harmonics, when we get down to basics. This applies to the spiritual worlds as much as in the physical world, where their manifest perception is in terms of colour, sound or tone, through the sensory perceptions of the body.

And you can be induced to vibrate at a higher level. Thus you are wise to choose the company you keep, the environments you frequent, at least until such time as your own mode of vibration, your personal colour and tone so to speak, are well enough established and stabilised to hold their own, and you can be a radiating creative force that raises others and their environment up to your level, rather than being yourself dragged down. You can be raised up by association with others of higher tone, or purity and delicacy of spiritual colour, if they allow you into their company. Spare a thought at times that this may be something of a sacrifice and burden to them, even as the company of those of lower tone may be something of a burden to you - assuming you have risen far enough for the lower modes not to be a temptation.

It is realisation of this that caused some medieval spirituals to despise and flog the body in an effort to kill out desire. This is not an attitude or process that we recommend. The supreme example of radiating spiritual influence upon the physical plane is the Resurrection Body of the Christ which served to galvanise the disciples into the beginnings of spreading the word, (and indeed this was a spreading of the Word quite literally, for it fired others with the rate of His vibration).

This had been foreshadowed on the mount of Transfiguration, a vision accorded to three of his leading disciples. But it was also at work in the whole of the ministry of the Christ, which is what rendered Him such a charismatic figure.

{The Philosopher, 11.10.93}

81

The simple kite shaped structure of a "countenance" gives a picture to your mind's eye of the principles that are dynamically operating, at whatever the level.

Thus there is the level of the Logoidal impress. In the language of *The Cosmic Doctrine* this is the conscious recognition by the Great

Entity of an individual Spiritual Atom within its being, within its aura if you like, or within the cloud of glory round its head. All of these are inadequate images but the best that can be devised to strike tangentially upon your consciousness, thus rendering formless principles into form ideas.

The pros and cons of consideration whirl around within the Mind of God as he contemplates each such Cosmic Atom. The Wisdom and Understanding of God in the Highest, work through the dual principles of Mercy and Severity, which are two very inadequate terms in this context, and would perhaps be better called the Love of God and the Purity of God. These bring about a conception (Knowledge) in Daath. Recall the phrase "to know even as you are known". There is no greater knowing, no expression of love more all-embracing than this. All of this powers into the Tiphareth point, the expression of Beauty, of the Child and of the Sacrificed God, images of great relevance, even at this level.

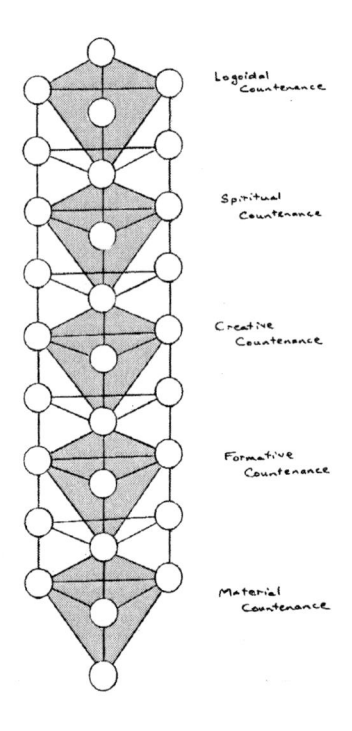

And so we have the phenomenon of the impressed Cosmic Atom. That is to say, one that is empowered with the principles of form creation, that can manifest a Spark by its activity, and that can develop or attract around itself the impressions of the Logos, which are expressed as the required bodies of form and experience. Through these are gained viable experience of life in the worlds of form.

{The Philosopher, 12.10.93}

82

In looking at this diagram two other things should become apparent from its form. One is of a kind of Archimedian screw that descends through the planes. This is an image of a vortex that is effective upon several planes (or sub-planes).

In another way of looking at it you may see a vertical series of cups or chalices, with the blade of a spear descending into each. This series suggests at each level the descending blade twisting, and forming a circle of turbulence around it, of the matter into which and through which it penetrates.

The intermediate Spheres on each side, represented at the different levels of the Sephiroth Chesed and Geburah, represent the positive and negative principles that institute the turning.

In the case of a vortex formed by the co-operation of two people such as an inner plane communicator and an outer plane mediator, they can be represented, one upon each side, as "bearers" upon an armorial heraldic device, between whom the pattern of manifestation appears. Indeed the basic pattern of such armorial bearings is also instructive. The crown, helmet or similar symbol of rulership is found at the top, with the bearers on each side contributing stability. The real force comes from the crown above - (albeit to a certain extent from the crowns of the bearers themselves). The field of activity between them is represented on the shield. And beneath, the motto encapsulates in words the aspirations of all who bear that armorial shield.

Thus another way of looking at the "countenances" of the soul upon the Tree of Life is to see them as a series of shields. The devices upon the shield will then be the individual's form of expression at each level. This can be a useful exercise of personal meditation.

Let us therefore create a specimen armorial bearing by way of example. There is also some importance in the order in which we shall list its parts.

1 - Of the two bearers, one is the "initiating" bearer. The communicating adept on the inner planes, for example.

2 - The other is the "co-operative" bearer, the mediator tuned in to the inner plane adept's aura of ideas.

3 - The Crown - or armorial crest - is their coming together, which enables the higher to manifest, to be the fount for a reservoir of higher energy.

4 - The detailed picture that is built up on the surface of the shield is the expression of the incoming force that the bearers hold in balance between them.

5 - The summing up of all that is depicted on the shield is expressed in the motto below. This is "the Word" made manifest. It is an expression, at a lower level, of the crest or Crown. This motto can act as a fount of force in itself, for it encapsulates on a lower plane all that has gone before.

You should now see the importance of human and indeed any other spiritual beings, and the reason for their creation. By their own initiative and co-operation they prepare the conditions for divinely inspired higher forces to flow and to make patterns in creation. Thus is the law created, the Word made flesh, made manifest.

Thus all are co-operators, ultimately, with the God-head. This applies at every level, whether one is thinking in terms of the earlier hierarchies and the Lords of Flame, Form and Mind who laid down the conditions of material being, or the later human development from that, which is the record of cultures and civilisations.

Nothing exists above the basic material level in the world that did not come into being through the active co-operation of human beings. This includes even the biological perpetuation of the race. Each and every child is the result of two coming together - with or without the desired element of responsibility. In that, or its lack, lie the seeds of the Fall, but that is another matter; the fundamental principles of creation in form still hold good.

In this sense, all human co-operation is, in essence, a magical act. Giving, or making, or even initiating in form, the conditions for higher or spiritual forces to make themselves manifest.

The reading of the motto, which is another aspect of its formulation, is the reading of the spiritual essence in form expression or experience. What might be regarded as notes of the Recording Angel, to use a somewhat simple analogy.

The process of assimilation, or meditation over that which has come to pass, (which is enjoined upon you to perform in the exercise of the evening review), is a desired and indeed required condition after death. The memory of the meaning of the motto lingers on. It is taken as a realisation into the higher worlds and remains as a potential that can be reactivated in any future manifestation of spiritual expression.

We speak in cosmic terms that can hardly mean very much to you, but shall we say that the garnered realisations of experience enhance the potentiality of heaven, increase the bounds and the potential of the heavenly kingdom. If these seem high claims for the significance of mere mortal man, ask yourself for what other purpose could creation be for?

Is it a gratuitous meaningless act? No, surely in such a perfect being as God there must be a divine purpose. So we are all, as the children of God, co-operators and collaborative builders in the Heavenly Jerusalem. Words of course break down here, like old and crumbling plaster. But the sense they try to convey before they disintegrate forms a useful platform for the training of your higher mind, which is real enough at the next "shield" up, upon the serial Tree.

{The Philosopher, 13.10.93}

83

There is, between any two people or spirits who come together in any form of co-operation, an "understanding". What may have been two individual subjectivities, based upon past personal experience and assumptions and realisations arising therefrom, becomes, in the relationship, a dual subjectivity. A field of inner awareness not only of shared perceptions but a field of vision to which each may contribute and from which each may draw. This shared awareness, this pooling of vision, is more than the sum of its parts. This is because, as we have seen with the coats of arms, their coming together and formulating a field in this way opens a channel to the hitherto unmanifest crown above. And this creates a channel of inspiration, so to speak, not directly to the individuals, but to their shared vision.

This will grow in a perfectly natural and organic way, and with a dual horizontal polarity between itself and each of the two bearers. In this, you may realise, there is a link with the early form of the Tarot Trump of the World, wherein two cherubs hold between them a sphere, in which the world can be seen. For completion there should be a crest device above and a scroll below, and although to some extent the name of the card performs this function, it were better if it had been incorporated as part of the design.

Thus you might conceive of instructive magical designs being formed by the co-operation of the two bearers. These appear on the shield or medallion between them, drawn from the higher power-source of the crest, and summarised and expressed in the motto beneath, the comprehended and pronounced Word.

Indeed you could take this a little further by visualising a single entity, the initiating entity to begin with, and visualising the type of being that is likely to appear in the role of co-operator.

Thus if we were to take a simple example, think of Adam, then the natural bearer opposite him becomes Eve, and the God-head, the Great Countenance, appears above. The conventional manner of old bearded man, either head only or full figure, has perfectly respectable antecedents, either in the Head Which is Not in the Qabalah, or in legendary figures of ancient hermits, patriarchs or magicians, as representatives of God.

Indeed, following this line of thought and imagery, one can conceive of many other instances. In Arthurian legend for example, wherein you may see the knight and the lady who shares his adventures, with the initiator Merlin, (often the controlling entity behind the adventures), represented by the crest. The adventures are then depicted upon the shield, and the lesson to be learned is indicated by the motto below.

In the case of Adam and Eve seen as bearers one might see depicted upon the shield the Garden of Eden, perhaps with the crucial scene of the Tree of the Knowledge of Good and of Evil and the Serpent upon it. Alternatively one might see a quartered shield with four sequential principal scenes. Indeed one might divide the shield still further, as in traditional heraldry, and then it might start to become a picture strip that moves, taking us towards the principle of the moving scenes of Qabalistic "path working".

Also consider how many adventures, in Arthurian legend for example, have the title of two characters - Eric and Enid, Launcelot and Guenevere, Tristran and Iseult. This is because all are demonstrations of basic principles of manifestation.

Much the same principles are to be found in formal dance, and particularly in circle dancing. Here the circle represents the turning of the vortex, and power is brought in from above, and often with an effect upon, or an answering resonance from below. And you may thus realise the importance and significance of the "caller" in certain types of communal dancing. Also think upon the fact that although the whole of the dance may be a communal activity, it is always based upon the principle of pairs.

But the principal lesson I want you to learn in all of this, because it is the key to further realisation, is that of the four-fold flow of force. This is when two upon one plane get together, and through their conjunction and co-operation open a channel for higher force to flow between them. This can be represented by the contents of a cup or the pictorial surface of a shield, and when all of this is realised and resumed in a particular statement, the Word is expressed.

Let us take a personal example in which you can visualise two bearers, Dion Fortune and "A.V.O.", (C. T. Loveday), who between them formed a cup that became realised as the device of their Community and Fraternity. You can see them each side of a great Cup or Grail with the Dove of the Holy Spirit descending into it. Then a motto could be envisaged as engraved upon the rim of the base of the Cup, summing up all that they have achieved. I would not care to write that in just yet, for a great deal that they started is still in course of achievement. But as representing one aspect of this you could envisage something specific that they achieved, "The Inner Light". This is a name that is frequently used or lightly mentioned with little reflection upon the great assumptions and aspirations that it implies and contains.

{The Philosopher, 14.10.93}

84

You need also to disabuse yourself in these matters of a sense of remoteness. Imagine all as being like a great lake in which many levels of life are present from the simplest micro-organisms to fish, frogs, mammals, even humans, such as yourself, swimming in it. The inner worlds are just like this, with many sub-creators, co-operators such as myself, those of the angelic realms and orders, the inner elements of yourself to which in your present focus of consciousness you are blind, and even up unto the Godhead. All are present, all of the time. You know the phrase, "closer than breathing, nearer than hands and feet". You simply have to expand, or to tune your consciousness, and you will find all are there. The Quest is therefore, to that extent, within you. You are the Grail, the bearer of the Divine Grace.

It can be helpful therefore to see the five countenances of the diagram of the Tree of Life in the form of Jacob's Ladder, further integrated, so that each Countenance lies over the other like a series of masks.

The process of "raising consciousness", is in reality expanding it, or clarifying it, or letting the light within shine. In another sense it is therefore a question of seeing the countenance that lies behind each "mask" - the mask of the Personality, the mask of the Soul, the mask of the Divine Spark, (the manifest Spirit), the mask of the Cosmic being that indeed you are, and then the real, the one and only Countenance of Light, the face of God, that also is your own.

The Divine Imprint is not an abstract thing, as may seem from a bald reading of *The Cosmic Doctrine*. It is not a cosmic rubber stamp, but a Divine Union. It is the "temporary" merging of two entities so that the receptor is never ever quite the same again; is empowered with principles and potentials as a result of the Divine gift and grace, leading to degrees of freedom and expansion of existent expression undreamed of within the confines of mere human universal consciousness.

This is the difference between the experience of the Rings and Rays of the Cosmos, and the experience of just one Ray, or a limited part of it as is described within *The Cosmic Doctrine*. But remember that these are merely magical images - structures in the form levels of the imaginative faculty of the currently limited human brain.

We aim to make that brain resonate to something of these higher, more finely tuned realities. The purpose is nullified if they resound, not with the clear tones of the harmony of the spheres, but with the dull clank of cracked realisation, unable to resonate freely because of a mind intellectually bound with mathematical abstraction. Let the images ring, radiate to your inner eye. Do not limit them.

And here is a useful exercise to break free of the limitations of intellect, which is simply a protective shell around the imaginative egg. Try to change perspective on the images described. Identify at times with them, either in the role of an Atom, or an Entity, feeling the swirling of the tides, rather than seeing all from above as from the eye of some remote and abstract uninvolved geometrician. Even a draughtsman is sufficiently involved to wield pencil, compass and square himself.

You see the popularity and the impact of Abbott's account of *Flatland*, wherein a two-dimensional universe is expressed in human terms. It is not entirely consistent or successful, but it is the kind of technique that you should use.

The Tarot has, in its ways, solved this problem, in clothing abstract archetypal, spiritual forces in concrete and personal images. These are alphabetic building blocks for spiritual babes, but they are the first step to being able to read the textbook of the skies, and the meaning of your own existence and the purpose of the cosmos. Let your mind, your imagination, run free. Do not fear running into the realms of illusion. Without freedom of thought, movement or action you are stuck fast within illusion anyway. But free the mind, to talk in imagination to gods, to great entities, to angels. For from this freeing of your mind, and of your conceptions, real resonances may start to chime.

This is the importance of visionaries such as Swedenborg, or Blake, or even Bunyan. They take the imagination out for a ride, whereby it can resonate. You simply have to let yourself, with willing suspension of disbelief, go with them. And if this induces you to undertake your own journeys then so much the better. It will contain truth for you.

It is much the same for symbolic diagrams of a Rosicrucian or Qabalistic nature, although here there can be trammels imposed by intellectually biased dogma. There is no point in substituting one dogma for another in the so-called pursuit of wisdom.

The true principle and practice is shown forth in story, and particularly children's or even childish story - in which much space or fantasy fiction is cast. Stories written for children are purer, for any number of reasons. Those that aim to extend space for adults can be more limiting, bound by barriers within the human mind.

There may also be the perverse and pernicious reflections of thwarted or misdirected desire, for just as the angelic may be readily portrayed to you in this guise, so too can the demonic. But at least it gives you a vision, a sight of the enemy, and what to avoid. Read enough, immerse yourself enough, in the realms of free flowing story, and the truth, the true and the good, will be revealed. The perverted, the inadequate, the evil, disintegrate by their own disruptive forces, or become as pillars of salt, bereft of all reality and life.

The scenic realms of story give a freedom without responsibility, a chance to extend your perceptive inner antennae. Let that faculty run free. Do not simply try to analyse the findings, the experience, the stories of others. Go with them. Flow with them. That is the essence of Quest. And you will find that you will be left with the residue, the golden grains, of reality.

{The Philosopher, 15.10.93}

85
{The Soldier resumes}

You have gone about as far as you can with the Greek philosophical service and its moving pictures of the cosmos. A lot of that applies nearer to home, with your head focussed squarely between your eyes looking at things from a personality level. Because that is where you are focussed, just one or two steps up Jacob's Ladder. And that is what makes you valuable to us. Not just to us of course, we are all mere stepping stones. Humble rungs upon the ladder of creation, and sub-creation too. For we all have our part to play upon the divine creative step ladder. Even if at times it seems that all you are called upon to do is stand up to your knees in the mud, holding the darned thing steady.

Believe me it can sometimes be not so comfortable even a few rungs up. Quite windy and wobbly it seems at times, particularly if those above are cooking up something new, and those below, ourselves and you, are uncertain of what we are supposed to do. Not at all unlike moments on the Western front.

But high up above they say, the sun ever shines, the birds sing, the buds burst for joy in the perpetual sun, and the Armistice has broken out. And we know this ourselves if we attain the presence of mind, the inner calm, to raise our focus a few steps up the ladder. We are never left without some guidance, a vision of permanent Blighty, even if our present focus of attention, our principal mode of being, seems to be floundering around in the mud trying to fry eggs in a mess tin over a candle flame, while all kinds of unholy star-shell display goes on overhead.

Talk about the earth moving too. Have you ever thought about the vibes a shell makes when it lands? It is not just the crater that feels the shock. It spreads all around too, especially noticeable if you too are underground. But then, being in the trenches gives you another perspective of the Earth, nice, kind, sheltering Mother Earth. Refuge from the slugs of lead whining overhead. No wonder lead is said to be the lowliest metal. Homicidal stuff. Brings out the worst in man. Doesn't put too much beneficence into him either!

Read a few war poems of the boys of our era. Talk about the importance of literature! If all had read what our generation had to say about what life is like when human inner conditions are taken to their logical outer conclusion, then maybe later, things could have turned out a bit different. But that is an even bigger earth moving job. It needs an explosion as big as an atom bomb to make the necessary crater, the required waves for a shift in human consciousness.

Did you know, did you realise, that the discovery of splitting the atom, of making the bomb, of the long held secrets (and I mean long) of the Lords of Flame and Form, were permitted to humankind in our era only as a means of helping it to a realisation? Otherwise things would have gone on in the same old way, but going from bad to worse, as technology outstripped morals. Belsen, and Auschwitz and all that, the Burma railway - it was all getting more and more easy to set up.

Organised iniquity, man's inhumanity to man, let alone what he has felt towards lesser man, or to the beasts, has always been there. It is a faculty of human nature, of the conditions engendered by the Fall. This is no mere theological abstraction. The increase of the creative faculty, and its application, upon the level of mind, without attendant higher realisation, was bringing about a situation that could not be countenanced by the Lords of Civilisation (optimists if ever there were any, by reason of their vocation).

Hence, or so it seems to me, they took a risk. To release yet more power and energy, secrets of a higher creative hierarchy, so as to give mankind a shock. Frighten him with his own destructive capability. An increasingly God-like responsibility.

As I say, that seems to me a risky policy, but who knows but that those a little higher up the ladder may know things that we do not, and that the risk is not so great as we suppose. But the battleground, you will appreciate, is within the soul of man. I think the Easterns call it *kurukshetra*. But what it means is that the pursuit of inner truth, of self realisation, is no mere weekend trip for high minded intellectuals. It has a wider application. It is a question of the lower Adam Kadmon, of the fallen Adam (and Eve). The serpent's venom, ingested with the apple still works within them, and the long struggle we have is curative, healing the maimed king, and with it the Waste Land, which in another sense is Eve.

In the end these seemingly high and abstract things come closer to hearth and home because we have the means within us for the cure. But this isn't glamorous and it isn't easy. It is downright overwhelming and terrifying at times - like being a field stretcher bearer. How to cope with all that carnage? But try to cope is all that we can do.

In terms of the contemplative orders of the church, it is boiled down to essentials - of poverty chastity and obedience. That is in order for the spiritual shock troops. For lesser mortals such as ourselves, we seek another way, and one that reaches out into life, not negating life by reaching up into the heavens.

Look upon yourselves as the Service Corps. Not heroic, not glamorously special, but needed everywhere. And it is by your inner realisations, your devotion to a specialist cause, that you are enabled to go where others cannot. Your realisations are needed, whilst in incarnation, of what conditions are like upon the inner planes and sub-planes immediately around the Earth. For in the smoke and confusion of this murk is where the battle lies. And you bring back intelligence from your "recce" on the lower planes, that can inform the higher generals. And at the same time you provide a little succour to those who are immersed in the lines of battle without benefit of the higher vision or wider meaning behind it all. Those who serve by only standing waiting and suffering upon the physical plane.

Sorry to be a bit downbeat on this occasion. But we need to set the scene for that which gives upon another horizon, and the principles and practice in another field of action.

{The Soldier, 16.10.93}

86

The kind of scene we set is associated with magical images, whether they come in the form of a high watchtower or by way of an underground passage into the Earth. In the latter case they may seem to be more historic, of a past era, but their presence, (allowed and released by the Masters, the Lords of Civilisation, and their initiates and helpers who control them), relates to matters or conditions that are in the present - otherwise they would not appear to you. Look upon this form of magical images as being like the safety valves that prevent a steam boiler from exploding.

They can be strongly and closely associated with place, as for example the old Stuart stronghold of Traquair, and indeed places all along the Borders of England and Scotland, of what is broadly speaking the valley of the Tweed. It is from being close to such sources that Sir Walter Scott derived a great deal of his imagery and the power of his imagination, whether or not you judge what he wrote as great works of literature. He was, and indeed to an extent still is, acting as a safety valve, a means of expression, to much that was and is seething beneath like the bubbling lava beneath the cap of a volcano.

This has erupted in physical terms in the centuries of bloodshed over the borders, which goes back to Roman times and beyond, and in the great crises of pitched battles between the emerging nation states of England and Scotland. In one sense the emergence of nations is like the crystallisation, the solidification of continental crusts, which then scrape and graze against each other, clash or drift apart.

You will find therefore that all magical images of this nature are expressions of national identity. One thinks of Drake in relation to England, Mary Queen of Scots in relation to Scotland, Joan of Arc in relation to France, William Tell to Switzerland, and one could go indefinitely on. Look to any series of national heroes and you see the expression of a particular segment of the group soul of humanity at large, expressed within the Globe of Earth upon the psycho-physical level. (That is to say, the Tree of Life in

Yetzirah, the world of Formation, that is, for those in incarnation, conjoined to Assiah).

Now you will begin to see the nature and importance of our task as servers of the light, and of the Lords of Civilisation, in the greater wider sense. For each nation, each portion of the crust of earth consciousness so formed, has its higher countenance - its extension of Jacob's Ladder, both upwards and down. Downwards it is to the genes and physical characteristics that differentiate tribe, family, and all that is associated with racial characteristics upon a psycho-physical level. Going upward however we achieve the sphere of angels and archangels and the spiritual realms of conglomerate or associated sparks and their Cosmic Atoms, and the Mind and Will of God beyond.

Now at these levels we do not say there is no division. For character and self-expression and free will are as fundamental upon the highest plane as they are upon the planes of form. On the planes of form they may be seldom fulfilled, or fulfilled in unregenerate ways. But on the higher planes, differentiation there may be, but conflict no. However there can be problems of adaptation.

Thus upon the physical plane, two lovers, however much they loved each other and intended no harm, could not walk into each other, could not occupy one anothers' space. Even though in some respects, expressed in its ultimate level in the act of love, they might try. Some bumps and bruises would be sustained in the process, if they did seriously attempt it. To some extent the disharmony between nations is a result of a higher intention that clashes with a lower custom or mode of existence or expression.

For instance you have had a problem with black immigration. I use this simply as one example among thousands the world over. Parts of large cities, London for example, are full of West Indians, or those of West Indian descent - many of course now born here. And in the first instance they were invited in, only a small proportion are "illegal" immigrants.

This came about as a consequence of war, and mutual need, and indeed high ideals before that. The colonies had fought alongside the Mother Country (in the terms of those times) in time of international war. Black blood was spilled along with white in what was at its root a European cause. And in the years of reconstruction, when hands were short to man or maintain health or transport services in the hub of empire, (or Commonwealth as it began to be called), so were there hands without work to do in the Caribbean islands.

And many were the high ideals and expectations of those times. Many who expected and dreamed of an opening up of opportunity, not realising the rejection, the prejudice, the conflict that would be caused, and that they would confront. Those of the host nation were in many ways as idealistic as well, not thinking that they, or the people of these islands, were capable of such base reactions as those which characterised what they saw as the less mature and tolerant white inhabitants of South Africa or the southern United States.

However there was soon a rude awakening, an awakening to reality upon both sides. And this is but one instance of a division between the operation of higher and lower "natural law". At one particular level things are expressed from the highest intentions, at a lower they are suffered in terms of conflict.

As an example, the idea of "empire" itself is an extremely high one. It is at root the ideal of a unification of the world, the re-establishment of a single human family. And if one reads the statements and ideals of many of those at the time who played a part in the establishment or maintenance of empire, some of the motives were of the highest. Sometimes naive perhaps, but not always self-seeking or base.

{*The Soldier*, 17.10.93}

87

And so we can have a conflict of ideals. Some may be out of time, because time is an important factor the lower one comes down the planes; even if at a higher level it is seen to be, or becomes, illusory. That is, rather like seeing a slice of cake from above, as a single piece existent in itself in its own reality, as opposed to the serial linear view of time taken by a worm burrowing through it.

And ideals may be out of place, or perverted into hate, sometimes even it has to be said with due reason or just cause. For iniquity breeds iniquity, stupidity breeds stupidity, insensitivity breeds insensitivity.

Hence the words of the Christ about forgiveness and turning the other cheek. Impractical and idealistic though this may seem, and honoured more in the breach than the observance, at some point it has to be the only way to stop the rot, to damp the momentum of reaction, vengeance and reprisal. Someone has to see this attitude of forgiveness not as a weakness, not as an act of treason. It is the Hanged Man of the Tarot once again.

Otherwise it becomes accepted purely from exhaustion, physical and emotional, of horror piled on horror, in an ever increasing pyramid of futility, a hellish version of the Tower of Babel. Something of that was seen for four years by those who served upon the Western Front, but there have been many other horrors, before and since. And man's increasing domination of the natural world by means of his technology tends to increase the field of misery rather than diminish it. The roots of conflict are within the human mind, the human heart, the human soul. And as has been said before, conflict will exist, will go on, be expressed upon the physical plane, as long as the inner conditions feed it and cause it.

Now some of the reasons for all of this, as we have said, emanate from higher beings upon the inner planes, and sometimes larger beings too. In this respect they may resemble the effects of natural law. A herd of elephants can be destructive, so can an earthquake or a volcano, but not necessarily from any malicious intent or aforethought. It is simply a relieving of pressure. Whether that pressure be of hunger, or of living space, or of the more basically physical problems of volume, temperature and pressure under the laws of chemistry and physics upon a geophysical scale. These things are not necessarily evil.

For instances of that one might turn to pestilence and plague, war and famine; some with neutral elements within them but also an expression of the destructively parasitic or of the self-centred and gratuitously and sadistically malevolent. As has been also said by the Master, "It may be that evil must come into the world, but woe unto him by whom it cometh."

In this we all have the question put to us, particularly in life within the lower worlds. There is often a stark choice between following a course of good or of evil, and an infinite scale of more subtle choices between bad and worse, good and better, better and best. None of us come out with a hundred percent marks in all of this, by the very nature of things. The odds are stacked against us, and to make the omelettes we have to break some eggs.

However it is not a treatise on the nature of good and of evil that I seek to give, even if I were qualified to give it, and you were wise enough to understand it. But as stretcher bearers and reconnaissance scouts upon the lower planes of existence, we can simply try to do our best to alleviate what problems lie before us, in whatever way we can.

Insofar that your eyes are turned towards the dynamics of the inner planes you can help to serve in this direction, just as your outwardly directed fellow citizens serve by doing their best upon the outer planes. There is no monopoly of good intentions or of virtue within the esoteric community. You have only to look at the squabbling that goes on to prove that. And many within the world, whether in the field of human charity or simply in making sure that things work so that civilisation goes ahead, are equally performing the work, as servers of the Lords of Light, of the Lords of Civilisation.

So it is a matter of specialisation, that which we call upon you to do. Not because you are superior beings, but because of your interest and expertise.

You simply have to be intelligently aware, upon levels of which others are unconscious, or to which they respond in an unbalanced and unregenerate fashion. That is to say, those who are swayed by the heavy strong-running currents and tides of emotion that is the sea of human consciousness, when it is surveyed in the mass.

This is like the great oceans upon the physical plane, and have been described to some degree by various thinkers, in psychological terms, as the collective unconsciousness of C.G.Jung, or in more philosophic/naturalist terms as an element of the noosphere of Teilhard de Chardin. It is a basic element of human sociology, of anthropology, and it crystallises as the history of the nations. Public opinion forms a part of it, but that is often a passive, or passively reactive factor, the real origins coming from another level, another plane. The movements of peoples in terms of aspirations or of ideas may be the expression of Principalities and Powers. Some are intelligent and ultimately what might be called "pains of growth"; others more or less accidental as might be envisaged by the concept of "the giant Albion stirring in his sleep".

Your part in all of this is, under guidance, to be aware of the conflicting forces, or of those to which your attention is directed. The world is too full of problems for you to find your own way through the labyrinth. And this you will become aware of in terms of magical images. It is your reaction to these, and your handling of them, that is the purpose of your receiving instruction. For training in this particular role in the Mysteries is in the nature of an Expeditionary Force of the Masters. And not, I hope, though it may sometimes appear so, Fred Karno's esoteric army.

{Here the communicator was seen to salute, in a slightly mocking but cheery way. Fred Karno was a comedian of the 1st World War period who ran a concert party whose brand of humour was chaotic slapstick comedy, thus "Fred Karno's Army" became a jocular reference to army organisation}.

{The Soldier, 18.10.93}

88
{The Chancellor resumes}

It is within the Formative World, in terms of the Tree, that magical images arise, and once again you can think of this in terms of a vortex. One that is set up with you, in the role of observer/participator, as one of the bearers. The originating force comes from a source of pressure upon the inner planes but will be connected in some way to some physical event in the past, or to a physical location, that may be neglected, ignored or even ruined in the present, but which has definite and lively past links. Whatever in fact may serve as a focus, however small or trivial in itself, to stir and work upon the imagination, and so be the cause of a vortex.

That, if you like, is the link between you, the seed image. So in diagrammatic terms, you may see the Initiating Bearer upon the left, holding the seed image or object. This may be large or small; a minor artefact, such as Queen Elizabeth's gloves perhaps; or a major site, such as the Cosmati paving and its surrounds in Westminster Abbey. The effect upon you will act as a part of a link which will consist of some kind of connection with your physical body and consciousness.

This connection may be of blood, as a member of the nation, or in terms of having physically visited a place. This in itself, trivial though it may seem, is generally evidence of some interest or connection within you that is deeper than the accidental. Although of course even the accidental is capable of being manipulated in case of need by those who are skilled upon the inner planes. But this generally needs to be helped by some factor in the person being so "manipulated" (the word is a little strong in this context).

The chord of "recognition" that may be struck by the object, or a sense of its significance in some way, forms the focus for a fount of power, the initiating point, of a spiral of descending force. You can think of this as coming from the place of the crest, in terms of the shield imagery, above the heads of the two bearers. You will note that a triangle is so formed, resulting in a downward flow, and already you may recognise the kind of pattern to be seen upon the Tree of Life.

There then forms in the stimulated imaginations of both participants, of both bearers, the pattern upon the shield, or the contents of the Cup. You will note how on a shield the pattern of the shape of the top indicates a three-fold involvement which culminates in their coming to a single point below.

Should the shield be quartered, the central point equates to that of Tiphareth. The centre upward point of the top of the shield is Daath, the bottom point Yesod. The scroll or motto below is in Malkuth. Again you will see curlicews of the scroll beneath each bearer, indicating their importance in all of this. Nothing in this imagery is merely ornamental or accidental.

The side bearers can also be developed in terms of the side pillars of the Tree. Head, heart and feet, being in each case Binah, Geburah, Hod in the Initiator; Chokmah, Chesed, Netzach in the Observer. You will note that the Initiating party takes the part of the Black Pillar. This is because the Observer, although not the activating party, needs the stimulus of the form to be put up before him. This is one of the secrets and subtleties of Binah, and the interaction of the Supernal Triad. The Tree of Life, as life itself, is full of subtle cross polarities.

You will appreciate also, that being on a higher plane, there is considerable pressure behind the crest or fount. You have heard speak of a square law in relation to potencies between the planes. This is a protection really. Four times the force upon the higher plane, when brought down to realisation upon a lower plane, by the act of crystallisation, becomes the equivalent, in power terms, of only two. Thus one is having to deal only with "roots", square roots, upon the lower level. High amounts of force to be contained are the concern of those upon a higher level, when what has been contained is released from its constraining form. Then you have trouble, problems squared, in terms of ascending powers.

So the degradation of a force, (I speak in technical terms) is in many ways a "containing" of it. And this is a part of the work you may be called upon to do. And it may be that you are acting as a safety valve, or overflow container, for some other problem related to it upon another level. It might have happened that some other vortex has become unbalanced and "blown up", releasing lots of pent up force into the upper ethers or higher planes. You, by co-operation with one of the relevant Masters or their servers, may be able to form a stable reservoir or receptacle, by your combined realisation, for much of this force. It has to go somewhere. The law of the conservation of energy applies on the inner planes just as much as upon the outer. Everything is in accord with law. It is our task and problem to render things stable, in accordance with the process of law, within and without. This is not always an easy matter. But that, I suppose, is the challenge of creation, and also part of its excitement!

{The Chancellor, 19.10.93}

89

To some extent some of these images might be said to be hanging in the aether. This is particularly the case in relation to particular historical sites, but it also applies generally. It is almost like washing being hung out to dry.

This, in part, is on account of great pressure upon certain levels of the planes, that seeks relief and redirection by the consciousness of those who are currently in incarnation.

In some cases this can even be the consequence of deliberate ill will. This could be malicious intent by certain beings upon the inner planes who have picked up the necessary inner technology, so to speak. Or those who have been swept into forming a vortex with those on the outer plane by the bias of their own being, upon more inner or upon more outer levels. By that I mean a recent incarnation, or perhaps even a more remote one, where major experiences, possibly traumatic, possibly triumphant, were suffered or experienced.

Eventually all form experience will be absorbed by the Higher Self (or Evolutionary Personality) and thence by the Spirit, of which the Higher Self forms an outer expression. Nonetheless there can be major experiences that are not so easily absorbed. And if they are only partly so, may give a bias to the Higher Self itself in its gathering of more experience upon the lower "personality" planes. Indeed it is possible to have the somewhat unhealthy situation of an element of unabsorbed personality experience being attached to the Evolutionary Personality (Higher Self) which can also have a somewhat disturbing effect upon the Incarnationary Personality. This has been covered in a previous teaching upon "the Ghost" which consists of this kind of unabsorbed material, and constitutes a kind of overshadowing.

This can be an almost obsessive presence to a sensitive or passively oriented personality - or can become a daimonic driving force in one who is also sensitive but capable of positive outer expression.

This, at its highest aesthetic level, can manifest either in works of art or literature, or in works of polemic at a lower level, or indeed a life of considerable unbalanced action. Here you have the source and driving power of much revolutionary activity, as well, and indeed more commonly, of various cranks and faddists, and movements that are "out of their time". There are also, it must be said, certain elements within the esoteric world that might accurately be described in terms such as this.

What we seek from those who co-operate with us is for them to be sensitive enough to pick up on these images that are blown about and inflated by inner currents of force, to recognise them for what they are and work with them in a way that helps to relieve the pressure and so render them harmless, or redirect them into more positive ways.

As far as you are concerned this is done by meditative realisation, and then casting this into a balanced ritual form. A great deal of energy is expended (or drawn off) in the individual meditative process, but when this can be channelled into work within a sympathetic group, when realisations are shared and visualised in concerted, disciplined and organised fashion, particularly in physically expressed patterned action, of light, speech, and motion, (that is to say, ritual), then very considerable curative and remedial action can be effected.

Again according to the numbers present you have another expression of a square law, although this tends to blur with a greater increase of numbers, (conforming then more to the laws of sonics, which prevents a 100 strong orchestra from being 100 times louder than one instrument.) Nevertheless large numbers do have an effect, as in the case of mass movements and public opinion. But so do small highly organised, concerted bands of people such as ritual groups, particularly upon the inner planes.

Indeed with the co-operation of inner plane assistants to the Masters, who may be human, angelic or elemental, the patterns formed by realisation and ritual can be maintained more or less permanently, in terms of inner plane energies and forms, and so help to contain the inner pressures that were a cause for concern.

You may now see the relevance and reason for the figure of Mary Queen of Scots to have appeared in some workings, even unexpected and unannounced. Such visitations are controlled however by those who work with you and behind you on the inner planes.

Also the phenomena associated with workings concerning Eastern Europe. I know that some may query whether, in the light of events you may not be working more harm than good. Let me tell you that work of this nature, under direction, is good. But in some respects, in the nature and the size of the problem, in its ancient roots, and the clash of cultural continents, all you can possibly achieve is perhaps a minor alleviation of suffering and strife. And otherwise things might even have been far worse. Who knows but what you may have helped lift a straw that otherwise could have broken the camel's back? We all know what events in that part of the world have been capable of blowing up into in 1914-18.

Similar comment could be expressed about certain doubts expressed about the wisdom and right of performing workings pertaining to the Middle East. This, as you may well know includes the area where Abraham emerged from Ur of the Chaldees, besides being an ancient frontier of cultures and "continental clashes". It is an area, as in Jerusalem and Palestine, where very ancient evils and human problems, resounding through the millennia, can be expressed.

However, have no fear. All you do, whether you consciously realise it or not, is under hierarchical control. And any member of a properly contacted group who appears to be in danger of becoming unbalanced can very quickly be isolated and ejected from all possibility of harm - to him or herself or to others, or to the work of the Lords of Civilisation.

{The Chancellor, 20.10.93}

Postscript

The bulk of what we desired to communicate is now accomplished. You have a quantity of material which we suggest you should now work upon yourself, to render into a form that is suitable and appropriate for wider dissemination. At the same time you can add, if you wish, exemplary material from your own experience, of working with a group in a magical way, in the practical handling and application of magical images. We have sought to lay down some principles, and a general theoretical structure of how you can and should work with them. It is up to you to provide the experience of application, as seen from the pole of physical plane consciousness, which is where of course you have, to an extent, the advantage of us.

At the same time in your working over the material, you will be in a position to assimilate it more yourself. This will put you in a position to receive more advanced work, building upon what we have told you and shown you. It would not be good practice, however, for you or for us, or for the work itself, to continue to load matter and knowledge upon you that you are unable to assimilate and distribute.

In your work upon this, which should be regular, and, ideally, fitted to an appropriate time scale, you will find you expand in knowledge and wisdom and grow in the process, even if we are not (at any rate so obviously) in daily communication.

Take a holiday now from detailed application to this work. This fallowing period will allow a number of realisations to crystallise within your inner consciousness, and for you to make the necessary change in polarity in relation to the work in hand. Your role now being no longer entirely receptive, but in an active mode upon what has been received.

In this cessation of daily communication, it does not mean that our work together has finished. This remains as long as you maintain the reciprocal good will to cooperate with us in the work of the light. This of course is very extensive in its calls upon our abilities, and wide in its ramifications, as we answer the calls of the moment, of the hour.

And remember that although we are no longer in regular disciplined communication by transmission of wedges of material, we are still in touch with you, our auras interconnect. More teaching upon what we mean by that remains for the future. And we remain available for any interrogative work, on points that evade your understanding or upon which you desire amplification. Although much of this may well come from your own resources, for in our communications with you not all has been consciously received. There is what is nowadays called I think a sub-text, a number of not directly stated but implied considerations, that pass from mind to mind and are available for later realisations. Thus if communication were visualised in terms of material being poured down a chute, this can be thought of in terms of osmosis through the walls of the chute, were it made of semi-absorbant material.

However, a more appropriate, pleasing and accurate metaphor would be the interlinking of the auras of those concerned, which is very similar to the linking that exists between members of a family, or the emotional and intellectual bonding between good friends. In the case of the Masters particularly, and initiation in general, this bonding, this fellowship, extends up the planes beyond the mere emotional and intellectual levels, to a unity of direction and of colour or type in the ways of the Spirit - the conformation and alliances made between Divine Sparks. But much of this, again, can be expanded later. Here ends our first text, or the draft thereof, on our teaching on Magical Images.

{The Chancellor, 21.10.93}

THE ESOTERIC STUDIES OF
THE SOCIETY OF THE INNERLIGHT

DION FORTUNE, founder of The Society of the Inner Light, is recognised as one of the most luminous and significant figures of 20th Century esoteric thought. A brilliant writer, pioneer psychologist and powerful psychic, she dedicated her life to the revival of the Mystery Tradition of the West and she left behind her a solidly established knowledge of many systems, ancient and modern.

This special edition brings together two immensely valuable classic books which make the complex foundations of psychic development accessible to all readers.

ESOTERIC ORDERS AND THEIR WORK examines how occultists have jealously restricted admission to their secret societies and schools and shrouded their practices in mystery. Dion Fortune here uncovers the workings of these secret organisations and describes their operations in detail.

THE TRAINING AND WORK OF AN INITIATE shows how, from their ancient roots, the Western Esoteric Systems have an unbroken tradition of European initiation that has been handed down from adept to neophyte. This book indicates the broad outlines and underlying principles of these systems in order to illuminate an obscure and greatly misunderstood aspect of the Path.

ISBN 0 - 85030 - 664 - 7

APPLIED MAGIC is a selection of Dion Fortune's writings on the practical applications of magical and occult techniques. Written from the point of view of a gifted psychic, they provide invaluable and suggestive pointers to anyone intent on increasing their inner awareness.

ASPECTS OF OCCULTISM looks at nine specific aspects of the Western Mystery Tradition, including God and the Gods, Sacred Centres, The Astral Plane, The Worship of Isis, Teachings Concerning the Aura, and the Pitfalls of Spiritual Healing

ISBN 0 - 85030 - 665 - 5

DION FORTUNE AND THE THREE FOLD WAY

When she was twenty, Dion Fortune found herself the subject of a particularly powerful form of psychic attack, which ultimately led to a nervous breakdown. With the benefit of hindsight, and her experience as a practising occultist and natural psychic, she wrote *Psychic Self Defence*, a detailed instruction manual for protection against paranormal malevolence.

The chapters in this book consist of articles that appeared in the Inner Light Journal, house journal of the Society of the Inner Light, between Spring 1997 and December 2001. They have as a common theme, aspects of the life and work of Dion Fortune, founder of the Society.

Dion Fortune and the British Mysteries was first given as a talk on 15th September 2001 to the Wildwood Conference, Conway Hall, London, organised by Atlantis Bookshop.

ISBN 1 899585 70 2

THE WELLS OF VISION

The chapters in this book consist of articles that appeared in the Inner Light Journal, house journal of the Society of the Inner Light, between Spring 1997 and December 2001. They have as a common theme, aspects of Gareth Knight's own magical work and experience.

Awen, the Power in the Magical Cauldron first appeared as a Foreword to the book Awen, the Quest of the Celtic Mysteries by Mike Harris [Sun Chalice, Oceanside, Cal. 1999]

Qabalah and the Occult Tradition was first given as a talk on 30th May 1999 to a conference on Kabbalah and the English Esoteric Tradition, at the Ashmolean Museum, Oxford, organised by the Kabbalah Society.

ISBN 1 899585 65 6

THE MAGIC RAILWAY

Fairy story or esoteric pathworking - following a long tradition!

The lives of the Selby children are threatened with disruption as their Media World parents part. They are consigned to the care of the fearsome Gerda in Notting Hill. The previous owner has mysteriously vanished. Mr Pretorius it seems was a great traveller on an extra dimensional magical railway from Nothing Hill Gate. Together they follow in his tracks and the youngest, Rosy, finds herself the centre focus for a life and death struggle involving the Grail and the restoration of order and balance to the world.

ISBN 1 899585 61 3

GRANNY'S PACK OF CARDS

There is much more to the Tarot than a curious game as Rebecca and Richard discover. Illustrated. Publication 2003

A children's fantasy story by Gareth Knight. Richard and Rebecca meet the Joker of their granny's magic pack of cards and, assisted by his dog, meet many of his friends on a hair raising cycle of adventures that takes them to many strange worlds such as the Mountains of the Stars beyond the Gates of Time and thence to the Wondrous Island at the Heart of the Rainbow.

Any correspondence with the figures they meet and the pictures in the Tarot pack are entirely coincidental – but we all know
what coincidences are – and they receive much fascinating instruction on this and that by characters as diverse as the Star Maiden and the Great Emperor, having evaded such dangers as the DarkTower and the Desert Reapers. All ends happily with their triumphant return to Myrtle Cottage having made some
acquaintance with their True Names and Essential Goodnesses.

ISBN 1 899585 85 0

DION FORTUNE TAROT CARDS

Strangely the Society of the Inner Light did not produce a Tarot pack although its symbolism is a feature of her classic MYSTICAL QABBALAH.

Now at last is a version of the Tarot in line with Dion Fortune's understanding and that of the Order of the Golden Dawn. All the suits of the Lesser Arcana have been illustrated with images reflecting their symbolism from classical times to the present day. The explanatory booklet also gives guidance on Tarot pathworkings, which are valuable psycho/spiritual exercises and a very positive use of the Kabbalistic Tree of Life.

ISBN 1 899585 75 3

THE DEMON LOVER

Young and innocent Veronica is taken on as Mr. Lucas' secretary though he has other plans for her... Without fully realising just what is going on Veronica finds herself involved in the work of a mysterious sinister male-only magical Lodge. In spite of Lucas' ruthless exploitation she falls in love with him and becomes an accessory in his occult workings.

To try to protect her from the wrath of the Lodge because of her unlooked for and unwanted attraction, Alec Lucas is immersed deeper and deeper into the darkness of the Underworld, ever struggling to free himself from many hells.

This was Dion Fortune's first novel, based on real characters and experiences. It offers many insights not only into the inner nature of the Mysteries and the dangers of Black Magic but also defines aspects of the sacred nature of love.

When it was published the Times Literary Supplement considered it to be 'exceedingly well-written', and it has stood the test of time.

ISBN 1 899585 30 3

THE ESOTERIC PHILOSOPHY OF LOVE AND MARRIAGE

Dion Fortune's basic esoteric textbook on the psychology of love and relationships gives a simple explanation of the universal factors governing interaction between masculine and feminine from the 'lowest' to the 'highest' level of the Seven Planes.

This sensitive and authoritative account, written by a distinguished woman who combined uncanny intuition with "hands on" psychological experience clearly states the principles of polarity underlying all relationships between men and women with insight and sensitivity.

These principles remain as true today as when this classic guide was first published, at the time it was fully realised that a formal marriage contract or ceremony would in no way neutralise or diminish the tensions of sexual incompatibility caused by temperamental differences, conflicting goals or destinies.

Sex is a function, not an ideal and there are other factors producing harmony or otherwise. The feminine is 'positive' on the Spiritual Plane and that of the Emotions. While the masculine tends to be more 'positive' on the Mental and Physical planes. In a proper union, these aspects are harmoniously complementary so the relationship remains in balance. Where these aspects are unrecognised and are denied free expression, disharmony can often result. Needless to say the physical expression through sex will also suffer, since attitudes derived from the 'higher' levels control or inhibit the 'lower' physical aspect.

THE ESOTERIC PHILOSOPHY OF LOVE AND MARRIAGE also includes Dion Fortune's teaching on some of the esoteric principles behind abstinence and asceticism, contraception and abortion.

ISBN 1 899585 25 7

THE COSMIC DOCTRINE

Seventy two years ago a remarkable event took place beginning at the Vernal Equinox in Glastonbury. For very nearly a year Dion Fortune received communications from the Inner Planes concerning the Creation of the Universe, which later became a classic.

THE COSMIC DOCTRINE remained a closely guarded secret until 1949 when a closely edited version was privately printed since Dion Fortune's successor considered the original "a most dangerous book".

It is now available for the first time in its entirety in the original text in this definitive edition.

This full text examines the no man's land where Science and Magic interact. The Cosmology of the "Big Bang" and Chaos Theory running parallel to the evolutionary process. Each Human Spirit volunteering to learn the lessons and acquire the experience going hand in hand with the physical Universe.

But a cryptic warning accompanies these clearly outlined concepts; this book is designed to train the mind rather than inform it. In other words it is intended to induce a particular attitude both to the inner and outer world. Most must realise, words can hardly describe the immensity of the Cosmic creative process and the manifold complexity of our planetary and atomic systems under the jurisdiction of the Solar Logos.

THE COSMIC DOCTRINE further illustrates the true nature of Good and Evil which man generally views from his own highly subjective and very personal perspective. There are further insights into the interaction of positive and negative polarity within the universal scheme of things.

Besides the Creation of the Universe and the evolution of Mankind the COSMIC DOCTRINE has much to teach about Natural Law, the evolution of Consciousness and the Nature of Mind.

Illustrated with diagrams by one of Dion Fortune's closest collaborators.

ISBN 1 899585 0 52

GLASTONBURY, AVALON OF THE HEART

Dion Fortune first visited Glastonbury while Bligh Bond was still uncovering its past with his amazing psychic investigations into the Abbey ruins. It was at Glastonbury also that she received her first major and dramatic Inner Plane contact in Chalice Orchard close to Chalice Well.

Later she acquired the plot of the land and established a retreat, where it had all happened, under the shadow of the Tor.

AVALON OF THE HEART is her personal account of the love affair with Glastonbury that drew her back repeatedly across the years.

Her description remains one of the most evocative and poignant accounts of this wild yet holy place; a power centre polarising with distant Jerusalem and linking and harmonising the Christian way with the primaeval and pagan past.

She includes as a background time honoured legends of Joseph of Arimathea, the Grail and Arthur the King with special insights since she, more than any other, re-established these long overlooked historic matters of the Isles of Britain with special authority.

AVALON OF THE HEART is besides, both lyrical and poetic, recapturing the timelessly inspiring mood of Glastonbury, as she knew and loved it.

To pilgrims of the Aquarian Age her account is a precious reminder of Britain's heritage and its deep roots in the past. Not only that, but a gateway to the future.

With black and white illustrations by Peter Arthy.

ISBN 1 899585 20 6

MACHINERY OF THE MIND

"One of the shortest and clearest of the many popular books on modern psychology which have been published."

When she was barely twenty Dion Fortune was working in London just before the 1914-18 War as a lay analyst and so obtained first hand practical insights into that aspects of the human condition. Her subsequent esoteric work placed a heavy emphasis on the unwisdom of embarking on the Mysteries without thorough inner preparation. In a perfect world this would mean that candidates for initiation would present themselves with a clean bill of psychological health.

MACHINERY OF THE MIND was considered sufficiently important to form part of the standard background reading for the Study Course offered by the Society of the Inner Light that Dion Fortune founded.

ISBN 1 899585 00 1

THE MYSTICAL QABALAH

Dion Fortune's THE MYSTICAL QABALAH remains a classic in its clarity, linking the broad elements of Jewish traditional thought - probably going back to the Babylonian Captivity and beyond - with both eastern and western philosophy and later Christian insights.

Dion Fortune was one of the first Adepts to bring this 'secret tradition' to a wider audience. Some before her often only added to the overall mystery by elaborating on obscurity, but her account is simple, clear and comprehensive.

The Qabalah could be described as a confidential Judaic explanation of the paradox of 'the Many and the One' - the complexity and diversity within a monotheistic unity. Whereas the Old Testament outlines the social and psychological development of a tightly knit 'chosen group' culture, the supplementary Qabalah provides a detailed plan of the infrastructure behind the creative evolutionary process.

A major limitation of the Authorised English Version of the bible is the translation of the many Hebrew God-names by the single name "God". THE MYSTICAL QABALAH devotes a chapter to each of the ten schematic 'God-names', the qualities or 'Sephiroth', which focus the principle archetypes behind evolving human activity: the Spiritual Source; the principles of Force and Form; Love and Justice; the Integrative principle or the Christ Force; Aesthetics and Logic; the dynamics of the Psyche and finally, the Manifestation of life in earth in a physical body.

THE MYSTICAL QABALAH works in a profoundly psychological way. Its lessons for the individual are invaluable and this book is a must for all who feel drawn to getting to know themselves better so that their inner world and their outer world may be at one.

ISBN 1 899585 35 4

PSYCHIC SELF-DEFENCE

When she was twenty, Dion Fortune found herself the subject of a particularly powerful form of psychic attack, which ultimately led to a nervous breakdown. With the benefit of hindsight, and her experience as a practising occultist and natural psychic, she wrote Psychic Self Defence, a detailed instruction manual for protection against paranormal malevolence.

Within these pages are amazing revelations concerning the practices of Black Lodges, the risks involved in ceremonial magic, the pathology of non-human contacts, the nature of hauntings and the reality behind the ancient legends of the vampire. In addition, the book explores the elusive psychic elements in mental illness and, more importantly, details the methods, the motives, and the physical aspects of psychic attack - and how to overcome them.

Dion Fortune was born Violet Mary Firth in LLandudno, 1880. A brilliant writer and pioneer psychologist, she became increasingly interested in her own psychism and the study of magic. She went on to become a powerful medium, mystic and magician and devoted her life to her role as priestess of Isis and founder of the Society of the Inner Light, until her death from leukaemia in 1946.

ISBN 1 899585 40 0

MOON MAGIC

BEING THE MEMOIRS OF A MISTRESS OF THAT ART

The Sequel to The Sea Priestess

The manuscript of this novel was found among the author's papers and tells the return of Morgan Le Fay, the bewitching, ageless heroine first met with in The Sea Priestess. This fiction classic is last in the series planned by Dion Fortune and which was designed to impart much of the teaching of the Western Esoteric Tradition.

The story centres round an enchanting love affair that will appeal both to those searching below the surface for the principles and tenets behind the Western Esoteric Tradition as well as to the connoisseur of good fiction. Both will be fascinated by this modern tale of Magic and Mystery, with the Old Gods as Archetypes and demonstrating their power to affect us in the world today.

For a mysterious cloaked figure continually haunts the dreams of Dr. Robert Malcolm, a caring, successful yet unfulfilled medical practitioner: The image grips his imagination until it becomes close to a reality, ever moving softly ahead of him at dusk through the damp London streets, and mirroring the reflection of his nightly dreamscape.

...Until late one fateful evening, the substance of his dreams enters his surgery, unheralded yet in person... the unforgettable and eternally attractive Morgan Le Fay.

Then as Priestess of Isis she gradually returns him to the Natural World he has for so long abandoned. Taking on the painstaking task of renewing his soul and masculine power within the confines of her secret magical temple.

As time goes on, the chemistry between them stabilises into a clearly defined polarity and Dr. Malcolm is transformed in the process.

MOON MAGIC is a classic account and exploration of the interplay between masculine and feminine, anima and animus and a searching study of human and superhuman relationship.

ISBN 1 899585 15 X

THROUGH THE GATES OF DEATH

The text explains the stages in the natural process of dying that every departing soul passes though from this world to the next. The correct attitude being that death is simply birth into a new form of life and therefore to be regarded as a joyful and positive event.

Dion Fortune further sets out the requisite states of mind as well as the necessary actions by which those closest to the deceased can speed and smooth their passing and which should accompany the natural progression of death, laying out, burial and mourning.

This handbook has proved to be an invaluable aid and comfort to all confronted with bereavement, whatever their situation; whether seeking to do what is best for a departed loved one or to widen their own perception to bridge the mysteries between Life and Death.

ISBN 1 899585 10 9

THE GOAT FOOT GOD

Desperate and wretched after his wife's death at the hands of her lover, Hugh Paston turns to the Ancient Mysteries in search of Pan to re-establish and confirm his own manhood. With another seeker, Paston acquires an old monastery intending to convert it to a temple of Pan. The building is troubled by the spirit of a fifteenth century prior, walled up for his heretically pagan beliefs, who also searched for the goat-foot God. This entity plans to take over Paston's body to pursue his unremitting quest and it is left to Mona, Paston's partner's niece to help solve the problem of human love in this case, when in reality man and woman become representatives of the God and the Goddess.

'Shoots with remarkable success at a most ambitious target.' – The Guardian.

ISBN 1 899585 06 0

THE MAGICAL BATTLE OF BRITAIN

Immediately following Germany's invasion of Poland, which resulted in Britain's declaration of war, Dion Fortune, the founder of Britain's foremost magical order - The Society of The Inner Light - initiated a magical programme designed to thwart the expansionist intentions of the Third Reich, and thus the invasion of Britain.

Now, fifty years on, those instruction papers have been released from the archives of her school. Accompanied by a commentary from Gareth Knight, himself a student of Dion Fortune's fraternity, these teachings offer the reader an astonishing insight into the workings of a genuine esoteric school and their - until now - hidden yet significant contribution to the Nation's war effort.

ISBN 1 - 899585 - 00 - 1

THE SECRETS OF DR TAVERNER

Based on real people, this collection of short stories, presents Dion Fortune's teacher (said to be Dr Moriarty) with herself cast in the role of his assistant, Rhodes. Taverner uses his abilities to cure the severely mentally disturbed by esoteric techniques. By technical work on the inner planes he frees his patients from frustration, misery and worse. Rhodes, though just a learner, becomes more and more engrossed in the work until the day she overreaches herself, just like the Sorcerer's Apprentice; only just escaping terror-drenched disaster.

Each story highlights a psycho-esoteric aspect; vampirism, astral journeying, karmic repercussions, demonic interference; and this edition includes a previously unpublished story.

ISBN 1 899585 02 8

THE SEA PRIESTESS

In Dion Fortune's own words; "This book stands on its own feet as a literary Melchizedek."

It is a book with an undercurrent; upon the surface a romance; underneath a thesis upon a theme; "All women are Isis and Isis is all women."

Further, it is an experiment in prose rhythms which beat upon the subconscious mind in the same way as the Eastern Mantra, which, because they are archaic, speak to the archaic level of the mind whence dreams arise.

Dion Fortune considered with some reason, that the psychological state of modern civilisation was hardly much of an improvement on the sanitation of a mediaeval walled city. So she dedicated this work to the great goddess Cloacina, whose function it was to cleanse the drains of the Ancient Rome.

Wilfred Maxwell, a 'wimp' by any standards, learns to assert himself, his creativity and full masculinity under the tutelage of the mysterious Vivien Le Fay Morgan. His asthmatic condition has induced a certain psychism and he has a dream vision at the full moon of his patroness as the High Priestess of the Ancient Moon cult who has returned to calm and control the sea by the house he is now embellishing.

ISBN 1 899585 50 8

THE WINGED BULL A ROMANCE OF MODERN MAGIC

The message of the book concerns the spiritualising of sex. But not the spiritualising of sex by sublimating it onto other planes than the physical, but the spiritualising of sex by realising its profound spiritual significance and far-reaching psychological values.

The man whom Ursula Brangwyn loves becomes involved in Black Magic and drags her after him. Her brother, a student of strange arts, knows that the only way he can rescue her is to make her transfer her affections to someone else. He chooses his man and sets to work on his difficult task, making use of certain aspects of the sex relationship that are the carefully guarded secrets of the initiates. The story shows the deliberate building of a curious magnetic rapport between two people who do not attract each other. A highly strung, highly cultured sophisticated girl and an unemployed ex-officer, hard bitten and disillusioned.

ISBN 1 899585 45 1

THE SOCIETY OF THE INNER LIGHT

The Society of the Inner Light is a Society for the study of Metaphysical Religion, Mysticism, and Esoteric Psychology. Their development of their practice.

Its aims are Christian and its methods are Western.

Students can take the Correspondence Course for training in Esoteric Science and developing the daily discipline which can lead to Initiation. Application forms and a copy of the Society's WORK AND AIMS are available from;

>The Secretariat
>The Society of the Inner Light
>38 Steele's Road
>London NW3 4RG
>England
>
>email - sil@innerlight.org.uk